35

Duane L. Gibson

THE POLLS AND
PUBLIC OPINION

THE
POLLS
AND PUBLIC
OPINION

The Iowa Conference on Attitude
and Opinion Research Sponsored
by the State University of Iowa, Iowa City

Edited by NORMAN C. MEIER
and HAROLD W. SAUNDERS
State University of Iowa

Henry Holt and Company
New York

THE IOWA CONFERENCE ON ATTITUDE AND OPINION RESEARCH

The Aim of the Conference

In a democracy, public opinion, expressing common attitudes widely held, is basic to effective self-government and to the general functioning of organized mass society.

Techniques for the ascertainment of attitudes so held are the concern of social science. The development and refinement of techniques are now in an early stage of progress and subject to tests too severe to warrant final evaluation. Yet scientific method is so important to the democratic process and to the advancement of knowledge about contemporary society that a conferring of scientists and survey directors for an examination of its present status and future improvement is opportune.

Because Iowa has produced many of the persons now prominent in the field, the University has arranged the Conference on Attitude and Opinion Research. To the Conference have been invited experts representing different backgrounds, interests, and experience who do not ordinarily meet together, for discussion together of problems which transcend the full understanding of any one individual or group.

It is not expected that easy answers will be forthcoming to the difficult problems of how mass opinion, prevailing attitudes, and impending behavior may best be measured. The problems, complex to an extreme, are still before those whose responsibility it is to restudy them with renewed zeal. Are there better methods suitable for the peculiar requirements of public opinion measurement? How can theory be tested in the crucible of actual use? These and a multitude of other problems of broad scope in social science constitute the constructive objectives that need full and unhurried discussion by those who can contribute with factual material, knowledge, and research experience.

PREFACE

Plans for the Iowa Conference on Attitude and Opinion Research took form shortly after November 2, 1948, when the need and desirability of a stock-taking of theory and methods in social science were apparent. Though the interests of the Conference and the *Committee on Polls and Election Forecasts* of the Social Science Research Council were never considered duplicative, the Conference deferred its original date of December 9-11, 1948, to February 10-12, 1949, in order better to supplement the work of the Committee and for the more cogent reason that it envisaged a broader coverage of social science interests.

The wisdom of the postponement appears in the better perspective which the passing of time provided, permitting more study and presentation of data not earlier available. Its participants represent a wide range of interests, including the views of some of the poll-takers themselves, and bringing together theoretical and technical aspects. It attempted further to outline and define some of the problems now made acute by the experience of 1948 and to provide suggestions and ideas which can be followed up by social science researchers in the future.

For the most part the Report is essentially as taken down during the Conference sessions by stenotype recording. The main presentations have been revised by their authors. In a few sections where insufficient time precluded the full presentation because of the necessities of a crowded schedule, the material is included here in full. Permission was granted to publish several papers in journals whose readership is particularly interested in those portions of the subject matter.

The Conference planning committee made an earnest effort to include in its invitations individuals representing a wide variety of interests, including many whose known views differ from others equally active and competent in social science research. It was intended to be a Conference inviting full discussion in the interests of clarifying moot points and enlarging understanding of the problems. Should any reader not find certain names on the roster of participants, let him be reassured that the omission was in no instance intentional but rather was due to inability to attend at the date set, which was the time when most of the group considered could attend.

The University offers its facilities of an atmosphere of full and free discussion, following the principle that only in such circumstances can helpful advance be made toward some degree of eventual clarification of the difficult problems of attitude and opinion research. This Conference is the first of an annual series with the prospect of resuming in subsequent years more deliberations of this nature. It is hoped they may serve a useful purpose in the young field of social science where research is greatly needed.

N. C. M.

The Planning Committee:

Harvey H. Davis, Executive Dean and Dean of the Graduate College
James Jordan, Director, Information Service
Norman C. Meier, Director, Bureau of Audience Research
Harold Saunders, Chairman, Department of Sociology

Merritt Ludwig, Assistant to the Committee

Iowa City
April 15, 1949

CONTENTS

Directory of Participants

* **Albig, J. W.,** Head, Department of Sociology and Anthropology, University of Illinois

Bachelder, J. E., Co-Director, Washington Public Opinion Laboratory, Washington State College, Pullman, Washington

Beiler, Ross C., Assistant Professor of Political Science, University of Miami, Miami, Florida

Berelson, Bernard, Dean, Graduate Library School, University of Chicago

Cahalan, Don, Director, Opinion Research Center, University of Denver

1 **Cantril, Hadley,** Office of Public Opinion Research, Princeton University

Casey, Ralph, Director, School of Journalism, University of Minnesota

* **Chapin, F. S.,** Head, Department of Sociology, University of Minnesota

Clark, Carroll, Head, Department of Sociology, University of Kansas

Crossley, Archibald M., Crossley Inc., New York, N. Y.

* **Davis, Harvey H.,** Executive Dean and Dean of the Graduate College, State University of Iowa

Dodd, Stuart C., Director, Washington Public Opinion Laboratory, University of Washington, Seattle

Gallup, George H., Director, American Institute of Public Opinion, Princeton

* **Hancher, Virgil M.,** President, State University of Iowa

Hansen, Morris H., Statistical Assistant to the Director, Bureau of the Census, Washington, D. C.

* **Hart, Clyde W.,** Director, National Opinion Research Center, Chicago

Kennedy, Frank R., Associate Professor of Law, State University of Iowa

Kroeger, Henry, Director, Research Department, *Des Moines Register* and *Des Moines Tribune*

Lazarsfeld, Paul F., Director, Bureau of Applied Social Research, Columbia University

* **Meier, Norman C.,** Director, Bureau of Audience Research, State University of Iowa

* **McCormick, Thomas,** Head, Department of Sociology and Anthropology, University of Wisconsin

* **Moeller, Leslie G.,** Director, School of Journalism, State University of Iowa

Nafziger, Ralph, Director of Research, School of Journalism, University of Minnesota

Russell, Francis H., Director, Office of Public Affairs, Department of State, Washington, D. C.

* **Saunders, Harold W.,** Chairman, Department of Sociology, State University of Iowa

1 **Schramm, Wilbur,** Director, Institute of Communications Research, University of Illinois

* **Sears, Robert,** Director, Iowa Child Research Station, State University of Iowa

Seymour, Gideon, Vice-President and Executive Editor, *Minneapolis Star* and *Minneapolis Tribune*

Shewhart, Walter A., Bell Telephone Laboratories, New York

* Section chairman.
1 Paper read.

* **Spence, Kenneth W.,** Head, Department of Psychology, State University of Iowa

Stock, J. Stevens, Opinion Research Corporation, Princeton, New Jersey

Stouffer, Samuel A., Director, Laboratory of Social Relations, Harvard University

* **Stuit, Dewey B.,** Dean, College of Liberal Arts, State University of Iowa

Part One

SOCIAL SCIENCE
RESEARCH

SOCIAL SCIENCE RESEARCH

Dean Harvey H. Davis, Presiding
President Virgil M. Hancher

MR. DAVIS: To open this conference it is my privilege and pleasure to present—I do not need to introduce to this audience—but to present to the audience President Virgil M. Hancher, who will give us a word of welcome.

PRESIDENT HANCHER: Dean Davis, ladies and gentlemen of the audience. I note that on the program I am listed to deliver an "address of welcome," and Dean Davis used the happier terminology "a word of welcome." I had assigned myself the more pleasant task of giving you a brief greeting.

I am happy to greet you at this conference on the measurement of opinion and the social implications of that measurement. Although I suppose it might be a little inept to mention the late election to this audience, I want to tell you an anecdote related by a friend of mine who was recently in Washington for the inauguration. While there she met at the hotel door a woman who told her she had just had a very interesting experience. She had been at another place, had attempted to get a taxi, had been unable to do so, and being in a great hurry had given some evidence of her agitation. A very kindly disposed gentleman who was standing in the group happened to have his car and chauffeur at the curb and he offered to have her driven to her destination. She got into the car and proceeded toward her destination and, being a very chatty person, she engaged the chauffeur in conversation. She said, "My, isn't the weather lovely? The weather man predicted we were going to have rain and very disagreeable weather, but it's really very nice." The chauffeur agreed. Then she added: "It was also predicted that Mr. Truman wouldn't be elected." "Yes," said the chauffeur, "that man *certainly has contacts.*"

Knowledge of such "contacts" might be very useful in these days in the measurement of opinion, because in addition to measuring people's attitudes, it is now necessary to know something about "contacts" and "headquarters," and about just how an organization is going to direct its members to vote. At least I have heard some very interesting stories, and not too long ago, about sovereign representatives of the people who sit in their hotel rooms and speak very frankly about their attitudes on various public affairs until a little release comes from the headquarters of the organization with which they are concerned—and when they vote their vote is opposite to the opinion they have been expressing.

Even as a layman, therefore, I can see that there are tremendous problems in this measurement of attitude and opinion and particularly in the prediction of election results. There certainly is, as we know, greater difficulty than we had anticipated in predicting the outcome. Many of us, particularly in positions such as mine, are very anxious to know why people are elected—not only *who* will be elected but *why* they will be elected—and the arguments, true or false, which control the minds of the voters in selecting certain candidates in preference to others. And if that problem should ever be solved, then I would submit a third problem in which I would be even more acutely interested, and that is *what will they do* after their election. You get them elected, you find out the reasons why they were elected, but can you predict what they will do after they are elected?

I speak only as a layman and in a very amateurish fashion, but I am concerned, as I believe all thinking citizens of this country are concerned, about public opinion measurement and its social implications. As a layman and without any right to do so, I certainly make the prediction that polls are here to stay. We have been predicting in an unscientific way for many years. Perhaps in another twenty years we will think of what we are doing now as still unscientific. But I am sure we are going to keep at it until it is scientific; and therefore I take it that the major problem before us is not whether polling will continue, but how we can make it effective so that it will be accurate and scientific. And most of all, how can we make it socially useful and desirable?

In your deliberations here I sincerely hope that you will progress toward solutions by a frank interchange of ideas, and that this conference may contribute largely to your thinking as experts and ours as laymen about the common problems in which we are engaged.

1

THE ROLE OF THE UNIVERSITY IN SOCIAL SCIENCE RESEARCH

Dean Harvey H. Davis

MR. DAVIS: The university's responsibility to society in general and to the state in particular (that is, for a state university) or to its service area (or whatever it may be) is that of disseminating knowledge, adding to the store of knowledge, and preparing servants and leaders for society. I say "servants" and "leaders" deliberately because the institutions, be they state or private, are established largely in order that society may have doctors, dentists, lawyers, political leaders, statesmen, and so on.

Now, along with that responsibility for preparing leaders and servants for the state goes the responsibility to youth, for making the preparation of their talents in life. Whether you are addressing a state-supported institution or a philanthropically supported institution or a municipally supported institution, I think you will agree with me that in the minds of the people who establish them, their objectives are to give young people a chance in the world or prepare them to serve society in one way or another. Therefore the university has a triple role of teaching, research, and service. Research happens to be the one that we are to discuss particularly today because of the three, research has a key position. By this means, the teaching and the service are kept fresh and up to date. We find out new things and then teach them to people; we find out new truths and disseminate them through conferences and the like.

The university is able to bring to bear on research problems a wider array of talents and facilities than most research agencies have available. For example, in connection with research in the field of aviation—a little better illustration than others—the university can bring to bear a variety of talents. The aviation industry is concerned with research about the flying machine as such; it is concerned with the fuels that propel it; it is concerned with the persons who operate the flying machine; it is concerned with the medium in which it operates. Only on a large university campus can that kind of array of talents be brought together: the engineering resources and physics resources that have to do with the perfection of the flying machine as such; the resources in chemistry and other fields that have to do with the perfection of the fuels, whether jet propulsion or whatever it may be; and the resources from the physiologists and the psychologists that have to do with the individual who flies the machine (because in modern aviation, as you know, the machine will often do things which the pilot cannot stand; it will change altitude more rapidly, and make turns more quickly than the human can endure). It is obvious that a whole cluster of things revolve around aviation—problems of meteorology, problems of the upper air, problems of the medium in which the machine is working.

Therefore, a university campus is the only place where you can bring all that array of talent to bear on a given problem. You can find any number of other illustrations if you wish to do so, but aviation will serve as a sample. That is why the government and the aviation industry frequently bring their problems to university campuses, because you must integrate and correlate those researches in order to help solve the problems before you.

It seems to me that the university's role with reference to social science research is particularly vital for three reasons: first, the increasing realization of the importance of social science; second, the fact that this field is less well covered by research in industry and institutes such as the Mellon Institute in Pittsburgh or the relatively new Midwest Institute in Kansas City; and third, the need for improved techniques in social science research.

The increasing importance of social science is attested by your presence here today. If you didn't think it were important you wouldn't be here; if we didn't think it were important we wouldn't hold the conference. It is also attested by the enterprises you represent. You have come from institutes of various kinds and universities of all sorts, leading in fields of social sciences. It is also attested by the attitude of industry. Many large organizations are saying quite frankly that they are better prepared to meet the technical problems of production and distribution than they are in human relations as between industry and labor or between industry and the consumer and the public. We have had two or three examples of that this fall with representatives of large concerns who have said, "We know fairly well how to meet our technical problems. Naturally we can do better, but we know fairly well how to go about it. But the problems of relationships, human relationships, between the folk who are working for us and the people who direct the enterprise, and the people who own the enterprise and the customers served by it—all those problems of human relationships we are less well able to manage."

It seems that man does well to study himself. About the first science that man studied was astronomy, for a number of reasons I suppose, but it seems that he began with the thing that was furthest away from himself, just as far from himself as he could get. After a while he crept up a little closer and began to study geology, and mathematics, and geography, and only with a considerable reluctance did he begin to study even his own physiology and anatomy. For example, you know it was not so very long ago we learned that the blood circulated. People have been very reluctant to study their own physical features, and apparently even more reluctant to study their own psychological phenomena. The science of psychology is a very new thing. I don't know that psychologists would agree with me, but only in the last fifteen or twenty years has psychology begun to come into its own as a serious and scientific thing.

Man, therefore, began away out, about as far from himself as he could get. He studied the stars, then the earth, then chemistry and physics and what he called "natural philosophy," and finally and very reluctantly did he come down to study himself. You can see it is only recently that this study of social science has come into prominence.

As to this second point, the fact that we do not have as much resources devoted to the study of human relations as we do to the study of various other things, it is only in the past few years that money has been devoted to social science studies, and it is still true (I am sure from considerable contact with research enter-prises in various universities) that it is much easier to get money to study the materials and processes of industry than it is to get money to study human relations. We are just beginning to get to the point where foundations and governments in general will vote money to it.

I remember four or five years ago attending a meeting of the American Management Association in Chicago. Corporations put a great deal of money into contributions to universities to carry on research in the processes of industry and in materials with which those processes work. At that time I was with Ohio State University, and I said to this group in the little conference that had been set up on education, "Would you be as interested, or anywhere near as interested, in putting money into a study of human relations, a study of the kinds of things that are concerned with the people who carry on industrial processes, with the people who work with those materials, as you are in perfecting the materials and improving the processes?" They studied a moment about it and some of them said they thought they would be, so we did establish the division or board of personnel research there, and a sizable sum of money has been put into it. That is a personal illustration but I use it to show that industry is becoming conscious, rather rapidly in the last year or two, of the importance of social science research as well as other types of research.

Furthermore, this third matter to which I wish to address a few moments of time, that of improving research techniques in the social sciences, is peculiarly the province of the university because it comes extensively under the head of pure research, and the university likes to think it devotes a good deal of time to pure research. Industrial organizations and industrial research foundations in general are concerned more with applied research. To some extent your public opinion institutes and the like must also be concerned with the applications of social science research. The endowed and publicly supported universities, on the other hand, find their part of their reason for existence in the responsibility for carrying on pure research, research merely for the purpose of adding to the sum total of human knowledge without any assurance that it will mean a thing to people eventually, or that it will have any practical application at all. Therefore the university is particularly concerned with this phase, the development of improved research techniques in public opinion and social conditions generally.

In order to manufacture large new machines it is usually necessary first to make another manufacturing machine. And before a very good job can be done in social science research, there must be some improvement in the techniques for doing it. It has seemed to some of us that the social scientists have been a little prone to borrow the techniques of the natural scientists. The natural scientist has a tremendous reputation in our society. He has shortened our day of labor, he has lengthened our life, and he has done all sorts of things for us. Therefore, why shouldn't we in our research in social science try to copy the very successful methods of the natural and physical scientists? Some of you have probably read McCall's book in which he said in substance that whatever exists at all exists in some amount and can therefore be measured. That sounded like a good doctrine, and he wrote a statistics book about it.

The social scientists have borrowed, and properly borrowed, a good many things from the physical scientists. The techniques of statistical management and so forth have been properly borrowed. However, in many respects the techniques of the natural scientist are not suited to the social scientist. Physical phenomena have no volition of their own and can be depended on to act the same from one time to the next providing the conditions are the same. They can't just change their minds or get out on the wrong side of the bed or have a bad breakfast. There isn't any question of free will involved in dealing with these materials. There is no problem of values or morals when chemicals are combined or operated. DDT kills mosquitoes and honey bees alike; TNT will blow up an ice jam or destroy a church with equal efficiency. There is no question of values or morals, but when you get into the social sciences, that isn't the case. Furthermore, another problem in the social sciences is that of propaganda and counter-propaganda. When two physical scientists set up two experiments on each side of a room, they do not send out propaganda to try to interfere with the other man's job. Scientists just don't operate that way in physical science, while social scientists find themselves confronted not only with difficulty in finding the true results but by some tendencies to have propaganda A on this side and counter-propaganda B on the other side, a tendency to prove not the truth but the thing they want to prove.

Furthermore, in developing techniques in social science we will of course—as President Hancher indicated a few moments ago—need to go beyond finding out *what* people think, which is very important, to finding out *why* they think as they do. We would like to know also, to use a slang expression, "What of it?" Does it make any difference what they think? Your social science techniques will need to be developed in such a manner as to find out not only what the people think but why they think as they do, and the implications of their thinking in that manner. That problem is peculiar to a democracy because the government of the people rests in the hands of the people, and in social science research you find out things about that. In a dictatorship the situation is reversed. All dictatorial leaders have to do is to decide what they want the people to think, make up their minds in star-chamber session that this and this and this is what they want the people to think, and then start out on a propaganda campaign of wrong information or withheld information, a campaign of stimulus of one kind or another, to bring the people to think what they want them to think. That isn't social science, of course.

In a democracy and in a university, and in a company of distinguished social science researchers such as we have here this morning, the problem is not to direct the thinking of the people, not to compel them to think this way or that, but to find out what they are thinking, and to find out why they are thinking as they do. Furthermore, the problem is to find out what implications arise from the fact that they think as they do think, and to work through research methods not to modify their thinking in terms of saying this is what they should think, but to modify the sources of information and methods by which people arrive at their thinking so that their thinking may be more sound and based on more important facts. Here, as in the case of aviation which I cited as an example, we have another instance of the responsible role of the university in doing this kind of work. (I am speaking for any large university and not for this one uniquely; I would be happy to do so, but you represent many universities and are equally concerned.) We are able in a large university to bring to bear on problems sociologists, psychologists, anthropologists and political scientists, journalists—a long array. I am not deliberately leaving anybody out, but I am indicating that there are many types of authorities, many types of resources, and many kinds of facilities on a large university campus which can be brought to bear upon these questions of social science research, and that the university has a responsible role to bring those things to bear. In so doing we must develop social science techniques which will give an appropriate place to values, to norms, and to human freedom of action, and which will at the same time give reliable indices of behavior. That this is a difficult assignment cannot be denied, but such conferences as this can help the university, and we hope the participants, in making headway toward meeting that assignment.

2

BASIC SOCIAL SCIENCE RESEARCH

Samuel A. Stouffer

MR. DAVIS: We shall next have the privilege of hearing a discussion on basic social science research, in which the items which I tried to mention briefly and untechnically will be developed by competent persons.

We shall hear first from the man who is a Professor of Sociology and Director of the Laboratory of Social Relations at Harvard University, formerly with the University of Wisconsin and the University of Chicago, and who was a member of the Social Science Research Council Committee to study public opinion polls—Mr. Samuel A. Stouffer.

MR. STOUFFER: We who are social scientists feel that the University of Iowa is to be congratulated in sponsoring this conference at this time.

After some events which transpired in the first week of last November (*laughter*), there has been a certain amount of triumphant glee, not only on the part of the layman who always likes in our culture to see the expert debunked, but also on the part of some academicians who never did believe in social science and who now see themselves vindicated.

Some of us who do believe in social science think that what has happened may be a blessing in disguise—rather thickly disguised, some will admit!—and that we can use that experience constructively.

Now, my mission is not to talk about the polls—we will hear at length about them at later sessions of this conference—but to talk about research in the basic social sciences relating to attitude and opinion studies.

I suppose the main reason why anybody thinks there is or can be a social science is that all around us in our everyday behavior we see not only how necessary prediction is, but also how successful

11

it is. True, we take most of the successful predictions for granted. Our very living from hour to hour is based on it. I happen to have been born in Iowa—a fact of which I am very proud—but I did not have to be a native Iowan to predict that Dean Davis, the chairman of this meeting, would be wearing a necktie (*laughter*). Now, that prediction is a bit on the trivial side, but it is symbolic of thousands of things we can say with confidence ahead of time. While we drive a car down the street only a few blocks we may make a score of predictions about what other drivers will do—and we are hardly conscious of any of these predictions until one of them fails and we have a smashup or near miss. Indeed, all human living is possible only because a large part of our daily activities permit us to make successful predictions.

Of course, even in our daily life there are areas in which it is dangerous to admit that one can be too successful in prediction. It's quite important to us, apparently, to have our little mysteries. Did you ever know a woman, for example, who was unhappy to have you tell her you couldn't quite figure out what was on her mind? All of us need such reassurance from time to time as to our private right to behave in unforeseeable ways. That's possibly why, incidentally, there was so much gloating last November. Let me read from *The New Yorker*, a great scientific journal (*laughter*), dated November 13, 1948:

"The total collapse of the public opinion polls shows that this country is in good health. A country that developed an airtight system of finding out in advance what was in people's minds would be uninhabitable. Luckily we do not face any such emergency. The so-called science of poll-taking is not a science at all but mere necromancy. People are unpredictable by nature and although you can take a nation's pulse, you can't be sure that the nation hasn't just run up a flight of stairs; and although you can take a nation's blood pressure you can't be sure that if you came back in twenty minutes you'd get the same reading. This is a damn fine thing. We are proud of Americans for clouding up the crystal ball, for telling one thing to a poll-taker, another thing to a voting machine. This is an excellent land."

Now really, right down in our hearts, I think we all—even possibly Arch Crossley over there—feel a little tingle of approval ringing in our bosoms at words like these. At the same time we know that we couldn't live without being able to predict reasonably well how the other fellow will react to something we say or do. Indeed, when our batting average gets too low we are locked up in a mental hospital. And also we know that business and government depend on prediction. There are big businesses which are based solely on very explicit probabilities of human behavior—for example, the insurance business when it insures against theft or embezzlement.

Of course, nobody dreams of a science of human behavior which seeks to predict each private thought any more than one dreams of a science of hydraulics which would predict the location and duration of each little eddy in a Mississippi River flood. But a science of human nature or of social relations must be based on the solid fact that there are regularities in man's behavior which do admit of actuarial prediction. That is the first point I want to make.

However, prediction is not in itself science, even though a science should be able to improve predictions. Basically, science is a system of theory of interlocking propositions whose implications have been tested empirically. Now, it is important here to make a distinction between science and engineering. Science sets up and tests theories; engineering selects among theories those which are applicable to the solution of a practical problem. The better the theories, the better chance the engineer has of finding a good solution. If the theories aren't too good, the engineer can make some bad blunders. For example, there has been almost nothing in the theory of political science or social psychology to help in the analysis of the conditions under which a given type of political campaign might or might not be effective. In the absence of tested theory, the best the engineer or practitioner can do is usually to use his common sense.

In the Roosevelt elections it seems to have been the historical fact, insofar as data are available, that few voters changed their minds during the campaign. One common-sense conclusion, in the absence of a theoretical analysis, was that this observed experience would repeat itself. It didn't. History, naked, is an unsafe guide. I think that if social science had been ready with a body of theory— even if inadequate in places—the practitioners at least would have been better sensitized to ask, "What elements in this election are different from other elections? What are some of the possible differences in voting these differences could make?"

It must be said very frankly, however, that theory in the social sciences is still pretty primitive. We have some exceedingly useful general orientations, but we do not yet have systems of interlocking propositions which have been tested by anything like the same rigorous criteria as those used in some of the more mature sciences.

Well, let's take a look at this. What are some of these general orientations which are helping shape, let us say, the science of social psychology? Now, may I mention briefly four streams of influence, all of which are contributing and will contribute to better socio-psychological theory?

One is what is called "dynamic psychology." The implications of the classic experiments in post-hypnotic suggestion were devastating to the older concepts of rational behavior. Even though little of Freud has been verified with the rigor that we would like and even though much of psychoanalytic thinking may eventually be superseded, nobody can doubt the profound importance of the Freudian insights. Psychoanalysts, particularly, tend to be sloppy scientists but they do tell us certain things to look for and, often enough to be useful to us, we think we find it when we look.

A second stream of influence is what may be called "learning theory." There are various schools of thought here, just as in dynamic psychology. Some of the simpler Pavlovian concepts of conditioning may now be obsolete, but there can be no doubt as to the value of the orientation we get. Moreover, students of learning theory have the excellent habit of being experimenters. Unlike all too many social scientists they know what constitutes proof; they know the enormous labor involved in designing a good controlled experiment but they do design it, not just talk about it which is the fashion I may say too often in social science. Their influence therefore on methodology is likely to be equally important with their influence on theory.

I have mentioned so far dynamic psychology and learning theory as influences on social psychology. A third stream of influence is from social anthropology. From comparison of peoples all over the world we see the astonishing plasticity of the human infant and the power of culture in producing an animal who possesses the peculiar values and conforms to the peculiar conventions which his social milieu decrees.

A fourth stream of influence is from sociology, which, among its numerous contributions, has helped us see more clearly the significance of social roles and of role expectations. In our western urbanized society especially, we find ourselves a member not of one social group but simultaneously a member of many. There is a strain for conformity to each of these, and there is conflict within one's self when the values and expectations of two groups to which one simultaneously belongs conflict. This is seen dramatically in the children of immigrant parents—who are often cited in discussions of the marginal man. But it occurs to all of us in our daily lives. It is amazing how much talk there has been about this. How long ago was it, Mr. Chapin, when you drew those intersecting circles in that book of yours? About twenty years? And we still hardly know very much about what the theory is.

Now let's take an example. There are probably some students here, graduate or undergraduate, of Iowa, and some of you may have served as proctors of examinations. Let me ask you a question: Suppose you caught your best friend cheating? Would you turn him in? Anybody who has been a foreman, or a non-com in the Army, can think of numberless examples of role conflict. The concept assumes high importance in attitude studies. (See, for example, Lazarsfeld's studies of cross-pressures in voting behavior.)

Anyone could extend this list, but these illustrations of our indebtedness to dynamic psychology, to learning theory, to anthropology, and to sociology indicate that social psychology is not bereft of invaluable orientations.

Now, an effective social science, as I have sought to point out at the beginning, must depend on the existence of sufficient regularities and replications in its subject matter to make a high batting average of prediction. That was my point 1. My point 2 was that it must consist of logically consistent theoretical propositions. But neither a predictable subject matter nor insightful theoretical orientation is enough. Something more is needed, and that is techniques of investigation.

There are some social scientists—there may be some in this room—who sit comfortably in their armchairs and watch the blue smoke curl heavenward as they think, and who pooh-pooh techniques as "mere gadgeteering."

I suspect that the so-called gadgeteering is as important in the development of a science as is the dreaming up of theories. Look at the scientific work which has made the modern conquest of disease possible. I'll agree with you that we've got to watch out about our analogies in physical science, so let's take medicine. Sure, there is theory. It is relevant to note, parenthetically, that it was as futile in medicine as it is today in social science to look for one simple general theory which would be the key to everything. A century and more ago Dr. Benjamin Rush thought he had the answer in a theory of convulsive action, and enthusiastic disciples suggested that monuments be erected to him in all the capitals of Europe as the Newton of medicine. We know, of course, that not one theory but many specific theories are needed to account for diseases. Germ theories, deficiency theories, theories of cell growth, psychogenic theories—each of them has a place. But the without-which-not of the advance in medicine was techniques of investigation. First, the clinical methods, and much more recently, controlled experimentation. And above all, instruments of observation and measurement—gadgets, if you will. It is inconceivable that medical research could have made more than a few inches of progress without the compound microscope, the thermometer, and scores of other gadgets. How recent some of these are is suggested by the historical report that at the start of the Civil War only six clinical thermometers were available for use in the Union Army.

Now it is obvious to some of us that progress in the development of tested theory in the social sciences has waited on the development of adequate measuring instruments, just as progress in aviation, for example—many of whose theoretical principles were known to Leonardo da Vinci—waited on the development of an efficient internal combustion engine. We talk about attitudes, we talk about role expectations or social norms—we keep drawing Chapin's intersecting circles over and over again—but how can we study or classify or theorize convincingly unless we can identify and preferably measure the objects of our study?

Let us take an even closer analogy than medicine. Let us look at the progress psychologists have made in the study of intelligence. Before World War I there were many theories of intelligence and endless philosophical quarrels about its nature, not unlike quarrels in social science about the nature of the democratic process. Along came the gadgeteers. Whatever the theories, there was a recognition of the fact that men differed in abilities and that it would help the Army in World War I if men could be classified and assigned in a way which would maximize their skills. The Alpha test devised was a pretty crude instrument but out of that old wartime experience came a vast amount of testing in the public schools and everywhere, and techniques were improved.

The new techniques led to direct studies of controversial theoretical points. Was the IQ a constant? Could it be altered by environment?—Stoddard's studies here at the University of Iowa were among the most important. Then it became apparent that what we call intelligence was not one ability but several abilities. New techniques arose to describe and isolate these abilities. Factor analysis, which is a sophisticated mathematical device for this purpose, using Matrix algebra and n-dimensional geometry, is still a controversial subject. But hundreds of research papers have now been published and the whole emphasis is changed. We now don't quarrel about the constancy of the IQ; instead, we have controlled experiments to determine which of the primary mental abilities are more easily educable and with what kind of people. Thus Thurstone in his studies of Chicago school children is finding that with respect to at least some of the abilities, the more of a given ability a child has the more he can improve it with intensive training. Factor analysis, with all its beauty, is a crude substitute for the more elegant and less empirical formulations we may expect in the future. But the important thing to note is that, thanks to tests and to mathematical models for analyzing them, controversies can be settled by experiment and not get lost in the dismal swamp of verbal futility.

Just as World War I gave a new impetus to the development of techniques for the study of *abilities,* so it may be that World War II gave a new impetus for the study of *attitudes.* Here again the technician has moved in on the theorist. Government agencies like the Treasury in the selling of War Bonds, the OPA in restricting consumption, or the Army in facing morale problems among its soldiers, needed quick and reasonably accurate readings of the pulse of opinion. Fortunately, in spite of the fact that theoretical progress had not been remarkable in the period before the war, there were techniques available. The experience of practitioners of opinion research in sampling, question construction, and analysis was to be of inestimable value. True, the instruments were crude, the sampling procedure was often inadequate, and the need for speed was not always consistent with ideal work. But the engineering value of these tools hardly can be denied. In the Army alone we made about three hundred studies based on samplings of an aggregate of half a million soldiers. The first two of four volumes funding that experience will be published in April by the Princeton University Press.

As might be expected, the glaring inadequacy of some of these tools in current use became all the more conspicuous as efforts were made to employ them in novel situations. There were fires to be put out; we could not divert all our energies to developing a new chemical extinguisher; it was necessary to use water and sand. But progress was made in the war and has been made at a geometrically increasing rate since the war in studying the basic logic of socio-psychological measurement.

Building on the work of Thurstone and others, the development of scale theory by Guttman, and more recently the work by Lazars-feld, has opened a new vista of possibilities for empirical attack on theoretical problems. Some of the most exciting new leads have not yet been published. We can expect what is done today to become obsolete tomorrow; what is done then to become obsolete the day after tomorrow. That is good. That is the way of science.

My emphasis on the role of techniques would be misleading if my emphasis or my tone is suggestive that I believe that techniques alone will build a science. I hope I have been clear on that point. But I do not want to be misunderstood, since one of the evils of our day is the demand for social engineering based on techniques but lacking the solid base of tested social theory.

May I give a homely illustration? During the war we were asked to find out whether it was a good idea to train men to meet terroriz-ing situations (a) by exposing them gradually to such situations, (b) by shocking them from the start, or (c) by evading the problem altogether. We called in a group of exceedingly competent psychol-ogists for advice. They argued for two days and could come to no agreement. It turned out that there is no basic knowledge of fear, adequately formulated theoretically and tested empirically, from which one could even deduce that it is better for a dentist to tell a nervous patient that (a) maybe this is going to hurt a little, (b) surely it is going to hurt a lot, or (c) it isn't going to hurt at all.

Now, fear and anxiety are not easy to measure, but theory and measurement must go hand in hand if a problem like this is to be solved. We certainly must have measures which will distinguish between adaptive and maladaptive fear, but we also must have theoretical models to put to critical test with the aid of such measures. And where possible, the critical test must be through controlled ex-periments.

Moreover, what if the concrete data which we work on are trivial? Mendel did not study the wheat crop in Europe; he studied wrinkled peas. The criterion of scientific importance may be far different from what appears important to us as citizens.

The great danger we face—in fact, I think the greatest danger we face, in spite of what happened at the recent election—is that the public demands for our services as citizen engineers will be too great, rather than too little, and that there will be too few competent social scientists free to work at the basic problems of formulating better hypotheses and devising the gadgets and the experimental designs to test them.

We have come a long way. Our progress is not always swift. There are accidents along the way like the little affair of last November which, while it was in the engineering field rather than in basic social science, can affect public confidence. But if we are modest in our claims, if we concentrate on fundamentals, if we draw into our group increasing numbers of hardheaded students all of whom know what proof is and some of whom are not afraid of mathematics, and if we have faith and daring, we can contribute mightily toward building a science of man and society. To that high aim I wish to believe this conference at the University of Iowa is dedicated.

DISCUSSION—Stuart C. Dodd, Clyde W. Hart; General Discussion

MR. DAVIS: We shall have the discussion of this very stimulating and very challenging paper by Dr. Stuart C. Dodd, Director of the Public Opinion Laboratory at the University of Washington.

MR. DODD: There are a number of points in Sam Stouffer's discussion that I think are very fundamental and that we want to follow up. The chief emphasis upon prediction is, I think, the most fundamental thing that the polling world and the social scientists in general have to emphasize very much more than we have in the past. In fact, I'd go so far as to say that the whole business of the scientist is to predict and control phenomena in his field, and that insofar as he increases man's ability to predict and control phenomena in his field, through the aid of laws or techniques or whatever devices increase prediction and control, he is accomplishing the science of adjusting man to himself and his environment or whatever purposes man wants. These ultimate ends lie outside the field of science, which deals with the relation of means to ends.

In our polling we have been concerned very largely with measuring people's attitudes, opinions, behavior, and conditions as they are, and have been content on a descriptive level—simply stating what the conditions are in the sample of the public that we have observed. We have not gone far enough into the field of trying to use those descriptions for predicting what public behavior will be in some important line in the future.

Now, one of the fields in which prediction has been going on is, of course, in elections. Another is in market research, with pantry-shelf checks and things of that kind. But we haven't consciously held before ourselves that ideal of using our techniques for predicting future behavior and checking and improving our techniques by that test. In fact, we can know whether or not a technique or any method is good scientifically, depending on whether or not it helps us to predict future behavior better. Now, to do that, I suggest that you might carry out some of Sam Stouffer's principles in this form: that we use a "predictance coefficient" much more than we have. In fact, many of us are hardly aware such a thing is usable. By "predictance coefficient" I mean any kind of correlation between a predicter index and a predicted index. It may be a contingency coefficient or any one of the different kinds of correlation that measure the degree of agreement between an index of one earlier situation and the index of another situation later in time. If we develop such a predictance coefficient and use it routinely in our studies, we then begin to know when we are using good scientific methods, when we are improving our scientific methods, and how much.

It would be possible, for instance, to develop such a predictance coefficient between what the polls say before an election and what the outcome of the election is, and to have it in a fairly standardized form that can be used in different polling situations and different elections by different agencies anywhere in the country. Or why shouldn't we test ourselves by our ability to predict people's going to church next Sunday and then measure the actual attendance in all the churches in the community, and find out how our prediction from sampled assertions checked with the actual behavior of the public, and so on? You could list thousands of other things of social significance in which some prediction can be tested by measuring both the earlier polled assertions and the later outcome in people's behavior.

If we had such a predictance coefficient more in use, it would mean that all of us in the polling world and in research in the social sciences would definitely design our experiments and our investigations to try to calculate such a predictance coefficient. Then any definite technique we were in controversy about, we would check up on by its predictance coefficient. If the area sampling method or the quota sampling method or any other is in controversy, let us compute the predictance coefficient for each method. Whichever method gives the highest predictance coefficient would be the best scientific method in that situation. If we did that, it would take a lot of the controversy out of the "area *versus* quota" issue and out of various other issues. We wouldn't argue about them; we'd appeal to controlled experiment; we'd have a definite technique for settling the argument; and that is the scientific method.

Now, going further than having a definite technique as Stouffer was recommending, there is another implication that it seems to me we should follow out. This implication is that every study should involve two studies: a study of the predict*er* variable that we now do all the time, and along with it, designed as part of the same study, a later study of the predict*ed* variable, so that we can calculate predictance and improve our methods. We shouldn't be content with taking a poll and saying the situation is thus and so; so many people prefer Brand A and so many people prefer Brand B. We should go ahead and try to devise situations and measurements which will test the outcome of those predictions.

Why shouldn't we, for instance, in any opinion test, try to see whether there isn't some behavior that can later be measured in a second poll at some later period, and have the two polls designed with the same sampling and so forth to check each other? It means that every study then would involve two studies, and insofar as we do that, we'd really be getting on with the testing and improving of our methods by scientific methods themselves.

If you learn to measure the outcomes later, you have to start in at the beginning and decide what kinds of public behavior are worth measuring—what kinds of mass behavior are of sufficient social significance to invest the research funds that society has given to us (insofar as we have money in our possession—and we hope for more in the future). We don't want to spend money on trivial things that are perhaps very easily accessible; we have to spend it on things that are of social importance to predict. I think a good example of that sort of thing is what Stouffer's outfit did during the war, in predicting the behavior of some twenty million GI's, several years in advance, as to their use of the GI Bill of Rights. These predictions were for a kind of behavior on which there are no actuarial routines available, a new kind of behavior. Has that result been published yet, Sam? I believe there was a prediction about the eight per cent of the GI's that would use their Bill of Rights for education under certain conditions. Are you going to tell us something about it before these meetings are over?—I think it is one of the most striking cases of the social scientist's use of prediction.

MR. STOUFFER: The first two volumes will be out in April. Those two volumes are the first of four.

MR. DODD: There is a case of an attempt to predict the behavior of a large mass of the public. There was a definite measurement of the predicted variable—the actual behavior of people in going to school under the GI Bill of Rights after the war was checked against the earlier prediction. That is the kind of thing we should consciously set out to achieve wherever we can with our polling techniques.

Then I think Sam went on to talk about the definite techniques that are needed. There will always have to be specific methods for carrying out these principles and scientific dreams that we have. One of the techniques I would like to emphasize is *formulating hypotheses.* In our polling work we are still too content with merely exploring a situation, asking questions, probing people's opinions, trying to find out what the facts are, who feels this way and how much so, and not with setting up definite hypotheses to be tested.

Now, I mean by definite hypotheses, stated in advance, much more than the null hypothesis that "a significant number that is not zero feels this way." That is an essential hypothesis but it is often a rather trivial one, because you know in advance that the number is going to be something more than zero. If it is worth investigating at all, you have some knowledge that there is an opinion of this kind among the public. I mean hypotheses such as: "the correlation between this Opinion A and later Behavior B will be above .5," or "The correlation between those two will be raised to .7 by Technique X," or "If variable Y is taken into account (or, 'If this complex of five variables is taken into account') the correlation will be raised by Z points."

In a great majority of cases we simply don't know enough to express these hypotheses as definite correlations or as regression equations; we have only a vague idea of what variables would increase the correlation. It is a commentary on our ignorance or on the undeveloped state of our science that we can't state hypotheses exactly even within very broad limits. More exact statement of hypotheses is what we have to work for; we have to think more in those terms. So we set out to say, "This is the hypothesis: Factors A, B, C, and D are involved to such an extent," and we test it out to see whether they were actually involved to that extent. We will get on with formulating definite conditions under which given results can be expected, and we will be getting on with the fundamental job of all science—to determine that like events can be expected under like conditions—by defining just what are those "like conditions" and the "like events" and what their limits are.

Now, if we get on with trying to formulate written hypotheses in which we declare ourselves in print beforehand, and then check up on them later, it will mean that we will very much sharpen our knowledge of the conditions under which these variables vary as they are observed to do. And I think that the practice of formulating quantitative hypotheses—the better to check what factors we expect to find, or to check how good or poor our techniques are in hunting for them—would be one of the most healthy stimuli to good scientific work that we could possibly introduce into our profession.

Let me give you just one example of that kind of prediction from hypotheses. It is in the work that has been started by Zipf at Harvard and Stuart at Princeton and that some others have been doing. It is often called the "P P over D" hypothesis—namely, that "the interaction between any two communities will be proportional to the product of the populations of the communities, and inversely proportional to the intervening distance between them." That sort of hypothesis has many variations on it, including what Stuart called the "population potential," which is the population divided by the distance at which its effect is felt. It is a very important hypothesis, I believe. I shall describe it a bit more (with some evidence we have been getting on it in Washington) in a later session because in social affairs it is practically equivalent to the law of gravity. In fact, it is the same formula. You can say that one special form of this formula covers physical gravity; another, with an appropriate shift in your definition of units, covers interaction between human groups. This formula can be set up as a definite hypothesis, for polls to test as we have done.

Consider any kind of social interaction, whether it is intermarrying between groups, whether it is going to college between colleges in different states, whether it is newspaper notices of things happening in different cities, whether it is bus, train, or airplane travel between cities, telephone service between cities, or any other kind of inter-human action. When observed between human groups such as communities, in pairs—and take all possible pairs—that amount of interacting will be proportional to a certain set of seven factors that can be very objectively measured in advance. You might call these factors "dimensions." They are such things as the two populations involved (which can be counted well ahead of time), the intervening distance between the two, the amount of time or length of period in which that interacting is observed, the time of unit interacting, and two other "specific" coefficients that define the cultural "level" of those particular populations. These specific coefficients may split up into subfactors such as age or sex or income if they are correlated with the particular kind of interacting.

With a hypothesis that interacting is proportional to some set of given factors of that kind, you can go on and set up a situation to test that hypothesis. You can get plenty of kinds of interaction. In our polls we are all dealing all the time with human interactions, with people's opinions about each other, or things of that kind. It becomes then a test of our skill to isolate the different factors progressively and measure the amount of agreement between the eventual facts and the prediction by this formula of seven factors. We have been able to do that in one or two instances, and have come out with some very striking agreements between prediction and theory (as my paper at a later session will show).

This "interactance" hypothesis is a statement in terms of factors that are measurable ahead of time as predictors, predicting the number of interactions of two groups. These interactions can be observed independently and can be easily used as a check. This is a very fundamental hypothesis for the social sciences as it is a sort of law of social gravity. It means we will be able to predict increasingly the amount of interacting, whether the interacting is competitive or cooperative. It is a fundamental statement of the amount of human interacting that is to be expected under specified conditions. It may become one of the most basic laws we can expect to arrive at in the field of human relations. And this hypothesis is easily tested by polls. By going in and observing these things, we have the tools with which to test such hypotheses increasingly and to get on with the business of developing scientific laws or regularities in human relations.

There are a good many other points in Stouffer's presentation that might bear discussion, but I think probably the discussion from the floor might be best to bring out the ones the group here is particularly interested in. The information streams that he pointed out as contributing to the scientific development might, I think, be amplified. Some of us would like to emphasize some of those even more and perhaps add to the list of them. I think it might be best to let the discussion take its course.

MR. DAVIS: Our next discussant is Mr. Clyde W. Hart, Director of the National Opinion Research Center of Chicago. He was formerly a Professor in our Sociology Department here. With no more introduction than that, if you will feel free just to talk quite informally and extemporaneously as it were, I present Mr. Hart.

MR. HART: I just want to mention three or four things that have interested me for a long time, but particularly since I have been devoting practically full time to research in the public opinion field.

The first thing needed by way of basic social scientific research is research on substantive problems of attitude and opinion. There can be no doubt that we have made long strides during the last two decades in the development of method and technique, both on the theoretical level and on the level of application. I don't think we have made corresponding strides in understanding the phenomena in which the student of attitude and public opinion is supposedly interested.

The emphasis on method and technique is not wholly unfortunate. Perhaps the excessive—or I won't say "excessive"—the very large concentration on problems of method and technique has, on the whole, been good. It has brought sharp and general criticism to bear upon the design of research problems and upon the methods and procedures employed, so that we are now in a position, I think now, to do much more effectively whatever we wish to do in the study of substantive problems.

However, at Williamstown at the second conference of professionals in the field of public opinion research, there was one session devoted to substantive problems. As I sat in the audience listening to a panel and to the general, and sometimes heated, argument from the floor, it struck me that not a single idea was voiced that could not be documented to some well-known publication at least twenty-five years old. Most of them could be documented to Walter Lippmann's little essay on public opinion which came out in the early twenties. There was little or no evidence of any marked growth in our understanding of the processes of opinion and attitude formation, in any generic sense, during the intervening years.

Those of us who are actively engaged in what is called opinion research are culpable and are likely to be more culpable if we don't begin to use presently available tools in an effort to solve some of the pressing problems in social psychology, sociology, economics, political science, history and so on.

This kind of research, fortunately, is now developing. I know of at least ten or a dozen significant studies now being undertaken that take the tools of the systematic sample survey and other methodological devices and apply them to substantive problems in a systematic and determined way. Just by way of illustration, I may mention the studies that are being undertaken under the direction of the joint SSRC-NRC Committee on the study of attitudes, opinion, and consumer wants, the committee under the chairmanship of Sam Stouffer. While the grants approved by the committee were primarily for the study of methodological problems, in all of them a great deal is being turned up that has highly significant substantive implications. In the long run, I think, the contributions these studies make will be of a substantive rather than of a technical or methodological character.

We have a study, just beginning at the present time, which I might merely mention as another illustration of the sort of thing I have in mind. It is a study of the relation of businessmen's expectations to the decisions they make and the actions they take. It is a study, really, of the relation of the psychological to the purely economic factors in determining the level of economic activity. In the course of the study we will test some of the hypotheses derivable from economic theory that seem to be fairly well substantiated on the *a priori* level, as well as some hypotheses from psychology, social psychology, and sociology. More work of this kind is needed.

I think one of the most valuable contributions made by the American Institute of Public Opinion (the "Gallup Poll") has been the continuing studies, now with international cooperation from all the Gallup Institutes, bearing upon some important substantive problem. Happiness is one such illustration, but there are dozens that could be drawn from the work of the American Institute—notwithstanding the fact that the Institute, since it serves primarily a journalistic clientele, has naturally to put a good bit of emphasis upon the timeliness or the general reader interest of any subject that it undertakes.

One thing responsible to some extent for the lack of substantive contributions growing out of our work is the fact that nearly all of us have been concerned with *projects* rather than with *programs*. We have an idea; we select a sample of whatever kind or character; we go out and do an interviewing job, supplemented perhaps by some exploratory observational work and an analysis of documentary sources; we analyze the data; we derive all sorts of fairly precise measurements, including measurements of the relations, in this historic case, between variables, usually fairly crudely defined variables; and we publish the results. We then call it a day and turn our attention to something else. Anybody who knows anything about science knows that science grows not so much by what it learns definitively in any particular undertaking as by the new problems that it turns up.

I have searched the literature of attitude and opinion research for instances in which a study has led to substantial refinement of the conceptions of the variables that were involved in its initial design, to more precise definition of the universe of instances that need to be sampled, and to the formulation of new hypotheses in terms of which subsequent studies were undertaken; I have found relatively few. Studies are nearly always discrete projects. We need more research *programs* in which each project is merely an incident which leads to refinement of prior hypotheses, to development of new hypotheses, and to suggestion of new types of sample surveys or experiments. Only such *programs* of research will contribute to an accumulating fund of substantive knowledge of the scientific sort.

Just one other point. I would like to underscore what Mr. Dodd said about research that proceeds on the basis of a previously formulated hypothesis and to suggest that it is lacking in the substantive realm even more than in the methodological realm. Too much of our research, as he has indicated, has been rankly empirical, just exploratory, even though we were using relatively refined methods of exploration. We haven't been particularly ingenious in setting up hypotheses that we want to test. Consequently, in a great many of our studies we haven't known precisely what we were about.

But in this connection I would like to mention just one additional fact, Dodd: so frequently the hypotheses that we do work with, we test in terms of variables that are very crudely defined. Look through the reports on surveys that have been done and see how many of them get beyond correlations that run in such crude terms as socio-economic status, age, place of residence, sex, and so on—all, strictly speaking, common-sense categories but far from the precise variables with which science should be working.

Quite frequently people not directly engaged in attitude or opinion research criticize those of us who are. They say we have no theoretical framework, or if we do have one, it's wrong. We are accused of holding that public opinion is just the opinions of so many millions of individuals added together. We have no conception of an *organic* public opinion. Our samples are always samples of discrete individuals in a population; they are not samples of a public. We don't know any method for sampling a public conceived as an organic social system. And these critics say that we always correlate the attitude or opinions being studied with the same crude variables whether we have any reason for thinking the correlate has a causal bearing or not.

Admitted. But sociologists and other social scientists have done practically nothing to contribute refined conceptions of the social variables in terms of which we should be setting up and testing hypotheses. Certainly the fault doesn't lie altogether on the doorstep of people like Dodd, me, Ted Gallup, and the rest of the pollsters and surveyors present. Instead of this purely destructive type of criticism, the social scientists could do a great service to the whole field of research by putting their ideas in workable terms so that those of us who have the opportunity to do some systematic empirical studies wouldn't have to invent everything for ourselves—or, if we don't have time to invent, work with the crude concepts that we have.

For example, nobody believes that "education" is a unitary category. The only way it can be measured is in some such terms as the year of school completed—as though schools were all alike, and as though the experience of completing so many grades produced a condition within every individual that was like that in every other individual. What the precise elements are in this omnibus educational category that are responsible for such differences as a correlation shows, we simply don't know, and certainly the educationalists and socio-psychologists aren't doing very much to help us find out. Here as elsewhere, the emphasis upon hypothesis and the quest for hypotheses more refined than the crude ones we are now working with, or that come to us from other disciplines, are of paramount importance.

MR. DAVIS: Now we have had a very excellent paper presented and two very good discussions of the topic, and the time has come for you on the floor to have at the thing yourselves. Who wants to raise a question, or make a comment?

MR. HAUSKNECHT: I'd like to take a leaf out of the notebook, Stouffer's notebook. He has remarked on many occasions that science progresses by getting at the crevices between sciences. That is a standard principle, and it is the crevices between sciences here which I think are of some import. I think there ought to be a theme song for this conference, and the theme song is sort of a combination of what Stuart Dodd said and what Sam Stouffer said, and applies to what Clyde Hart said. Now that theme song, starting with the comment of the last speaker—Clyde Hart—would be, "We haven't got any real variables in sociology." Well, it's not alone embarrassing not to have any. In fact, there aren't any real variables anywhere. That is true of the physicist as well as anybody else. That isn't embarrassing. It's simply so. So the real variable is something we create, not necessarily one that exists. The difficulty there is not that there aren't any real variables at all, maybe, but that we don't have a very good method of specifying an error, *any* kind of an error, about our measurement of an attitude. Now, we have sampling error, which is all based on probability; we don't have any kind of a sampling error which is based on attitude; we write a report, plus or minus two percentage points of error. We have a frequency of attitude, and that is all. We count them. We may be wrong—we may be right. We simply count them. This is basic social research. One of the bases in social research is a concept, it seems to me, a concept requiring that a range of error be put around the measurement of an attitude. That is a notion, and it may not apply. Perhaps you have two systems of thinking. You have logic or mathematical logic, that is *a priori* as Sam talks about—the pipe smoke curling up—then you have the experimental notion. Then you may need another one that doesn't exist at the moment, perhaps a sociologic notion, but it seems to me that until you have that kind of sampling error for measuring an attitude you are reduced to the prediction system.

Now, some place there ought to be a field of applied research with respect to the measurement of attitudes and opinion, some approach that eliminates error. You use an indirect approach, after some spurious attitude, you use a scale that prevents you from using too small a number of samples of the human universe and mind. All those things are in one fashion or another short of the mark. None of them go clear to the point of providing an estimate of the sampling error of measuring an attitude. Now that is a social science research tool, and who is going to do it?

MR. DAVIS: Anybody ready to volunteer to do it?

MR. DODD: I think that is very necessary. I wonder if we aren't getting one partial answer to it in developing, in addition to theories of population sampling that have reached a rather high point of development, theories of sampling universes of attitudes within a person's mind or in a public's mind. This type of sampling might be developed a lot further and get on with very much the sort of thing you are after.

To be definite, let us define an attitude (as Guttman does) as being the responses to all possible questions in one field—say it is the field of anti-Negro attitudes or something of that kind. To take as a person's true attitude his responses to whichever of the questions we happen to pick out arbitrarily for a questionnaire is simply a rough approximation. If we define an attitude this way, we would have an operational procedure for testing it—namely, to get hundreds of such questions on statements collected from all possible minds that knew anything about that field and then test their intercorrelations and develop techniques for selecting a representative sample of statements from that universe of statements.

Of course, this would involve present sampling theory, but a lot more, because present sampling theory is based upon the assumption that the elements sampled are independent of each other, whereas these statements of attitude are all highly correlated and are not independent of each other. So formulas which involve the intercorrelations of the sampled statements would have to be developed. One result would be that we would come out with some smaller number of statements. By combining sampling theory and intercorrelation, we would come out with a smaller number of statements that we could, with a certain probability, say represented that universe of statements—namely, that attitude. And isn't that the way we are eventually going to get on with measuring all error, by analyzing out separately the attitudinal-sampling error, the population-sampling error, the interviewer-bias error, and so on for all the errors involved in polling, and later synthesizing them into a total error? To start with the total error seems to me the wrong end. We have to start by building up the measurement of each component error and then go on to synthesize them.

MR. LENTZ: Between attitude and measurement in two directions, or two fields—the field of public opinion, and the field of individual prediction. In prediction of individual behavior in our inventories for vocational guidance purposes, and that sort of thing, we have certified standard techniques, and one of them bears very much on what Hausknecht and Dodd have been saying. The technique is not to ask an individual one question and determine if Johnnie will be a candlestick maker instead of a lawyer. We insist on a sample, a considerable sample, and when we test the reliability of the instrument we never test the instrument, at least by measuring the test of only one item. If we want to know if the test is reliable, we say, "Let's compare it with another adequate sample of opinions or interests of the particular individual." It seems to me that in opinion and attitude research we have very little of that. The crevices between sciences, if acted upon, would give a greater margin, perhaps, between individual attitude measurement in terms of techniques, reliability and what-not in that field. This is the problem of real science in public opinion research.

To be more specific about it, we have had studies of individuals where we'd ask each individual three thousand questions—it is possible to do that—and I don't think there is any evidence to affect any breakdown in the validity of the responses under those circumstances when they are conducted.

It seems to me we have then a totally additional, a tremendously additional, dimension to the process of attitude study when we come to measure individuals. We ask each individual quite an array of questions; a hundred questions is not unusual at all in an individual attitude measurement and individual behavior prediction. When we attempt to measure the public, why couldn't we ask each individual as many as a thousand questions, or as a national average, three thousand persons, which we think is necessary for a valid sample of the population? Then why couldn't we add three thousand questions of a valid sample, psychologically? In other words, the concept as I see it is adding this matter of psychological samplings and the errors of psychological samplings to which Hausknecht refers, to the error of prediction in population sample. I suppose somebody will say, "We ain't got the dough or the resources to ask three thousand people three thousand questions."

MR. DAVIS: The speaker was Theodore F. Lentz, Washington University, and since I can't do that well in identifying everybody, please, if you will, give your name for the convenience of the stenotypist and the rest of us.

MR. HART: Mr. Chairman, I'd like to question Ted on one implication of what he said, that this kind of technique was not used in opinion research. Don't you think that the difference is not in the fact that the multiple-question approach is not used, but in the fact that we don't use it with nearly the sophistication with which it has been used in individual attitude studies. We test in advance the relevance of the items we want to include in a battery of questions or in an integrated questionnaire and consequently it isn't used—we don't have any sort of standardized list of questions. I think that, in part, is due to the fact that each study we do is an independent study—we are interested in the distribution of individual opinions in some historic public at some historic time with respect to some historic issue, and attitudes have gone a little farther than that. We have some abstract definitions, and consequently more work has been done in the selection and standardization of the interrelated items. Some of the kinds of things that Stuart Dodd talked about have been done in these attitude studies but I think we are getting more sophisticated about it in some of the scaling studies that are going on at the present time.

MR. DAVIS: Who else wishes to comment on this or related items? Mr. Guffy had some ideas along this line a long time ago in his story of the three blind men and the elephant. We are anxious to get more ways of finding out about the elephant than just one.

MR. DODD: On this whole question of basic research and just what we ought to do to develop it further, there are two points I'd like to pass on to the group here. In the questionnaires and polls that we put to the public there are certain standard kinds of questions that we ask which make a pattern like Gallup's "quintamensional design." This quintamensional design has five kinds of questions, and I think they should often be supplemented by two further kinds of questions.

These five kinds of questions are: (1) *information* questions that screen out the people who are informed and uninformed so we can classify their opinions separately; (2) *open-end* questions that draw the respondent out; (3) *closed-end* questions that present the specific alternatives; (4) any *reason-why* question which gets at the causes as far as they are conscious and can be stated by the respondent; and (5) *intensity* questions that ask how strongly the respondents feel.

Now, in addition to those five sorts of questions I think there are two other sorts of questions that should be added. The sixth type is connectedness or *membership* questions. What connection has the respondent with this question? What personal experience of his is connected to it? Is he a member of some group whose membership is correlated with the particular issue at stake? We ask this membership type of question in a crude way when we get his age or sex, economic or educational class, but we can go very much further with that question in searching out the connectedness of the respondent to the issue at stake. These connections, or memberships in relevant groups, may help predict his later behavior.

And then there is a seventh type of question which it seems to me should be a part of the standard pattern; it is a question on *activity* of the respondent. What has he done on this issue? What has been his behavior connected with this issue in the past? For instance, if you are trying to predict voting behavior, obviously his relevant acts are such things as: Has he registered? Has he voted in the past? Has he joined any party? Has he made any speeches? Has he declared himself in public, worn a button, asserted to his friends how he is going to vote? Has he taken any public stand? What actions has he taken that indicate both the strength of his feeling and the likelihood that he will behave later as he says he intends to. If we measure the past actions of the respondent relative to that question, we will be improving our set of predicter variables, the probability of predicting how he is likely to behave in the future.

I think other sorts of questions could be added to that quintamensional pattern but at least these two, the respondent's relevant *memberships* and *activity* could be made pretty much standard in our thinking.

MR. HART: I'd like to ask whether in using "projective techniques" on a mass scale we will get more valid and reliable answers.

Mr. Dodd: The question is whether we see a possibility of using projective techniques of psychologists on a mass scale in polling to increase our prediction. It is a grand field for research. Certainly, the projective techniques can be adapted to mass use. A poll interviewer can ask what the respondent sees in a queer-shaped ink blot, etc., just as in a psychological laboratory. It has been done on a small scale, and there is no reason why people's interpretations, and various other things of that kind, can't be done with interviewers on a mass sample just as well as in a laboratory with a single subject. The projective techniques, with proper adaptations, can be used, but their interpretation is still unstandardized. Whether they will be fruitful is a question for research to answer. The degree of promise they hold in individual investigations in laboratories seems to me to justify their exploration on a mass scale in polling. I should very much like to see projective techniques tried out in polls under controlled conditions and to find out just what there is in them, whether they do actually increase our ability to predict later behavior.

(Meeting adjourned.)

3

COOPERATIVE RESEARCH
IN THE SOCIAL SCIENCES

Kenneth W. Spence, Presiding
Samuel A. Stouffer
Robert R. Sears
Walter A. Shewhart

MR. SPENCE: This being the first time that I have ever been cast in the role of a luncheon chairman, I thought I should inquire from colleagues and friends just what one was supposed to do in such a circumstance. And after a few helter-skelter questions, it didn't seem that I was getting anything consistent, and, desiring to get the best answer possible, I naturally thought of using the technique of polling. So I worked up a rather systematic poll questionnaire and sent it around to my colleagues and after getting the results in and tabulating the data, I obtained this answer to the question: Should I tell a funny story or not? The results were as follows: 49% for telling a story, 2% against, and 49% undecided. The pollsters among you will be very interested in these results and will probably understand the reasons why I made the decision not to tell a story (*laughter*). Naturally the events of last November made me very hesitant as to how the undecided 49% felt about the matter.

The topic for discussion is "Cooperative Research in the Social Sciences," and instead of the announced single speaker we are going to have three. Naturally this will reduce the amount of time that each speaker will talk. The first speaker will be Professor Samuel Stouffer whom most of you—I think all of you—heard this morning, and whom I need not say anything more except to mention that he is at the present time Director of the Laboratory of Social Relations at Harvard University, a rather unique organization in academic environment in that it consists of cooperative researchers. It has one group of social anthropologists, a second group of sociologists, and I understand as a third component, the more sociable members of a department of psychology who decided that as their retrospective colleagues never communed with anyone but themselves, they might just as well move over to the Department of Social Relations.

MR. STOUFFER: The chairman suppressed some facts about the poll which I think I should report to you from his notes here. It seems that yesterday he took a poll on how long, if there were three speakers, the first speaker (who was to be myself) should be permitted to talk, and the median limit according to the vote here was twelve minutes. He took another poll after the meeting this morning and the median length of time they suggested that I talk is eight minutes (*laughter*). I shall try to keep, Mr. Chairman, within the time limit as required by public opinion.

I read in the paper a few days ago about how the Indiana Legislature rose for one minute of silent meditation in memory of Dr. George Gallup, and it struck me as a great tribute (*laughter*), particularly from the Indiana Legislature because it was this same Legislature, I believe, which something like a century ago is alleged to have passed a bill decreeing that pi should equal 3.14 in order to simplify arithmetical operation (*laughter*).

Now, that is one way to do research, by getting a legislature to decree methods of simplification, but I believe that we are supposed to talk this noon a little bit about some methods of cooperation which are likely to be more productive. And I'd like to talk briefly about two levels of cooperation.

One is the level of cooperation between the universities and the practitioners. Shortly after the war—largely, I may say, through the influence of Dr. Shewhart, who is with us today—the National Research Council and the Social Science Research Council appointed a joint committee consisting of several of the leading practitioners— Mr. Crossley, Mr. Gallup, and Mr. Roper—a number of academicians, and several people from government, in an effort to see what could be done in exploring the needs in this field. A little money was obtained from the Rockefeller Foundation about three years ago, and three rather excellent projects of cooperative research were undertaken; one in the field of sampling which has been under the general supervision of Mr. Frederick Stephan, at Princeton; another one on interviewing which has been under the general supervision of Mr. Clyde Hart at Chicago; and another one on panel techniques under the general supervision of Mr. Paul Lazarsfeld at Columbia. This research is progressing very well. There has been wonderful cooperation between the practitioners and the academicians in the pooling of experience, and the fruits of the work were seen in the excellent forecasts made by the polls last November!

The work, nevertheless, is going on and we have every confidence that there is an enormous opportunity for mutual education in the problems involved. I think it is rather shocking that the universities did not recognize as quickly as they might have the importance of this new tool of social research, whose development has so largely been a product of the blood, sweat, and tears of people who have practical problems to solve in the field. It was relatively late that the universities came along and began to see that sociology, social psychology, political science, and so on needed these methods if they were going to make any progress.

I well remember in the late nineteen-thirties I happened to be the editor of a series of monographs on the social effects of the depression. There were a dozen or thirteen or fourteen monographs written—Mr. Chapin and Mr. Queen here contributed to that series. I remember that Paul Lazarsfeld and I worked pretty hard on one of them, on *The Family*, and I remember how we sweated and sweated, taking census data and trying to infer very remotely from it some of the effects of the depression on the family. I think we did some rather clever work and it was hard work: we'd study marriage rates, etc., and we'd find a little shift of some sort, and then we'd try to figure out what it meant. We made a canvass of all the case studies that had been collected in a half dozen places over the country. Then we got these ideas together and managed to put up a monograph. Dr. Gallup was just starting his work at that time—too late for us because he hadn't started early enough. But if away back at the beginning of the depression the polling techniques had been available and could have been used, the information one study would have yielded in its contribution to sociology might have been greater than all of the stuff we collected by indirection in this single mono-graph on the family. The same would have applied to several other monographs.

That experience opened my eyes and I saw what we were missing. From then on I was convinced that we had here a tool, not only of vital importance for the development of democracy in America, not only of vital importance for making business run better or for giving the newspaper readers curiosa, but of vital importance in making —helping build—a social science.

Then during the war there were a lot of organizations that made use of these tools, and that brings me to the second level I wish to speak about in cooperation using social scientists of diverse backgrounds. It is very interesting that when these wartime organizations went to work they didn't usually ask, "Is this man a sociologist; is this man a political scientist; is this man a psychologist; what school of psychology does he belong to?"—that wasn't the kind of question asked at all. The question was, "Is this a bright fellow who is reasonably competent technically and who has some background of interest in this problem?" And granted that, then that was enough. In fact, we considered it kind of a liability if a person were too much of a conventional sociologist or too much of a conventional psychologist. As a result we brought together people with diverse backgrounds, people who were "rat psychologists," people whose training was primarily in psychoanalysis, people who had worked primarily in anthropology, people who had worked in sociology, and all worked on the same kind of a task. The result was that we had some very stormy times and I don't think we were as efficient as we might have been if we had all had exactly the same training. But I think the result was also that out of our work something new happened which could not have happened if we had all come up along the same groove.

I am very much impressed with the theory of inventions which my teacher Will Ogburn of the University of Chicago has propounded, and that is that an invention is not essentially a discovery of a new element but is rather a new combination of two well-known elements. He has illustrated that time and time again. Two things that are well-known by everybody are put together in some kind of a new combination. I am convinced that if we are going to make rapid progress in this field of ours, we might apply this hypothesis of Ogburn's in practice to this field. This method of bringing together two elements, well-known, into a new situation has more promise than any other single procedure for social research, and not only for research but also for training. In the institution where I am working now, we are trying an experiment of running a series of workshop seminars. We have one on learning, for instance, which is taught by three persons—two psychologists from different schools of thought and a social anthropologist. We have another seminar taught by a social anthropologist, a sociologist, and a clinical psychologist; we have another taught by a Ph.D. in mathematics, a statistician with training in sociology, a psychologist, and a sociologist, and all four are right in there pitching. The result is that there are all kinds of arguments in public, and all kinds of embarrassments in public, but I do think that students are becoming aware of the silliness of some of the compartmentalization which has been built up in the past.

This sort of thing is happening perhaps better at other schools, and it is a trend going on everywhere. A particular combination doesn't matter at all. I think some of the accidents by which combinations like this are made are historically interesting and quite irrelevant. Probably many of them happened because Professor A can't get along with Professor B, so they are reshuffled in some new way. It doesn't matter at all. The main point is—the thing I'd like to leave with you to keep in mind—is the Ogburnian hypothesis: "When you put two old things together, you get something new."

MR. SPENCE: Being a "rat psychologist," I have finally found out just how I came to be the presiding chairman at a talk on cooperative research in the social sciences. The second speaker will be Dr. Robert Sears, Director of the Child Welfare Research Station here at Iowa. Dr. Sears is a social psychologist, prior to his becoming a child psychologist, and now he is about to combine the two by going to Harvard as a child psychologist and also a member of the Department of Social Relations.

MR. SEARS: I started my graduate work in 1929 at Yale, in the Department of Psychology, under the apprehension that I would learn mainly psychology. But this was the time when Yale was starting the Institute of Human Relations. I soon became involved in that program, and for twenty years now I have been carrying on cooperative research in one form or another. I therefore can speak about this topic with some knowledge and a great deal of conviction.

I frequently find myself speaking publicly and with great fervor for cooperative science. On this occasion Professor Stouffer has done that so effectively that I am going to express some of the skepticism that I sometimes feel, but which most of us rarely express, and make a cautionary comment or two about cooperative science.

I don't know how many of you have ever tried to write a book with another person, or if you have, how many of you have tried to write a book with seven other people. I did. It was an experience. Although all of us are alive today, there are scars here and there in our psyches, if not in our epidermi.

MR. STOUFFER: Was the subject of that book "Frustration"?

MR. SEARS: The subject of that book was "Frustration." It is a very difficult thing to do cooperative research, and if we are to support such difficult enterprises, I think we ought to be perfectly clear as to just why. Professor Stouffer has said that you can put two old things together and get a new one. That's fine. The question is, What is this new one you get? Is it something someone really wants?

Cooperative research is sometimes the only way to get results. Therefore we say it is a "good thing"; it has the symbolic value of "goodness" about it. But I am afraid that too often we develop a term like "cooperative research" as a symbol, and then, finding the symbol good, we forget what it stands for.

There are examples of this in the field of child development. Back in 1920 the field of child development was started by a group of enthusiastic people who were drawn from different sciences, some nutritionists, quite a number of pediatricians, a few psychologists, a very few sociologists, and perhaps not more than one or two anthropologists.

These people were convinced that it was necessary to create a science around the developmental process itself. Over a period of some years, to the mid-thirties, child development as a field stuck pretty much to its last. Some of the work was of a cooperative nature; it went across the boundary lines of disciplines, and it went across for reasonably genuine reasons. Then the notion of cooperation began to be symbolic, and interdisciplinary research became a goal in itself even when there weren't any problems that demanded it. A rather substantial percentage of interdisciplinary papers in the technical literature of child development really have little excuse for being. Too often, two people have written two sections of a paper, and instead of putting a separate title and author on each section, one title and both names have been placed at the beginning of the whole thing.

Cooperative research has an excuse for being only when there is a research problem that requires it. If there isn't a problem there is no more reason for doing cooperative research than there is for doing any other kind of research. A man wrote me recently that his university was planning to set up a longitudinal child study program in order to have research facilities available for the theses of doctors' and masters' candidates. He asked, "What is the minimum number of tests and measurements that should be used in such a study?" The only answer I could reasonably give, of course, was that *zero* is the maximum number of tests that should be used unless one knows why he is using them. There is no point in carrying out so-called research procedures unless there is a specific problem to be solved. The mere fact of the researchers' being multiple, or of interdisciplinary membership, has no special virtue.

Now there are points in social science where there is an honest-to-goodness legitimate reason for doing cooperative research. One person doesn't carry in his head enough information to suggest all the kinds of problems that need to be solved. I can give you an example from some things we are doing right now. This is a narrow area of research, but one in which I think it is demonstrable that we have a genuine need for the skills and talents of three kinds of people. One is the child psychologist, another the social anthropologist, and a third the social psychologist.

We are working on a group of problems that relate to the social development of young children. We are concerned in such behavior as aggression, dependency, competition, and status seeking. These are four motivational systems that develop in children no matter what kind of a society they live in, what the nature of their culture is, or what kind of children are involved. These motivational systems are inherent in the very fact of social living. Take competition, for example. A child can't grow up without experiencing the situation in which he has to compete with somebody else for an unshareable goal. That is true of every child who was ever born; therefore competition represents a universal motivational system that is bound to the process of growing up, no matter what the culture.

The social psychologist or the psychologist of learning knows very little except what he may pick up casually from his colleagues about the nature of culture structure or social structure. He knows little about such things as roles, or role playing, about the organization of groups, or the interrelations among members of groups. The result is that the psychologist alone can do little research on problems that have to do with the development of competition or aggression or dependency in the absence of specialists who not only have an intimate knowledge of the subject matter of sociology and social anthropology, but who also have the skills which are involved in measuring those variables characteristic of their fields or disciplines.

Well, cooperative or interdisciplinary research *can* be a good thing. If it couldn't, it would not have such high symbolic value. But let's do it because we *must,* and not because it is virtuous. There is no getting around the fact that it is painful. When you get an anthropologist and a sociologist and a psychologist and a psychoanalyst in the same room, it is wise to have it soundproofed during the first three years of their association with one another. Our academic structure, with its departmental lines, is not designed to train a person to think easily in terms of the framework of more than one discipline. Psychologists always think about individuals, no matter what you do to them, and sociologists always think about groups, no matter what you do to them; they try to talk each other's language, but so far, in my own experience, I have found that twenty years is not quite sufficient to create, in me at least, an easy transfer from one frame of reference to another.

MR. SPENCE: The third speaker will be introduced by Professor Stouffer.

MR. STOUFFER: Bob Sears said that after twenty years he was just beginning to appreciate here some of the difficulties involved in the kind of problem that we are discussing this noon. It happens that just about twenty years ago I first heard a lone voice crying in the wilderness who was talking the idea of the application of modern methods in mathematical statistics to the control of production in industry. I remember he came over to England at Karl Pearson's laboratory, and gave a series of lectures there which were met with a good deal of skepticism at the time. This idea of statisticians telling engineers anything, or being able to, was just a lot of nonsense. And later there were long years in between, years in which there was opposition and in which it was felt by people who had chronic jaundice—not acute jaundice—that this sort of idea just couldn't take.

Well, during the war, all over America there were hundreds—in fact, thousands—of people in our war industries who were statistically trained to operate these new ideas of mathematical control of inspection, production, and so on. I believe that in Chicago alone they had a professional society during the war of several hundred members, of engineers and statisticians, varieties of engineers and varieties of statisticians, sitting down together and discussing the kind of problems that were involved.

And I think it is very relevant today to have with us the man whose lengthened shadow is represented in that work, a man who is now concerned particularly with promoting, in the field of consumer standards and a number of fields relating to market research, the importance of the ideas that we are discussing at this meeting. It is a particular pleasure to introduce Dr. Walter A. Shewhart of the Bell Telephone Laboratories.

DR. SHEWHART: I wonder if Professor Sears ever had an engineer in that group, or a natural scientist? Because it has been my experience beginning thirty-odd years ago, as Professor Stouffer said, to find a great clash between the engineer and anyone who would consider himself interested in any of the social sciences. And at that time, statistics was considered, and is considered in some places yet, as a social science.

I think that it may be interesting just to state briefly how the prosaic problem of quality control really—if it is going to be solved—must have the cooperation not only of natural scientists but of the social scientists. What is now known popularly as the application of quality control deals primarily with the application of mathematical statistics in inspection and production, but this is only a part of the brand theory of quality control.

In studying the legal status of the standard of quality, it was necessary to go through the treatises on the theory of law. We found in doing so that the contributions of the European scholars and men like Roscoe Pound, Charles Evans Hughes, Brandeis, Cardozo, gave an important background for considering the fundamental status of a standard of quality. It so happened in that case that it was not simply a one-way exchange because the theory of control has, at least in the eyes of people like Dean Roscoe Pound, given a picture of a rational basis for law which has been lacking—at least he says it has been lacking—up to the present time. There was to be a book written on that subject just before the war, but the war intervened.

Another social science is economics. But that is only a part of the story because you cannot control anything unless you have a goal, and that goal is the satisfaction of human wants. We in the engineering field are only now beginning to appreciate many of the important problems to be solved in attaining that goal. In this connection such contributions of the social scientists as Ralph Barton Perry's *A General Theory of Value* have been very helpful.

As Sam Stouffer said a few minutes ago, it probably was somewhat at the insistence of some of us in engineering that we had a joint committee of the NRC and SSRC on polling public opinions, attitudes, and consumer wants. To get those two groups together required a lot of talking both to the social science people and to the natural science people. But it was felt necessary that something of that kind be done, so that there would be a body of people chosen from the different fields of the natural and social sciences to express a non-biased view on many mutual problems such as sampling involved in polling and in setting up consumer standards, should they come up later. I really think it very fortunate that we had that committee in connection with the study of the recent polls.

It was only about two months after it was agreed to set up that committee that both the American Standards Association and the American Society for Testing Materials decided to launch programs of consumer standards. But prior to that, as I talked with some of those who actually took the step, they did not know what was involved, and they said they didn't after we talked to them. And yet the times were such that engineers were being forced to think of consumer standards. But you cannot think of consumer standards without thinking of sampling, including design, experiment, psychophysical problems, and, for example, the studies that may even take you over to the field of brain waves, muscle potentials, and things of that kind in order to get back to objective measurements.

Hence, if we would look at the real problem of applied science, we start with the abstract—mathematical logic, and mathematics. A pure science, like physics, involves making use of certain physical measurements. As soon as science becomes applied, it takes in valuations. But valuation can be done only by the human machine. Finally, industrial production involves control, which means the setting of a goal, namely the satisfaction of human wants, and control within economic limits. Therefore, solving the problems of controlling the quality of manufactured products takes into account the contributions of many if not all social sciences, as well as every natural science.

It is a great privilege to have this opportunity of being here today and of meeting many that I haven't had the pleasure of meeting before. My own particular work at the present time is largely in connection with the study of new developments in measuring preferences in an objective way, which brings in psycho-physics and other kinds of studies that you people are talking about here, and that some of you have worked on—the ones that I have known, like Sam Stouffer here, George Gallup, Arch Crossley over on the polling side, and every one of the three subcommittees that Sam Stouffer mentioned under the NRC-SSRC Committee. Those people are contributing just the kind of things that we must have as engineers. But we, as engineers, are just beginning to wake up to the important contributions that are coming our way from the type of things you people are doing.

(Meeting adjourned.)

Part Two

APPLIED SOCIAL

SCIENCE

APPLIED SOCIAL SCIENCE

H. W. Saunders, Presiding

MR. SAUNDERS: It seems now to be appropriate and fitting to transfer our attention from what we have chosen to call "Basic Social Science Research" to "Applied Social Science." After all six speakers have presented their material, we will then throw the meeting open to questions and discussion from the floor.

We hope that as we put these two aspects side by side, basic social science and applied social science, and study their interconnections and interrelations, we shall be able to see the whole field in much better perspective. We assume that people who are working in the area which we have chosen to call applied social science are borrowing more or less heavily from the work of the people who are functioning in the other area of basic social science research. We hope that they are applying some of the theory as well as some of the methods that have been developed in the first area. But we also assume that this relationship is reciprocal. And we assume that the people who are working in the area of applied social science are making certain contributions to the growth of basic social science theory and are making contributions to the development and perfection of research methods in social science as a whole.

I think it is very fitting, then, that we open this afternoon's session by calling upon a person who has been working in the area of applied social science for a considerable period of time. He has pioneered in this area and therefore we feel that what he has to tell us about industry and marketing as an area of applied social science will be very beneficial and enlightening, and therefore, without further ado, because I know he needs no introduction, I am going to call upon Archibald Crossley, who will discuss industry and marketing as applied social science.

4

APPLYING THE SURVEY TOOL TO INDUSTRY IN TODAY'S MARKETS

Archibald M. Crossley

MR. CROSSLEY: The preliminary announcement that was sent out about this conference had in the middle of the cover, "How can we know what the people think?" I think that is still the password or watchword or theme of the conference. Well, last November I discovered a way. We carried on a poll, as you may know, and now I know what the people think (*laughter*).

After one of our polls, Mrs. Crossley and I were taking a trip to South America. We had had some pretty good success at that time with the poll results, and we were in a smoking room about to place a bet on the ship's run. (We had been written up in the ship's newspaper because one of the papers that carried our poll had a man present whose job it was to get publicity.) A man came up to me and, I thought with a certain amount of awe, he said, "Can you tell the ship's run just as well as you can tell what is going to happen in your poll?" I said, "Oh, yes." You can see I was right.

As a matter of actual fact, a man that is working for me has a great yen for horses. He came up to me a while ago and he said, "You know, if we study horses and find out everything we can about them, and put that on cards, and then just correlate and correlate and correlate, very soon we can find out which horse is going to win. What do you say we do that?" That was before the election. I have given up the idea now (*laughter*).

On January 26th the *Wall Street Journal* had this headline: "The Customers Have Turned Coy! Auto Buyers' Market Return Speeds Up. Dealers Blame Everything from Weather to Credit Curbs for Slump in Demand."

The second subhead is "Auto Men Rush to Salesmanship."

This is clearly something new on the horizon for an industry that hasn't had to pat a customer on the back for years. It is not so new for others. Ever since the war's end, the return of the buyers' market has been foreseen. Some are better prepared for it than others.

The return in 1949 has a particular significance. Last year industrial profits were high, this year they are the subject of attack. This year there are specters of higher taxes, labor demands, price ceilings, and price declines, continued high sales, merchandising and advertising costs. To the forefront of these come the costs of new competition for consumer favor—more aggressive selling, better cooperation with the dealer, perhaps redesign of the product for consumer favor, perhaps more advertising. The consumer has to be informed, and the consumer has to be impressed.

If all of these things add up to greater cost per sale, then industry has three choices:

(1) It can accept reduced profit.

(2) It can find a way to sell more.

(3) It can find a way to do its selling job more efficiently.

The ugly words "recession" and "depression" are on the people's lips, but America still has lots of money. Right now we are just being coy. Later, if we as customers are not catered to, our coyness may turn into resistance based upon actual inability to buy.

It is this consumer resistance which everyone is watching anxiously today. How far will it go? What form will it take?

To find out about it there are two courses open. One is to wait for statistics to accumulate and be released. The other is to make use of the sampling tool and to observe those facts in process of formation. It's pretty much like the choice between measuring the log-jam downstream *versus* checking the jam in its early stages upstream.

The *Magazine of Wall Street* says in the current issue: "The uneasiness of businessmen about recent trends in the economy is heightened by the absence of up-to-date business statistics. Most figures coming to hand apply to conditions that prevailed weeks back. The time lag tends to accentuate uncertainty, and may lead to greater psychological depression than warranted by actual conditions. We don't know today how far recessive trends have actually gone. We hear of rising unemployment, tumbling bank loans, price weaknesses, spreading buyers' markets, oversupply, price resistance. No one knows exactly what it means. The latest available FRB index is for November. It will take two months or more to learn what it was in January. Business is forced to mark time. Further price resistance *could* bring about a rather severe dislocation."

And a few days ago the *New York Times* said: "Some of the business statistics now coming through reflect the thinking and decisions made after the November elections. In striking contrast the news of the last week seems to offer an abrupt about-turn."

So, with statistical indices, where are we?

In this uncertainty the survey tool offers a means of very fast operation of repeatedly-proved reliability. We know that any lasting movements down or up must arise from a certain small number of factors. We know where those factors may be in operation. We know the points upstream where to look for the beginnings of the log-jams, and there are telegraph facilities not so far away with which to report what is happening. You don't have to wait long periods of time for census birth statistics to tell you how many baby carriages to make. A small number of doctors or hospitals can tell you all you want to know long before you have to buy the materials and hire the workmen.

Fundamentally, the survey tool is no different from methods used to select materials and to determine many processes of manufacture. Just as samples of materials are tested and processes are tested under typical conditions, so markets are examined under selected circumstances to show their characteristics. With the use of samples, accurate reports are obtained at high speed. Today they are used a great deal in industry for quality control and the maintenance of exact standards in the finished product.

In marketing the survey tool is about thirty-five to forty years old. It has spread widely in that time over many different types of uses. But it is still a long way from achieving its potentialities. We have seen the tool used successfully in measuring markets and their characteristics and in determining the best ways to reach those markets. To find ways to make more sales, it has had wide usage. To reduce the cost per sale, it has been applied only sporadically. To warn of the trend of coming events, its use has been extremely limited.

The fact that the tool has been used much more in certain ways than in others means simply that its other applications have not been considered. The same thing is happening with many products which are advertised for one purpose while other valuable uses are given little attention.

The need particularly exists in 1949 to apply the advantages of the survey tool to sales cost reduction and to fast reporting of log-jams while they are forming, as well as to the building of sales under the newly competitive conditions. This does not call for new tools but for new uses of those which have been amply tested. Measuring consumer resistance is an old story to most of us in marketing research. Operating at high speed in certain types of studies is nothing new. What we need to do is to apply speed reporting to known measurement techniques. For sales cost reduction we need some new tools, but mostly we need to interpret in dollar terms much of the type of information we have been accustomed to collect.

In simple terms, "buyers' market" means that now the buyer is once again beginning to dictate:

The price he will pay.
The product characteristics, quality, and service he will accept.
The place where he will buy.
The media, copy and sales talk to which he will pay attention.

The fact of this dictation does not necessarily mean, and must not be construed to mean, that the buyer dictates because of limitations of his pocketbook. That may be the fact today in some lines, and it is likely to be the fact in later stages. But today the dictation *could* mean only a buyers' strike or boycott, as, for example, a refusal to buy meat despite ability to pay for it. We haven't overnight lost a great part of the purchasing power with which to buy automobiles, houses, furs, etc. "Pricing out of the market" does not mean that bank accounts and wages collapse with the speed that has characterized the sudden drop of sales of some commodities. One look at television sales to middle living standard levels evidences that.

In the early stages of the buyers' market, we as consumers feel our power, back up, and say "no!" If we keep on saying "no" when we could say "yes," production declines and our "no" then stems from necessity. We are hardly very far advanced yet into the necessity-no stage. To prevent its onset American industry needs to cater to consumers, to find out and give them what they want while they can buy.

Log-jams are our danger-signs. If we find out about them downstream, we may be too late. If we wait for goods to pile up on the dealers' shelves, pass their story along to the jobber in declining orders and then to the manufacturer, or if in any other way we wait for evidence of consumer resistance to accumulate in statistics, we may be too late.

To tell the story of consumer resistance, much attention is being given today to retail inventories. They are not necessarily the expression of consumer attitudes, which will later accelerate or change the trend. But they are the expression of consumer buying actions. They show the first jamming of the logs, though not necessarily what is causing it. Retail outlets are being used more and more as the focal points for the collection of total statistics on consumption. To individual manufacturers they offer a source of very fast reporting of exactly what the public is buying and refusing to buy, what sales appeal is most successful, the extent of price resistance, the nature and effectiveness of competition week by week in today's markets, and many other things.

It is just as easy to report quickly, when conditions require, shifts in the relative buying power, the need, the buying desires and attitudes of any groups of consumers at selected locations. If, for example, there is reason to believe that buying attitudes may be changing quickly in certain areas due to sudden changes in local conditions or to the introduction of competitive products and advertising, shifts in the attitudes of people in those areas can be quickly tested and reported. In today's transitional market picture, such fast reporting will sometimes be desirable.

The many companies that have used marketing research know what it means competitively to cater to consumers. From experience they have learned that the consumer does not buy blindly but chooses what satisfies him best. In conditions of abnormally high purchasing power or of shortages, he will pay much more than a product is worth. But when shortages cease to exist and when buying ability is normal or less, he will buy for competitive price and value in many instances. Value to the consumer means not only intrinsic worth but the nearest approach to the exact kind of a product or service which fits his needs and desires, so far as he knows and so far as convenience permits.

Companies experienced with marketing research have learned its value competitively in almost every phase of the marketing processes. Many of them adapt every characteristic of the product and service to specifications known by careful testing to satisfy the consumer. Similarly, container styles and sizes are built to specifications. Consumer habits determine their distribution policies. Media are chosen only after consumer tests. And the many angles of sales and advertising appeal are based upon surveys to determine which are likely to be the most effective.

The millions of dollars which industry has spent in marketing research each year have paid off well in the competitive battle for the consumers' favor.

Research has contributed greatly also to the general development of total markets. It has located basic new uses for established products, whose original uses were approaching saturation. It has pointed the way toward multiple use per person or family—two or more radios, bathrooms, razors, more types of shoes per person, and so on. It has accelerated obsolescence and replacements—expanded the market for replacements of such articles as kitchen appliances, tires, radios, automobiles, furniture and floor coverings, etc., before the actual need is urgent.

Now marketing research is called on to widen its horizon, help industry go beyond the job of building gross volume, and attack the high cost of selling. This should be one of its greatest accomplishments. Today's selling dollar needs to be watched. Price resistance does not mix well with all the many attacks on profits—taxation, labor demands, transportation and warehousing costs, high advertising, sales and distribution costs, perhaps made higher to meet competition. Where costs cannot be reduced, they must be made to yield better results. How can the survey tool be of value to this end?

First, it can prevent unnecessary and unprofitable moves in the competitive battle. It can prevent unnecessary price cuts. It can prevent unnecessary expansion of lines and perhaps even reduce present lines. It can prevent unnecessary distribution costs, and perhaps reduce some present costs. It can seek out the product and container characteristics which will yield not only best sales results but best profit results.

Second, it can work toward stability of sales and cut down the costs of seasonal and other peak-and-valley operations.

Third, it can test every step of the marketing process to see that there is no better way to achieve the same volume at lower cost. This means comparative-effectiveness studies of each aspect of the sales program (staff, quotas, territories, appeals, etc.), of each aspect of distributor relations (merchandising, dealer sales training, and all the other factors), and of each aspect of the advertising program (media, copy and all the other factors).

This is not the place to go into detail on the specific applications of marketing research to selling cost. And even if it were, such detail would vary with the needs of individual manufacturers. Much of it will be handled purely by careful analysis of existing records—data from government and other public sources and data taken from files of the advertising and sales departments. Other material will have to be collected from distributors and consumers.

Today's need in industry is more than ever for factual research—the evaluation and interpretation of conditions as they exist at the time. We are not concerned with how people think they will act in the future. In the study of markets we are not particularly concerned with public opinion, except insofar as favorable or unfavorable reactions at the time may be considered to be opinion.

Industry today wants mostly to know for different segments of its market how well its products are known, how they are regarded competitively, and the comparative reactions caused by different promotion stimuli. Any projections that may be made into the future must take into account the way those stimuli may vary.

To do the job ahead well, marketing research calls upon its very successful past experience, gears to more flexible and faster operation, and now expands to the broader fields of evaluating promotion effectiveness.

5

MASS COMMUNICATION

Bernard Berelson

MR. SAUNDERS: Our next speaker is Dean of the Graduate Library School at the University of Chicago. At luncheon I overheard a remark by Mr. Ellsworth, who is Director of the Libraries at the State University of Iowa. He said that he believed that the librarian, the head librarian that is, on the university campus was probably the only university official who occupied a position that was completely administrative in character.

Now I assure you that Mr. Berelson, your next speaker, was not selected because of the fact that he occupied that position, especially not as an administrator, but rather as a person who has been associated with research in the social sciences. Some of you may recall that he was co-author of a work entitled "The People's Choice." He is qualified to discuss the area of applied social science with particular reference to *Mass Communication.*

MR. BERELSON: Discussion of the application of social science research to the field of mass communication could be carried on in any one of three ways. In the first place, one could deal with the practical application of the results of communication research in the operation of the media. This would involve a description of the ways in which such research has affected radio programming, or the content of certain kinds of propaganda, or the distribution of motion pictures, and so on. Certain contributions have been made by communication research, particularly in the commercial fields, to the operation of the mass media.

Or secondly, one could deal with the substantive contributions made by communication research to general social science literature. During the past decade or so, communications specialists have produced a series of generalizations which will have a place in the body of social science knowledge. As examples, one can cite propositions about the self-selection of communication exposure, the spiral of the reinforcing effects of communications upon social structure, the development of the control structure of the media, particular patterns of content emphasis in the media, and the relationship between the mass media on the one hand and small groups and personal conversation on the other.

Finally, one might deal with the application of social science methodology to the field of communication. One could indicate the extent to which the various methods and techniques of social science research have been applied in the field and suggest the kinds of methods which can be most appropriately applied to communication problems in the next few years. It is to this third area—and specifically the application of social science methods to problems in the audience and effect fields—that I shall address my remarks.[1]

There are three main areas of social science methodology: (1) the over-all formulation and design of social science studies; (2) the collection of social science data; and (3) the analysis of the data. In each of these three areas various social science techniques have been applied in the communication field, as this brief survey will try to indicate.

Formulation and Design

There are four general designs of social science studies which can be illustrated in the communication field. The first design involves *establishing relationships between crude communication data and various kinds of ecological data.* Just as the circulation and readership of magazines and newspapers used to be measured by ABC data, there have been studies on the composition of the audience and even studies attempting to get at the effect of communication materials which are based upon more or less elaborate statistical analyses of existing data. For example, one study of "who reads what" was done by correlating the gross circulation of various magazines in ninety cities with a whole battery of data referring to certain census-type characteristics of those cities.[2] By refining both the characteristics of the magazines and the characteristics of the

---

[1] Since I shall deal only with the audience and effect areas, I shall omit consideration of content analysis in this review. And since this is meant to be brief and general, I shall not go into the detailed techniques of audience measurement.

[2] Paul F. Lazarsfeld and Rowena Wyant, "Magazines in 90 Cities: Who Reads What?" *Public Opinion Quarterly, 1* (1937), 29-41.

cities, the authors secured some information to answer their original question. At about the same time, another study was done on the effects of Chicago newspapers upon elections in that city by correlating various kinds of election data (by wards) with newspaper circulation data, over a series of elections.[3] Such studies were quite rough since they were based upon large segments of the population within which there was a good deal of heterogeneity. With the development of the sample survey, allowing for the identification of personal characteristics and of communication behavior on the individual level, these gross ecological analyses have become largely outmoded for this purpose. Hence this first general design of social science study is now found only seldom in the communication field.

The second kind of design is the *case study* involving intensive analysis and documentation of the problems under investigation, usually in a relatively small number of cases. This method was applied in the communication field in the Payne Fund studies of the effects of motion pictures upon children. Long case histories centering upon the psychological function of the movies were secured from a group of children and young people.[4] More recently a variation of the case-study design was applied in an intensive analysis of the opinion determinants among a small group of men, with reference to their attitudes toward the USSR.[5] Because the case study provides a large body of information about a single subject, it is particularly appropriate in the communications field where many problems involve subtle and complex relationships. The more information one can secure on such problems, the better chance he has to establish sound relationships. Particularly, the case study makes it possible to trace communication effects over a period of time, through the career line of the subject. This is one research design which should be employed more frequently in the investigation of the effects of communications.

A third type is the *controlled experiment.* This is the traditional method of science in which an experimental group is subjected to a stimulus or experience which is withheld from a matched control group. Both groups are measured on the crucial variable before and

[3] Harold F. Gosnell, "Relation of the Press to Voting," in *Machine Politics: Chicago Model* (Chicago: University of Chicago Press, 1937).

[4] Herbert Blumer, *Movies and Conduct* (Macmillan, 1933).

[5] M. Brewster Smith, "The Personal Setting of Public Opinion," *Public Opinion Quarterly,* 11 (1948), 507-23.

after the introduction of the stimulus, and the residual differential is attributed to the action of the experimental stimulus. In the communication field there are many such studies of the laboratory (usually classroom) variety, e.g., studies in which an instructor uses a class of students to get at the effectiveness of a series of lectures or a set of propaganda materials. The literature is about as full of such studies conducted under artificial conditions and based upon dubious assumptions as it needs to be. However, the design itself is very valuable for communication research. One of the more notable experimental studies in the communication field was done as part of the Payne Fund series; the effects of motion pictures upon children's attitudes was carefully and systematically investigated, with a lasting effect measured months after the experimental situation.[6] Perhaps the most elaborate series of studies of this sort ever conducted is about to be published in the series "Studies in Social Psychology in World War II," reporting on the studies of the Research Branch of the Information and Education Division of the U. S. War Department.[7] These studies suggest that the experimental design is an extremely effective research instrument in the communication field, and much more work needs to be done with it.

The fourth research design is probably used in this field more frequently than all the others put together. It is the design of the *sample survey*. It is useful to distinguish two forms of the sample survey. The first is the cross-sectional poll, which is very useful in the field of audience measurement but which is able to contribute a good deal less to the field of response and effect.[8] That is, the cross-sectional poll is able to provide a fairly accurate picture of static or "frozen" communication behavior but it is less satisfactory as an instrument for getting at the dynamic quality of communication effectiveness. The second form has come to be known as the panel method, which involves repeated interviewing of the same respondents over a period of time. This method has most of the advantages of the cross-sectional poll (together with some disadvantages not found there) and, in addition, it has the important characteristic of fol-

[6] Ruth Peterson and L. L. Thurstone, *The Effect of Motion Pictures on the Social Attitudes of High School Children* (Edwards Brothers, 1932).

[7] C. I. Hovland, A. A. Lumsdaine, and F. O. Sheffield, *Experiments on Mass Communication* (Princeton University Press, 1949). Forthcoming.

[8] Leonard Cottrell and Sylvia Eberhart, *American Opinion on World Affairs in the Atomic Age* (Princeton University Press, 1948).

lowing the development of communication behavior and related variables through time. In a sense, the panel method can be considered an attempt to combine the better features of the cross-sectional poll and the case study. Among the examples of the use of this method in investigating the effects of communication upon opinion are the study of the formation of political opinion during the presidential campaign of 1940 [9] and the study of the development of political opinion among a group of college students during their undergraduate years.[10] If some of the major technical problems can be solved and particularly if the period of investigation can be lengthened, the panel method is another research design which will prove particularly useful in the communication field over the next years.

In summary, then, the statistical analysis of ecological and communication data is now pretty well outmoded in this field; the use of the sample survey is widespread and continuing; and the case study and controlled experiment need to be utilized more effectively in communication studies.

Methods of Data Collection

Just as there are various research designs in social science, so there are several ways of collecting data to test relevant hypotheses. The first method of data collection can be passed over quickly, since it is so widely used and so widely accepted within the communication field. It is, of course, the basic method of *interviewing*. The particular method of interviewing may vary from a relatively simple checklist schedule or questionnaire all the way to very intensive interviews lasting a good period of time. Special interviewing methods have been devised within the communication field in order to secure the most appropriate data. For example, the so-called focused interview has been developed in order to key the respondent's replies most effectively into the communication content itself,[11] and the so-called Program Analyzer and other mechanical devices have been developed in order to provide a running account of the

[9] Paul F. Lazarsfeld, Bernard Berelson, and Hazel Gaudet, *The People's Choice*, 2nd edition (Columbia University Press, 1948).

[10] Theodore M. Newcomb, *Personality and Social Change* (Dryden Press, 1943).

[11] Robert K. Merton and Patricia Kendall, "The Focussed Interview," *American Journal of Sociology, 51* (May, 1946), 541-57.

respondent's momentary response to a piece of communication material, synchronized with his exposure to it, as a basis for later interviewing.[12] There is hardly an audience or effect study in the communication field which has not utilized interviewing procedures to some extent, and most have used them to a large extent.

A second method of collecting data, which has been little used with this field and which probably has a limited utility, is the device of *participant or non-participant observation*. It is extremely awkward and expensive to observe communication behavior itself and it is difficult and even impossible to observe certain of the major related variables, like opinion and taste. Hence, there are relatively few examples in the field involving observation of communication situations or their outcomes. The observation method is particularly characteristic of the anthropologists, who have used it as a basis for describing the communication patterns of primitive as well as modern complex societies and in relating such patterns to the total cultures of which they are a part.[13] Or again, through observation, anthropologists have described the effect of the introduction of literacy upon the structure of a small primitive community.[14] Psychologists, too, have used this method, as for example, in observations of the patterns and consequences of interpersonal communication among children.[15] By and large, however, the value of this method of collecting communication data is probably quite limited.

A third method of securing data, which may be conveniently distinguished from traditional interviewing methods, is the psychological technique of *projective tests*. The two most prominent projective devices are the Rorschach and the TAT (Thematic Apperception Test). These tests provide the respondent with a highly ambiguous pictorial symbol which he then describes. What the respondent sees in the symbol forms the basis of what the psychologist sees in the respondent. Because of the time and expense involved in

[12] Tore Hollonquist and Edward A. Suchman, "Listening to the Listener," in *Radio Research, 1942-43*, edited by Paul F. Lazarsfeld and Frank Stanton (Duell, Sloan and Pearce, 1944).

[13] Margaret Mead, "Some Cultural Approaches to Communication Problems," pp. 9-26; and "A Case History in Cross-National Communications," pp. 209-30, in *The Communication of Ideas*, edited by Lyman Bryson (Harper, 1948).

[14] Robert Redfield, *Tepoztlan, a Mexican Village; A Study of Folk Life* (University of Chicago Press, 1930).

[15] Ronald Lippitt, "An Experimental Study of the Effect of Democratic and Authoritarian Group Atmospheres," *University of Iowa Studies in Child Welfare, 16* (1940), 43-195.

administering such tests and perhaps, too, because of the degree of skill and training required, such projective tests have not been widely used thus far in the communication field. There has been one study in which the "meaning" of daytime serials for their listeners was explored by means of the TAT device.[16] Because of the presumed capacity of such tests to tap relatively "deep" psychological characteristics of respondents which cannot be reached in a direct interview, they hold out a good deal of promise for effect and motivation studies in communication. Efforts are currently under way to adapt or modify such projective tests so that they can be applied to relatively large population samples by interviewers with normal training and under something like survey conditions.

Related to both interviewing and projective tests are the *clinical procedures* employed by depth psychology to secure intensive material on the respondent's personality structure. This method seems capable of providing useful insights and hypotheses on the psychological uses and functions of communication for the individual. And it seems a matter of some regret that systematic efforts to collect such hypotheses have not been made. Clinical procedures could undoubtedly be extremely valuable in the field of motivation and effect.

Finally, there has been a small amount—and as yet exploratory and not particularly fruitful—use of what might be called *psychophysiological methods* of collecting communication data. This method requires a mechanical recording of such measures as body temperature, skin conductance, heartbeat variability, body movement, and so on. Mechanisms have been developed by which such data can be secured in synchronization with the subject's exposure to communication materials, and thus the variations through time in such measures can be correlated with the content of the exposure. Studies exploring the "emotional" reaction of children to radio and motion pictures have been done by this method.[17] The adoption of such psycho-physiological methods was stimulated by the desire of objectivity and reliability in the measurement of emotional states. However, in the search for objectivity some investigators sacrificed

[16] W. L. Warner and William Henry, "The Radio Daytime Serial," *Genetic Psychology Monographs*, Vol. 37, no. 11, 1948.

[17] John J. DeBoer, *Emotional Responses of Children to Radio Drama* (University of Chicago dissertation, 1940).

R. R. Brock, "The Effect of Motion Pictures on Body Temperature," *Science*, *102* (1945), p. 259.

validity; that is, with this method there is still the problem of determining the extent to which such physiological variations are valid indicators of the emotional states they are taken to represent.

In studies of the audience to and the effects of communications, interviewing methods will undoubtedly remain the major device for the collection of relevant data. Participant or nonparticipant observation seems to be quite limited in its application to this field, and psycho-physiological measurement still needs to prove its utility. There is a need for greater use of clinical procedures and projective tests as the field moves into the more complicated and "deep" problems involved in the communication process.

Analysis of Data

The major method of analysis of communication data has been quantitative analysis. Such analysis ranges all the way from the use of simple frequency distributions to the application of quite sophisticated and refined statistical procedures. This is no place to go into the various techniques which are useful in this field. However, it may be appropriate to point out a kind of disparity between the training given students in this area and the actual use of the technical procedures of quantitative analysis. My guess is that a content analysis of communication research would show that there is a relatively insignificant use of highly refined statistical procedures and that for the most part such studies are reported in the form of cross-tabulations with perhaps one factor controlled. However, many students receive a much more elaborate form of statistical training in the graduate schools, which they do not have the occasion to employ later. It seems to me that there is an opportunity for the training agencies to instruct students in the intricacies of this more elementary form of quantitative analysis—which, though elementary, is by no means self-apparent.[18]

Finally—although this is not strictly a method of analysis—the relationship between analytic methods in this field and the construction of a body of social science knowledge must be mentioned. A good deal of analysis of communication materials is done on a descriptive and *a priori* basis. The analysis of various studies is done with relatively little relationship to a systematic framework of concepts and propositions, to the extent that that exists. All the more be-

[18] Hans Zeisel, *Say It With Figures* (Harper, 1947).

cause a communication theory is not now readily available, students in this field have a responsibility to formulate one (or several); yet most studies do not take the additional step at either the formulation or the analysis stage to relate the findings to general propositions of social science. For example, in a recent study of the effectiveness of one of Kate Smith's marathon bond drives, the author did not rest content with "explaining" on a superficial level why the drive was so successful, but for fuller understanding related the whole event to a general theory of American culture.[19] Here, then, is an empirical study on a communication problem which was made part and parcel of general theoretical propositions in the social sciences.

Next Developments

In summary then, it seems to me that there are five methodological directions in which communication research should go:

(1) We need more intensive studies of communication behavior, rather than additional extensive and relatively superficial investigations. This means greater use of the case study, projective tests, and clinical procedures in order to get at communication effects in a manner more sophisticated than the typical before-and-after study.

(2) We need more long-range studies. This means that we must keep respondents under investigation for a period of months and even years rather than a period of hours. The whole problem of the long-range effects of communication in determining the value frameworks in terms of which short-run decisions are made have simply not been attacked. Developmental studies of communication variables are needed.

(3) We need more experimental studies cast in real-life conditions. This means that researchers must be more ingenious and inventive in devising research models of this sort.

(4) We need to develop the inter-use of several methods at the same time. This means that the case study or the projective test should be used in connection with the techniques of the sample survey. The co-ordinated use of various designs and methods is needed to attack a full range of communication problems.

(5) We need to frame communication studies in such terms that

[19] Robert K. Merton, with the assistance of Marjorie Fiske and Alberta Curtis, *Mass Persuasion* (Harper, 1946).

they become relevant for the construction of a general theory of communication and society.

If the field of communication research can move in these directions over the next five to ten years, it will contribute more than its share to general social science and more than repay its indebtedness for the development of social science methods.

6

THE FUNCTION OF
PUBLIC OPINION ANALYSIS
IN THE FORMULATION OF
FOREIGN POLICY

Francis H. Russell

Mr. SAUNDERS: Our third speaker is a person who has something in common with the men associated with the public opinion polls. It seems that Mr. Crossley, Mr. Gallup, and Mr. Roper have been forced to take something of a ribbing since last November, but if my observations are correct, the Department of State of the United States government also takes something of a ribbing occasionally. However, that is not the main reason why the next speaker was invited to this conference. Rather it was because of the fact that his position puts him in such a relationship with the social sciences that he not only uses their contributions but he also, I think, has something very valuable to tell those persons who are perhaps a little more cloistered, should we say, in academic life.

I therefore take great pleasure in presenting Mr. Francis H. Russell, who is Director of the Office of Public Affairs of the Department of State of the United States government.

Mr. RUSSELL: During a round-table radio discussion the other evening, someone observed that in a democracy it is far more desirable to debate an issue without settling it than it is to settle an issue without debating it. In any event, the American people today are energetically debating issues of foreign policy and more than they realize, perhaps, helping to formulate foreign policy through their debates. I think it is also true that the policy makers in the government are in a better position than ever before to assess and give weight to public opinion in their efforts to find solutions to those problems.

The reasons for the current interest in foreign policy are obvious. Two world wars in a generation is one of them. Another is that the American people have come to recognize the importance of foreign affairs in their daily lives. We know that we are affected, directly and indirectly, by conditions abroad; that our employment, for instance, is bound up with the state of world affairs, as are the taxes we pay.

In 1925 only one bill in twenty-five that was enacted by Congress had any immediate bearing on our foreign relations. Most of those were of a relatively inconsequential nature. In the last Congress, one out of every seven of the enacted bills was related to foreign affairs, and many of them were of crucial importance. Congressional action not only reflects the requirements of our time, it usually reflects American public opinion.

How can opinion research help in relating public opinion to foreign policy formulation? To provide an answer we must obviously know how foreign policy is made. We must know the nature of the policy officer's thinking processes. What are the factors that are present in the mind of an officer who makes a foreign policy decision? A brief survey of the situation confronting such an officer may suggest to you, who are more experienced than I in survey planning, new projects and methods which could improve and sharpen the analyses which help shape our foreign policies.

In the first place, a foreign-policy question implies that there are conflicting considerations or factors which must be resolved. Without such a conflict there is no problem. If all of the considerations point in the same direction, no question arises. The task of the policy officer, therefore, is essentially one of making a decision on the relative weight to be given to the conflicting considerations that bear on his particular problem.

We may say to begin with that the task of the policy officer cannot be accomplished merely by taking a poll and acting in accordance with the results. He cannot abdicate his responsibility. The fact that it appears from a poll that 55 percent of the American people prefer one course of action and 45 percent prefer another is a very important consideration, but it is only one consideration. The American constitution provides for governmental action by representatives who are given authority to act. It does not provide for action on the basis of a polling of the American public, whether official or unofficial. The responsible officials must take action on the basis of all of the factors. What are these factors?

The factors that enter into almost any problem of foreign policy are two-fold: foreign and domestic. The *foreign factors* are obvious: the growth and spread of ideologies abroad which threaten the American way of life, goals and actions of foreign nations, foreign economic and political conditions, and a hundred other kinds of facts and developments beyond our borders that create problems in international relations and affect the solution of the problems.

The *domestic factors* are equally important. They include such *physical factors* as our military strength, the economic requirements of the American people, our industrial strength, the size and concentration of our national population, the extent of our skilled labor, our agricultural production, and so on.

No less important are the *domestic factors* which are *nonphysical:* various political beliefs, religious affiliations, nationality and racial differences, adherence to various organizations or movements, the attitudes of labor and management, different levels of education or economic position, for example.

It is impossible to understand, much less to formulate, any particular American foreign policy without analyzing the bearing of such elements as these on the issue in question. A country that differed from us in these respects would inevitably have a different foreign policy from ours.

Take a concrete case, the problems involved in planning the present Foreign Aid Program. When policy officers in the State Department began to deal with the problem of strengthening war-ravaged economies abroad, among the *foreign factors* with which they were required to deal were those relating to the kinds and amounts of aid needed to assure economic revival in various areas, balance-of-payments problems present and prospective, the effect on the program of the presence or absence of Eastern European countries, to what extent the program could be conducted inside the framework of the United Nations, and so on.

All these questions were intricate and delicate enough in themselves, but each also involved American public opinion, actual or potential. The role to be undertaken by the UN might affect the degree of support for the new program among the American people. If the Soviet Union were one of the countries in the program,

American popular attitudes toward it might be quite different than if it were not. American public opinion was important even in connection with such a technical matter as the kinds and amounts of aid to be provided, since the scale of the program and its impact on the taxpayer and on various economic interests might determine the response of important elements of the American public to the program as a whole.

When the policy officers turned to the *physical factors* in the United States which would affect the development of the foreign recovery program, they were up against such problems as available resources, the probable effect of large-scale shipments on the price-and-wage structure, and the effect on American national security. And American public opinion on these issues—quite apart from the economic or strategic facts—might also determine the fate of the plan. If Americans generally reached the conclusion that the recovery program would deplete our resources, precipitate runaway inflation, and impair our national defense, the program would be done for—whether or not these conclusions were correct.

In the third place, the policy officers working on the recovery program were faced with the importance of numerous *nonphysical factors* operating on the American scene. They knew that certain economic groups would be likely to support a foreign recovery program. Others could be counted on to oppose any plan to help foreigners at the taxpayers' expense. How numerous were each of these groups? Was the recovery program likely to become a partisan political issue? How would the college-educated, who supply much of America's civic leadership, respond? What would be labor's position?—the farmer's?

As you all know, a number of these questions were posed by the opinion survey organizations. The findings were of great assistance to policy officers.

Public opinion surveys are not the only means by which the State Department draws upon the American public for assistance in solving policy problems. Editorial and periodical comment is followed carefully. The Department makes an effort to keep in close contact with major national organizations. Nongovernment experts are frequently asked to consider a problem either as official or unofficial consultants. By these means the portion of the public which has given the greatest amount of attention to particular problems is able to have its considered views taken into account. Frequently the views of those who have given the greatest amount of attention to a problem differ substantially from those of a cross section of the public. The policy officer then has to balance these. The weight to be given to each will frequently depend upon the type of question involved.

(I have been referring to "the policy officer." In almost all important instances, of course, a number of officers will be involved— each, in view of his responsibilities, presenting various factors for consideration. Thus has grown up out of necessity the large number of committees for which Washington is well known.)

I have referred to some of the opinion surveys relating to the European Recovery Program. Most of these surveys were naturally taken subsequent to Secretary Marshall's suggestion of the program at Harvard in June, 1947; but it is clear that many of these issues had to be dealt with by policy officers prior to that time— that is, prior to the time when most Americans had given any specific thought to a long-term recovery program. This will frequently be the case in the development of American foreign policy. It means that much reliance has to be placed on survey results which indicate the changing moods and attitudes of the country. So we find helpful a continuous audit of the general mood of the people on such key attitudes as those toward the United Nations, toward Western Europe and toward the Soviet Union, toward international trade, toward the control of atomic energy.

We have often noted the utility of approaching an issue from different angles, of posing various types of questions in a particular field in order to make more sure that all the essential elements are incorporated in the final result. We appreciate not only the trends based upon repetition of the same question, but the variety which may be found in surveys by a number of different organizations.

A simple polling question usually cannot convey to a policy officer an adequate idea of the public's attitude even with respect to a comparatively concrete topic. To illustrate, suppose a hypothetical question would inquire whether people would favor or oppose a high tariff by the United States on goods coming from Iron Curtain countries and suppose we find that 55 percent of the American people are in favor of it, 35 percent are opposed, and 10 percent have no opinion. Do we conclude from this that a substantial majority of the American people are in favor of such a policy and that it should be immediately put into effect? Or do we go on to inquire how many of the American people know what a tariff is? Recent surveys indicate that only half of the American people have a clear idea of the nature of a tariff. Do we inquire how many people know the elements of this country's reciprocal-trade-agreement program and what the effect of such a reversal of this program would mean to the economy of this country and the general program of world economic recovery? Do we inquire how many people are aware of the relationship between the Tito regime in Yugoslavia and the Kremlin and what the possible effect of a lumping together of all countries behind the Iron Curtain might be?

While, therefore, it is important to know the general attitude of the country on a particular issue, we need to know much more than the specific percentages in order to evaluate the significance that should be given to them.

It is frequently as helpful to know about people's current ideas and expectations as it is to know their attitude preferences. What are the assumptions underlying their current attitudes? How are these attitudes interrelated? Fuller background material of this sort can give policy officers greater assurance that they have a fundamental understanding of the current attitudes of the American people.

Public opinion surveys should also be able to expand our knowledge of how opinion becomes public. Surveys can count the number of adherents on each side of the question—with due allowance for a margin of error. Can surveys tell us how many of these adherents have been won by the slogans or appeals of competing interest groups, or foreign propaganda organizations? There is room for many surveys to illuminate the processes of leadership and of education in foreign affairs—studies on a local, regional, group, or national basis.

Obviously a particular foreign policy action that may be favored by the American people may be impossible to carry out in view of the domestic physical factors in the case or in view of considerations arising outside the United States. Such a conflict between popular preference and practical possibilities is, of course, unfortunate. On the one hand, it creates a lack of confidence in the soundness of our foreign policy on the part of the American people, and on the other hand, it undermines the effectiveness of the policy that is followed. The State Department is striving to do all that it can to make sure that the American people have as much as possible of essential information so that the number of such conflicts may be minimized.

Summing this up, it seems to me that as a general matter, public opinion analysis can be helpful to those who are faced with the necessity of formulating particular elements of our foreign policy in the following ways:

In the first place, public opinion analysis can show the general mood or attitude of the country toward a particular line of policy. Such attitudes are not, under our form of government, determinative but they are a most important factor and frequently fix the limitations within which policy can be formulated.

Secondly, in addition to knowing the general attitude of the public, it is important to know the extent and intensity of the views of the contending interest groups that are involved, and also to know the intensity of opinions of non-self-interested groups.

Thirdly, it is important to know the extent and the accuracy of public information concerning the elements of the problem. This makes possible an assessment of the weight that should be attached to the views that are held. It may also be helpful in providing a guide to areas in which the government has failed in making available adequate information where that information is exclusively or especially in its possession.

The publication and discussion of opinion studies also make a significant contribution to the people's understanding of the foreign policy alternatives which are available to them. Thus, in a way, they steadily enable people to provide more intelligent answers to the questions.

Our national policies should reflect the will of the people, a will that is not distorted by false propaganda or slogans, that is based upon a solid knowledge of all of the facts, that has taken into account all factors and considerations, and has resulted from open and active debate so that all points of view have been thoroughly aired and discussed. Where a clear public opinion such as this does not exist, those who are charged with formulating policies can usefully sharpen their own thinking against the contending points of view that are held.

The United States government is engaged in an effort to stimulate interest and debate in foreign affairs and to learn what opinions

Americans hold on the important issues confronting us. But this is only part of an effort which must be larger in the interest of intelligent self-government. The contributions of individuals and organizations engaged in opinion analysis have been important and will undoubtedly be increasingly important as such studies are expanded and are based on a keener appreciation of the foreign policy officer's task.

7

CENSUS AND
GOVERNMENT

Morris H. Hansen

MR. SAUNDERS: We regret very much that Philip M. Hauser was
unable to be present. He was to have been our next scheduled
speaker. Though he is now back in academic life, the connections he
established as Deputy Director of the Bureau of Census seem still
to be in existence and fairly strong. Just a few days ago he informed us that the American representative who was to attend the
conference in Rio de Janeiro on planning the Census of the Ameri-
cas for 1950 was ill and consequently the Bureau asked him to serve
in that capacity. He felt that in the circumstances, he could not re-
fuse the request even though he had a prior commitment at this conference. We asked him for a recommendation as to a possible substitute, and we were very fortunate in obtaining one capable of
filling the need. Therefore I am very happy to present Morris H.
Hansen, Assistant Statistician for the Bureau of the Census, who is
going to fill in this afternoon and discuss with us "Census and
Government" as an area of applied social science. I think it goes
without much saying that we certainly appreciate the last-minute
arrangements that he has made to attend this conference and to help
us fill this gap. Therefore I take great pleasure in presenting Morris
Hansen.

MR. HANSEN: The question of applied social science research in
the government is an exceedingly broad one. The question as related
to the Bureau of Census is an exceedingly broad one, also, and I
want to confine my remarks to a limited but important phase dealing with the problems of research in methods of collection of information and with the evaluation of reliability of results obtained.
I think this may be the most relevant for the purposes of this conference. Actually, the whole activity of the Bureau of the Census,
and of similar types of agencies in the federal government, is directed

at social science research, at the evaluation requirements for data, and at the collection of information needed for dealing with social science problems.

I want to concentrate primarily on the collection process rather than on the broader aspects of getting data to serve needs. In particular, I want to concentrate attention and to discuss briefly precision of measurement, and techniques of measurement of social and economic phenomena. This measurement of social and economic phenomena and research in the precision of measurement involves prediction of behavior—behavior of the interviewer and the respondent and other people in groups that may be involved in the collection process when they come up against a particular situation.

I want to comment briefly first on the accuracy of survey-method results. We sometimes conceive of survey results, whether the results are from a sample survey or a complete census, as having a census value. That is, there are certain biases and response errors and other errors that occur in survey results that are of the same character, whether the survey is on a sample basis or a complete census basis. And the nature of these biases and response errors affects the reliability and the interpretation of results we get from surveys of small or large scale. In the Bureau of the Census, we are placing increased emphasis on evaluating survey techniques and the nature of response errors in survey results. We do this in order to be able to indicate the meaning and precision of the data we make available, and to work toward improvement of the data. In this type of research we bring together groups with different backgrounds—primarily with psychological, mathematical, and survey technique experience and backgrounds.

The first step we have taken in approaching this problem of precision of measurement and techniques of measurement of results is to begin to get some idea as to the magnitude of the problem involved, to get an evaluation of the accuracy of results that we may be getting from censuses and surveys that we take. Actually, I think many of you are well aware of such problems, and yet some of you may be quite surprised at the difficulties involved in the collection of what might be thought to be comparatively simple basic facts. For instance, the difficulty in getting reasonably accurate responses and measuring the magnitude of errors involved, in the enumeration of young children, particularly infants under one or children under

five years of age, has long been recognized. There are fairly serious
deficiencies in the enumeration of these groups in the census.

As another illustration, we have serious problems in identifying
veterans as a class in the population. In our surveys, both sample and
complete censuses, we have succeeded in identifying perhaps only
sixty to ninety percent of the veterans, depending on the care and
attention given to the job, and on other circumstances. Actually, the
only time we attempted to identify veterans in a complete census,
the proportion we were able to identify was a good deal smaller than
in some of our sample surveys in which bare attention can be given
to the problems. Thus, such a simple factual characteristic as veter-
an's status is difficult to establish though there appears to be no
strong motivation on the part of the respondents for underreporting
this characteristic.

Identification of farm residents and the accurate measurement of
shifts in population between farm and nonfarm dwellings are always
problems, and different approaches may lead to very different results. It is difficult to get comparable results between censuses of
population and censuses of agriculture, or between successive censuses.

In the last census we made an effort to identify "emergency
workers"—people employed on WPA and other work relief projects—and succeeded in identifying only about seventy-five percent
of them. This appears to be a simple factual matter, although here
one might see some motives for misreporting.

Even "counting" the total population involves very serious problems of accurate measurement. I have already referred to the incomplete coverage of infants. Actually, on the basis of comparatively
recent information available during the war from draft and rationing
registrations, and on the basis of some of our own field checks on
the accuracy of results, it appears reasonable to assume that we
succeed in covering perhaps 95 to 98 percent of the population.
The incompleteness of coverage of the population, whatever it is, is
not the result of what might be regarded as carelessness in the administration of the job, but it is because the job is a good deal more
difficult than has often been supposed.

It is not surprising, when problems of accuracy of measurement are
as serious as I have illustrated, that we are up against a situation
time and again where two different censuses apparently measuring
the same thing give strikingly different results. This is just by way of

indicating the problem, and the seriousness of the problem, of response errors in survey data.

There aren't very many census results on which we have reliable independent checks. Where such checks are possible, some of the census results look reasonably good but often there are quite serious differences. This is true for both sample survey or complete census results. Actually, with a sample one may, if he puts the resources into it, perhaps impose (at a price he can afford) better training and better controls on some of the work than in a complete census. However, the fact that this is possible with sample surveys doesn't mean that it necessarily happens in *most* sample surveys.

One of the techniques, then, of evaluating the accuracy of census or survey results is comparison with reliable independent data. That is what I have been doing for the most part. Another method is through the use of what we have come to call a quality check, a re-interview of the population, or of a sample of the population. A re-interview may be under one of two bases: (*a*) an effort to repeat an interview under the same essential conditions, or (*b*) an effort to repeat it under vastly improved conditions—better qualified and better trained interviews, with more time, and greater intensity of questioning. We have as a matter of policy adopted a procedure of intensive quality checking, through intensive re-interview of a small sample in each of the major censuses we take. The first such quality check was after the 1945 Census of Agriculture. We also conducted a quality check in connection with the 1947 Census of Manufactures. The 1948 Census of Business is now getting under way, and we are working on a quality check; and also for the 1950 Censuses of Population and Agriculture.

There are serious problems in determining what the techniques of quality checking should be in order to get at measures of reliability of the census results—serious problems that we are just beginning to explore. I can illustrate with two or three problems—there are a great many others. One of them is this: you send a carefully selected check enumerator out to re-interview a family or a person in an effort to get improved information from that person. Will the second interviewer do better if you give him the results of the first interview? If you do give him the results of the first interview, there may be a tendency for him to be guided by it, and thus to understate the discrepancies that may exist. If you don't give it to him, you may not resolve many of the problems of why the discrepancy existed, and thus may not get the improved answers that could come by trying to ferret out the reason for any difference between the two results.

Another type of problem is concerned with the sort of personnel that should be chosen and put into a quality-check procedure to carry out the job. Should it be an independent field organization? Or should it be one with personnel selected from the organization that did the original job? There are problems each way.

Again, what is the effect of using a more intensive questioning process? Do we get an answer which is simpler, different, or can we find more intensive procedures for getting closer to the true answers —that is, if we can conceive of a "true" answer to a question we are trying to get information on.

In our work on quality-check procedures I can say this: We are making efforts to carry through well-designed experiments with careful interviewing and sampling procedures and approaches which will give us an evaluation of the precision of the results.

In addition to this work on quality checking, we are engaged in a family comprehensive program of pretests or tests in connection with the censuses and current surveys that we take. We may set up an operation, a census, or a survey of a population, for the sole purpose of testing techniques. We have been doing a good deal of this in planning the 1950 census, and have learned a good deal from it. As a result, our census of agriculture will probably cost us a million dollars less. There are other less tangible results of pretesting the other aspects of the census from which we will succeed in improving accuracy and reducing costs. In these pretests we are sometimes able to use a controlled experimental design, to get at particular things we want to measure. They show us the impact which a particular change in procedure may have on reliability of results or on cost.

In dealing with these problems of response measurement, we need to develop some theories and background, some approach as to what are the important things to measure in connection with response errors. We need to classify sources of error in a useful manner that will make it possible to formulate effective programs for dealing with response errors and for interpreting results.

In this connection I should like to distinguish two major aspects of response error: response bias and response variation. Response bias is the net effect of response errors. Response errors may, and often are, compensating in character. That is, one person will overstate his age and another will understate his age, and the effect may be the same age distribution. Other aspects of response error will result in a net bias. It was the results of response bias, the net difference, I was quoting earlier on some of the problems of accuracy of enumeration on a census or survey. This distinction between response bias and response variation is quite important. The extent to which there is a significant bias or not, and the amount of response variation, have different kinds of impact on the meaning of results and on the steps that should be taken to control response errors.

For example, if we were sure we had only response variation and not response bias in our characteristics, it would seldom pay to put any money into reducing response variability. But if there is a substantial response bias, it might pay to put a good deal of money into reducing it if one is interested in measuring an aggregate value of a particular variable. If, on the other hand, it is desired to divide the population into income classes, as an illustration, then a large amount of response variability, even with no bias, may cause many shifts between income classes, and result in serious distortion of other figures summarized by income classes.

Another type of approach in dealing with response errors is concerned with the sources of response errors. Now, sources of response errors have been discussed a great deal. I will mention some of them briefly. Techniques of questioning—short answer, intensive questioning, open-answer questioning may have an important effect on the results. Also to be considered are the interviewer's characteristics, his training, the supervision he receives, and the control of the whole process. The respondent may be responsible for an important part of the response errors. Some of his responses can be improved by careful questioning—others may not be subject to change. There is no point in spending money on improving interviewers or on more intensive questioning in an effort to reduce response errors which are inherent in the respondent. However, various motivations and conditions have an important effect on response reliability and response bias, and these need study and control.

We are just beginning what I hope will be a good deal of work in this field. I mentioned a few of the types of things that are going forward. I mentioned the vehicles we are using for them—that is, experimental designs, projects carried on for that purpose only, and experimental work carried on in conjunction with surveys and censuses. We find that for many questions the accuracy we get from the questions depends essentially on the amount of money we want to spend on the question. For example, if we have two questions on age we can get a more accurate result than with one. I am not sure how much further we can go there in improving response, but there are a number of points on which extra resources will get extra reliability. In the 1940 census we had a question on migration: Where had this person lived five years ago? We found rather significant biases on this question. In some of our testing work since then we have learned how to reduce these biases substantially by more intensive questioning. If we want to spend additional questions, and that means additional money—often measured in millions of dollars when we are talking about the census—we can improve the answer to that question. An alternative is to avoid the use of certain of the questions for which the bias is particularly serious, and not get information on those uncertain subjects.

We have had similar results on some other characteristics we measured. Properly directed questions will improve the nature of the response, at least up to a certain point; it may not go all the way.

We are in the process of exploring some other hypotheses or response errors, as for example, the effect of the length of the questionnaire. There have been theories on the part of some of the people working in the field that too many concepts in a single questionnaire will lead to poorer quality of results all the way through, and that a few concepts will lead to better results. We have done only a limited amount of work in this particular field, without too many variations in the length of questionnaire; but with moderate variations we have found comparatively little difference in the reliability of results, except as we do more intensive questioning on a particular point as distinguished from just extending the concepts. When we do more extensive questioning on a particular point we can often improve quality, as I have indicated.

Another subject of study is self-enumeration in which the respondent himself fills out the questionnaire versus a direct personal interview. In one comparison as to the amount of cooperation received and the accuracy of results, we find that on some questions self-enumeration was better; on others worse.

Again, from the little experimenting we have done—it is comparatively little but enough to give some indications—we find that the length of the questionnaire has much less impact on whether you will get a person to cooperate in filling out a questionnaire left with him than we had imagined to begin with. At least, we got about the same cooperation from a quite short questionnaire as from a considerably longer questionnaire. It seemed that the will of the respondent to cooperate had more effect than, within reasonable bounds, the length or design of the questionnaire.

In some tests we have used what we call "hothouse" methods as well as field methods. These hothouse methods involve setting a group of people down in a room with an interview taking place in front of them and seeing how well and how accurately they understand and record the answers. We have used this technique in testing training techniques as well as format and the effect of format on accuracy of response. It is far from foolproof, but comparatively low-cost, and gets a lot of questions further along toward an answer than the same amount of money spent in the field.

Studies of characteristics of interviewers and their relationships to results involves randomizing enumerators in their work assignment. We have done a little of this and expect to do a great deal more in trying to ascertain the effect of the interviewer on the responses he gets, and the effect of training on the interviewer.

Another problem being studied involves isolating the cost associated with the various survey operations. How much more does it cost us in a census or survey to add a question? A point of view often expressed has been, "If you are going around and visiting the population anyway, an additional question doesn't make much difference." We find it makes a difference to the tune of millions of dollars when you add just one or two significant questions in a major census of the United States.

Effective use of response-accuracy measurement involves tying it in with sampling variability and with time studies getting an approach in sample surveys to minimize the total errors, and putting the right amount of resources into sampling and interviewing, interview training, and other aspects of design in order to maximize the reliability of results for a given expenditure.

Really effective development of improved survey techniques still waits on a good deal more research. Much of this research will come from many sources—government, private agencies, and the universities—and there is an urgent need for cooperation and joint development in this field.

8

APPLIED RESEARCH:
JOURNALISM [1]

Ralph O. Nafziger

MR. SAUNDERS: Our next speaker is aware of the fact that there is some unavoidable overlapping between the topic *Mass Communication* as a special area of applied research, about which Mr. Berelson, spoke, and his area, namely, *Journalism*. However, this overlap is not excessive. Journalism is a special field of endeavor in which considerable work has been done for some years, and one that is sufficiently able to stand on its own feet and to warrant a special treatment. I think that there is no one who is better qualified to discuss this particular area than Ralph Nafziger, who is Director of Research of the School of Journalism of the University of Minnesota.

MR. NAFZIGER: [1] Twenty years ago, Dean Eric W. Allen of the University of Oregon, reporting for a newly formed committee on research in journalism, asserted that media analysis and, in fact, investigation in the entire field of communications was a "poor relation" of research. Too little fruitful research was being done in proportion to the importance to society of the mass media, and those who held the money bags for research were reluctant to invest funds in this area of study.

Times have changed. World War I stimulated interest in public opinion propaganda and the mass media. But the development of radio and World War II gave a tremendous lift to this field of study, particularly to methodological aspects of it, and resulted in the training of a large number of students who have since applied themselves throughout the country to this sphere of investigation.

[1] I am interpreting my assignment literally by confining my remarks to the activities of men identified with schools of journalism and to publications in our journals. I am, therefore, purposely ignoring the rich contributions to the literature concerning the mass media of communication which have been made by men in various disciplines or which have been reported in journals other than those published by us. Others here, perhaps, will report on this additional literature.

Dean Allen also attempted to add up the various types of special studies that were being undertaken by staff members and students in journalism.[2] He and others noted that results of studies undertaken in the early decades of journalism-school history were likely to be circulated within a narrow field and not published in widely circulated journals. (The journalism teachers, incidentally, had no journal of their own until 1924 when a mimeographed bulletin was converted into the printed *Journalism Bulletin*.) His listings and other reports in the early issues of the *Journalism Bulletin* give some idea of the nature of study projects in journalism prior to 1930.[3] As a young field of systematic study, it was perhaps inevitable that research studies should have concentrated prior to 1930 on the history of journalism, including local and regional studies, biographical material, ethics, and aspects of control analysis involving particularly communicator management, legal controls, advertising. Experiments in journalism-teaching methods were also attempted and the results discussed in gatherings of the journalism teachers.

Allen's report for 1929 reveals, however, the attempts which were being made in the 1920s to extend the field of journalism studies into the areas of content, audience, and effect analysis. While the results of these efforts show that the investigators were groping for valid and reliable methods to apply to their projects, they were nevertheless manifesting considerable interest in evaluations of performance of the press. For example, Bleyer of Wisconsin, press historian, conducted a seminar which analyzed the content of newspapers in the nineteenth century and related the data to the events of the day. He also was concerned not only with means for categorizing newspaper content, but was attempting to give proper weight to display and prominence of the news items.[4] These projects complemented the Columbia content studies.

In rank order of frequency, the main research topics which appear in Allen's listing for 1929 were: history of journalism, readership of newspapers, newspaper content (often qualitative reports on the ethics of journalism), advertising and newspaper management, journalism-teaching methods, editorial methods, foreign-press organiza-

[2] Allen, Eric W., "Research in Journalism," *Journalism Quarterly*, 7:40-54, March, 1930; "Organization of Research," *Journalism Bulletin*, 5:10-18, January, 1929.

[3] See Index, Suppl. to *Journalism Quarterly*, 25:4, December, 1948.

[4] Bleyer, Willard G., "Research Problems and Newspaper Analysis," *Journalism Bulletin*, 1:17-22, March, 1924.

tion and content, specialized press, law of the press. The 1932 research council report reveals virtually the same sequence, except that "specialized press" had moved up to fifth place.

Among the influences which resulted in some change of emphasis of topics and methods after 1929 was an increase in activity of the journalism teachers' Council on Research and the *Journalism Quarterly* which in 1930, under the editorship of Dr. Frank Luther Mott, replaced the *Journalism Bulletin*. Dr. Mott, who was later to win a Pulitzer prize for his studies in the history of the American press, gave the readers of the *Quarterly* summaries of a wide variety of studies in journalism. Among these articles were many which were representative of widespread interest among readers in international news communications and the foreign press. Other contributions showed a continuation of deep interest among journalism teachers in the practical problems of producing a newspaper or a magazine, an interest stemming in part from the fact that staff members of journalism schools had usually served an apprenticeship for teaching by earning a living as members of the press. They had seen the communications industry and had witnessed its problems from the inside.

A broadened concept of journalism studies and closer association between journalism studies and the research needs of the press, parallel with the coming of new communications agencies and a recognition of the close ties between the social sciences and journalism, resulted in new approaches to journalism research. Volumes of the *Journalism Quarterly* in the early 1930s give evidence of these new tendencies.[5] Emphasis on communications research in the 1930s can be traced in the pages of the *Journalism Quarterly* and in the annual mimeographed reports of the Council on Research in Journalism entitled "Research in Progress." Dr. Ralph D. Casey became editor of

[5] Gallup, George, "A Scientific Method for Determining Reader-Interest," 7:1-13, March, 1930; Bleyer, Willard G., "What Journalism Schools are Trying to Do," 8:35-44, March, 1931; Nafziger, Ralph O., "A Reader-Interest Survey of Madison, Wisconsin," 7:128-41, June, 1930; Casey, Ralph D., "Journalism, Technical Training, and the Social Sciences," 9:31-45, March, 1932; Wilkerson, Marcus M., "The Press and the Spanish-American War," 9:129-48, June, 1932; Kingsbury, S. M., and H. Hart, "Measuring the Ethics of American Newspapers," 11:179-99, 276-300, 361-81, June, September, December, 1934; Sumner, W. A., "Reading Interests and Buying Habits of the Rural and Village Subscribers of a Daily Newspaper," 9:182-9, June, 1932; Taeuber, Irene B., "Changes in the Content and Presentation of Reading Material in Minnesota Weekly Newspapers 1860-1929," 9:281-9, September, 1932; Seebert, Fred S., "Contemporary Regulations of the British Press," 8:235-56, September, 1931.

the *Quarterly* in 1935. He was succeeded by Raymond B. Nixon in 1945.

Illustrative of stimulating articles which the *Quarterly* in the past fifteen years has brought to the attention of journalists and journalism teachers are many which tapped various research resources.[6] Several of these articles were later developed into books.

The *Research in Progress* report for 1947-48 of the Council on Research in Journalism showed some significant changes in the nature of journalism studies since the reports of the early 1930s. Leading research fields were in order: history of press and radio, readership and listenership, radio miscellaneous, advertising miscellaneous, management or control, instructional methods and education for journalism, communications law, media influence or effect,

[6] For example: Lasswell, Harold D., "Research on the Distribution of Symbol Specialists," *12*:146-56, June, 1935; Willey, Malcolm, "Quantitative Methods and Research in Journalism," *12*:255-65, September, 1935; Bush, C. R., and Jane Cook, "The Measurement of Editorial Attitudes," *12*:367-73, December, 1935; Gosnell, H. F., and M. Schmidt, "Relation of Press to Voting in Chicago," *13*:129-47, June, 1936; Kobre, Sidney, "Newspapers and the Zangara Case," *13*:253-71, September, 1936 (one of a series) ; Rosten, Leo C., "The Social Composition of Washington Correspondents," *14*:125-32, June, 1937; Coggeshall, R., "Was There Censorship at the Paris Peace Conference?" *16*:125-35, June, 1939; Hulten, C. M., "The Right of Privacy in California," *17*:133-8, June, 1940; Mickelson, S., "Promotional Activities of the Northern Pacific Land Department," *17*:324-34, December, 1940; Lasswell, H. D., "The Politically Significant Content of the Press: Coding Procedures," *19*:12-23, March, 1942; Lazarsfeld, P. F., and R. Durant, "National Morale, Social Cleavage and Political Allegiance," *19*:150-8, June, 1942; Wilson, Q. C., "Voluntary Censorship During the Civil War," *19*:251-61, September, 1942; Geller, A., D. Kaplan, H. D. Lasswell, "An Experimental Comparison of Four Ways of Coding Editorial Content," *19*:362-70, December, 1942; Tinker, M. A., and D. G. Paterson, "Differences Among Newspaper Body Types in Readability," *20*:152-5, June, 1943; English, Earl, "A Study of the Readability of Four Newspaper Headline Types," *21*:217-29, September, 1944; Mott, F. L., "Evidence of Reliability in Newspapers and Periodicals in Historical Studies," *21*:304-10, December, 1944; Kobre, S., "The Sociological Approach in Research in Newspaper History," *22*:12-22, March, 1945; Nixon, R. B., "Concentration and Absenteeism in Daily Newspaper Ownership," *22*:97-114, June, 1945; Schramm, Wilbur, "Measuring Another Dimension of Newspaper Readership," *24*:293-306, December, 1947; Kinter, C. V., "How Much Income Is Available to Support Communications?" *25*:38-42, March, 1948; Bigelow, C. L., "Some Suggested Refinements in Newspaper Readership Studies," *25*:349-53, December, 1948; Swanson, C. E., "Readability and Readership: A Controlled Experiment," *25*:339-43, December, 1948.
  Among examples of contributions to various journals by journalism teachers in the field of propaganda and public opinion are several, for example, by R. D. Casey such as: "The Press, Propaganda and Pressure Groups," Annals of the *Am. Acad. of Pol. & Soc. Sc.*, *219*:66-75, January, 1942; "Republican Propaganda in the 1936 Campaign," *Pub. Op. Quart.*, *1*:27-44, April, 1937; "British Politics—Some Lessons in Campaign Propaganda," *Pub. Op. Quart.*, *8*:72-83, Spring, 1944.

content analysis, propaganda and public opinion miscellaneous, international news and foreign press. The historical approach continued in the lead, therefore, although closer ties had been made by the investigators with the social sciences in the intervening years. Content analyses appear to have receded in popularity since the early 1930s, but an examination of the titles shows that the quantitative studies in the field had increased and the more descriptive and qualitative studies had decreased in number.

Parallel with this development of journalism research was an increase, decade by decade, in the cooperation of the schools and the media in instructional and research projects. Symptomatic was the creation of a joint council of newspaper men and journalism teachers and a similar radio council designed to improve the standards of journalism instruction.

Step by step the intuitive estimates of editors were subjected to research tests, until in recent years, scores of research projects annually have been set up jointly by the schools and the media. That the media, as well as the schools, have profited from this association and from the research procedures is shown by the increasing contribution financially by newspapers and other communication agencies to research projects in the journalism schools. Northwestern University, University of Illinois, State University of Iowa, Stanford University, University of Minnesota, Syracuse University, to name only a few schools, have organized continuing research projects which are being watched with interest by members of the press and by radio men. The nature of these activities and the methods which are being employed are suggested by the bibliographic references which have already been cited.

Studies of reading habits, content analyses, historical studies, experimental methods adapted to the field of typography, attitude surveys involving the activities and the influence of the media, public opinion polls, and studies dealing with the community environment of the media represent some of the areas in which these projects are being conducted. Illustrative are investigations undertaken by the newly developed Institute of Communications Research in the University of Illinois and a similar unit in the State University of Iowa. In California, Chilton R. Bush and his associates in Stanford University are studying reading habits and public attitudes toward the media in cooperation with the press. Charles L.

Allen and others at Northwestern University have for several years carried on readership, marketing and advertising studies in close association with the media. Earl English at the University of Missouri is continuing his experiments with type readability. Thomas F. Barnhart at the University of Minnesota, as consultant to members of the state press, has redesigned the typography of several newspapers in his and neighboring states. Our School of Journalism at Minnesota also established five years ago a Research Division which has carried out continuing studies of reading habits, content and attitudes in cooperation with members of the state's press. At the University of Wisconsin, Iowa State College, and elsewhere, programs of study involving the agricultural and industrial press were initiated years ago and have recently been accelerated. Individual newspapers have also profited from the development of research procedures by establishing their own research activities. The opinion surveys of the Washington *Post* are an example. Paul Trescott of the Philadelphia *Bulletin* has testified to the use which his paper has made of its Philadelphia Poll. Opinion and fact surveys have been made to establish backgrounds for the *Bulletin* editorial writers and to develop the reporting of public affairs of the community. The Curtis Publishing Company's development division tests working hypotheses of its editors as well as of its advertising department. Service of the Minnesota and Iowa newspaper-conducted state polls has been extended to public welfare agencies that are in need of local and state attitude, opinion, and fact surveys. *Wallace's Farmer* and *Iowa Homestead* has conducted opinion surveys and experiments on readability and readership.

Further applications of research procedures in journalism are as inevitable and potentially as ramified as are the same basic procedures in the social science disciplines in general. There remains the need for training many more adequately equipped young researchers in journalism. This goal is one of the objectives of the Council on Research of the Association of Accredited Schools and Departments of Journalism. Wilbur Schramm of the University of Illinois is now chairman of the Council.

The moot and unsolved questions facing the research workers in journalism are likewise as extensive as are those in each of the social sciences.

Kinter's exploration of the economics of communication media and Gerald's study of the recent interpretations of freedom of press [7] point to possibilities in control analysis.

Response analysis or the investigation of the effects of the content of the mass media on the public is an area of research which has not been thoroughly explored.

Although content analysis has a comparatively long history, it has not been carried to the point where it has become a meaningful index of media performance in terms of press and radio's role in social control and responsibility. Moreover, despite an interest displayed in content studies by practicing journalists such as J. Russell Wiggins, managing editor of the Washington *Post*, relatively few editors, publishers, and other communicators have cooperated in the advancement of this area of investigation.

Analyses of the audience or readers have stimulated scores of joint study programs between the practicing journalists and the schools. The close association of this field of investigation and the well-being and financial stability of the media perhaps accounts for its popularity among communicators. Recent efforts to examine unsolved questions in this area of study include studies which are designed to relate the socio-economic composition of readers and listeners to their reading and listening habits. For example, what are the conditions that account for widely read news items? Who reads what and with what degree of comprehension or understanding? What are optimum reading conditions for "significant," "important" articles or those that are related to public affairs? What really is the effect of prominent display on news articles? What accounts for exceptionally popular items on the inside pages of newspapers? What is the relation of social composition in readers and listeners to reading and listening difficulty among various categories of news and feature items? What else does the avid reader of sports (political news, society news, comics, etc.) read?

Corroboration of some evidence that top readers of any one category of news tend also to be among top readers of all other kinds of news (except perhaps sports and society) will have value to the editor, the information specialist, and the educator. That the top-news reader also tends to be the socially active, well-informed, and better-educated member of the community is a probability which invites deeper study.

[7] Gerald, J. E., *The Press and the Constitution, 1931-1947* (Minneapolis, 1948).

Basic among our social and political problems is the question: How shall we communicate subject matter involving serious thinking on important public issues, in view of evidence that many "significant" articles do not reach certain cultural frames of reference? When an answer to this question is closer at hand than it is today, then perhaps publics can be reached more effectively through integrated use of various information channels.

9

LAW AND THE COURTS

Frank R. Kennedy

MR. SAUNDERS: From the sequence of topics it seems we are going from one of the oldest and best-established areas of applied social science to an area which is just emerging, in the sense that it is now becoming cognizant of the existence of certain social science techniques and is demonstrating something of an interest in the possible application of these techniques.

We are very pleased to present a member of the faculty of this campus, an Associate Professor of Law in the College of Law in the State University of Iowa, who will discuss "Law and the Courts" as an area for the application of social science research methods and techniques. Mr. Frank Kennedy.

MR. KENNEDY: Man lives in a world populated by his own kind. Indeed the most important factor in his environment is his relations with other men. If men are to exist together, so that each can develop his individuality as fully as possible without hindering the efforts of others, limits of the activities of each individual must be recognized. These limits are established by law.[1] Law thus defined embraces many sanctions perhaps. In common parlance, however, law includes only the rules for conduct recognized and enforced by the machinery of the courts.[2] Nevertheless, one of the principal schools of jurists [3] insists that it is the social pressure behind legal rules that makes law obligatory; that the efficacy of the legal order rests on the sanction of public opinion, which is the source of the social standard of justice.

[1] This definition of law is Savigny's. 1 Savigny, "System des heutigen römischen Rechts § 52" (1840), reprinted in Pound, Outline of Jurisprudence 65 (1943).

[2] Gray, Definitions and Questions in Jurisprudence, 6 Harv. L. Rev. 21, 24 (1892).

[3] The historical school. See Pound, Outline of Jurisprudence 31 (1943).

The disaster that befell Prohibition with all the authority of a duly adopted amendment of the United States Constitution behind it is certainly a recent notable illustration in the documentation of the historical jurists. And it has been said that the best explanation for the rather amazing turn in the development of constitutional doctrines that occurred in 1937 in this country is that the Supreme Court justices, or at least some of them, read the election returns of 1936,[4] not to mention the reports of the polls that preceded the election.

I am not going to be so unorthodox as to suggest that the courts should abandon their traditional sources of enlightenment as to the facts and the law in the controversies presented to them,[5] in favor of a more direct investigation of the state of public sentiment by consultation with the polltakers. But I believe that a strong case can be made for considerably more extensive reference to and reliance on data obtained by survey technologies as an aid to the courts in the ascertainment of social facts relevant to the determination of many controversies.

In any law case, civil or criminal, the court must ascertain not only the law but the facts to which the law may be applied. The law is frequently—one might say generally at the trial-court level—not in dispute; but the facts, the true facts, may be exceedingly difficult to isolate. Researchers in social science need not be reminded of the difficulties inherent in the function of discovering unadorned truth.

The court's machinery for getting the facts in the Anglo-American system of jurisprudence is a product of centuries of development. Some may be inclined to say the machinery is outmoded; but it has been thoroughly tested. And while administrative agencies, arbitration tribunals, and other bodies have been assigned some judicial or quasi-judicial functions, there is no serious suggestion that I

[4] Corwin, Constitutional Revolution, Ltd. 73 (1941).

[5] But if we consult tradition as far back as the thirteenth century, we find that jurors were selected because of their personal knowledge of the facts of a dispute they were to decide. Their verdict based on such knowledge, especially in criminal cases, was regarded as "the voice of the country-side, often the voice of some hundred or . . . community. The justices seem to feel that if they analyzed the verdict they would miss the very thing for which they are looking, the opinion of the country." 2 Pollock and Maitland, History of English Law 624 (2d ed., 1899). The preference for twelve members for the body was apparently due to a persistence of an ancient belief in the mystic virtue of the number rather than to a calculated judgment as to the sufficiency of the sample. Lesser, The Historical Development of the Jury System 98 (1894).

know of looking to any drastic revision of the structure of our courts or to the substitution of any significantly different mode of hearing and settling disputes.[6]

In certain classes of cases, the court relies on a jury to find the facts, to which the court applies the law. Typically the jury knows nothing about the case except what is presented in court [7]—by oral testimony of witnesses, by transcribed testimony of witnesses absent from the court (called depositions), documents, photographs, etc. The court determines by reference to rules of evidence what the jury should be allowed to hear and consider in arriving at the facts to be found in its verdict. The purpose of these rules is not to keep the jury from learning all the facts, but to exclude irrelevant, prejudicial, and unreliable evidence—e.g., to exclude evidence that a man is a Communist from a trial of the issue whether he stole a factory payroll (the evidence may be reliable but it is irrelevant and prejudicial), or to exclude a statement attributed to someone not in court that a particular professor is a Communist in a criminal prosecution against him for conspiracy to overthrow the government by violence (the evidence may be relevant but it is unreliable).

There is another cause of cases where the court typically does not call a jury. In this class of cases, usually called cases in equity or chancery, the court must find the facts as well as ascertain the applicable law. But practically the same rules of evidence obtain in equity as in common-law jury trials. There is, however, as might be expected, somewhat greater flexibility in the application of evidence rules in equity.[8]

Even though certain testimony may meet all the tests of relevance and reliability that have been formulated through the years, it may

---

[6] Trial by jury, particularly in civil cases, was subjected to considerable critical discussion and debate a score of years ago. See list of fifty (then recent) articles advocating abolition, retention, or revision of jury trial in Moschzisker, Trial by Jury 395 (2d ed. 1930).

[7] Moschzisker, Trial by Jury 58 (2d ed. 1930). If a juror has personal knowledge relevant to an issue being tried, he may be called as a witness and return to the box after completion of his testimony, but he may not contribute his private knowledge to the other jurors in any other way, as by communications after retirement. 6 Wigmore, Evidence §§ 1801, 1910 (3d ed. 1940). Counsel can guard against being confronted with such a witness-juror by ascertaining the fact of his knowledge on the juror's *voir dire* and then having him excluded from the jury by exercise of the right to challenge.

[8] Thus, in equity an objection to an interrogatory will not prevent a witness from answering, but if the objection is well taken, the judge is required to disregard the answer in his consideration of the evidence on which his decision is based. See 1 Wigmore, Evidence 15 (3d ed. 1940).

be untrustworthy. The witness may be a downright liar. To discover the lie, the courts have long allowed cross-examination of adverse witnesses. Cross-examination in the hands of skilled counsel is an exceedingly valuable tool for testing truth. It has come to be regarded as so effective and indeed essential an instrument for discovery of truth that denial of the opportunity of cross-examination in any trial is basis for striking all the testimony elicited on direct examination.[9]

But the witness who is not before the court cannot be cross-examined. Whence cometh the most famous (or infamous) rule of evidence—the hearsay rule. This is the rule of evidence which poses the most serious hazard to counsel who would tender the results of a survey for consideration by the court or jury in determining the facts of a particular case. This rule excludes testimony in court by a witness of what he heard another person say outside the court when the out-of-court testimony is offered as proof of the truth of the fact asserted. There are of course many exceptions. But the general rule is—no hearsay will be admitted in evidence.

Its relevance to the issue before the court does not save it; for the justification of the rule is that the offered hearsay may be unreliable because of the lack of opportunity to test the evidence by cross-examination.[10] Of course, in our daily living we all hear and read many things second-hand and are inclined generally to believe and act in reliance on their truth. But in court where parties are disputing the facts in issue, reliability of the evidence to be weighed is a paramount consideration.

When the poll taker comes in to court to report what the public opinion is respecting a particular issue, the poll taker is reporting what selected members of the public have said. Applied in its pristine rigidity, the hearsay rule would exclude such testimony. Let Mrs.

---

[9] Thus, if after testimony on *direct examination* a witness becomes unable to submit to *cross-examination* because of illness or death, the testimony elicited may be stricken. Maguire, Evidence, Common Sense and Common Law 14 (1947).

[10] Additional objections to hearsay testimony sometimes suggested are the lack of confrontation, preventing observance by the trier of the facts of the demeanor of the witness while testifying, and the lack of the penal sanction of the oath. However, these are subordinate or incidental objections: confrontation may be dispensed with; and while the administering of an oath precedes cross-examination, testimony elicited under oath without opportunity for cross-examination is inadmissible. The danger of erroneous transmission of the absent witness's statements is not generally regarded as a significant factor in the exclusion of hearsay. The nature and theories of hearsay are discussed in 5 Wigmore, Evidence §§ 1361-3 (3d ed. 1940).

Jones, the interviewee, come into court and testify—so the court and jury can observe her demeanor when testifying and so counsel for the opposition can cross-examine her—prove, if possible, that her opinion is in fact contrary to that originally given, or perhaps discredit her opinion.

It can readily be seen that the rule if applied literally would simply make impossible the introduction of evidence of a public opinion held on a national or regional scale. The judges themselves would be the first to admit that trials cannot be protracted to permit the parade of a sufficient number of people to the witness stand to obtain a fair sample. That is not even to refer to the additional and perhaps more serious difficulty with such a procedure that subjecting members of the public to a barrage of questions, direct, cross, and re-direct, by a battery of lawyers, shrewd or stumbling, may not be the best way to discover what public opinion is on a particular issue. Lost would be the advantages and perhaps the indispensability of spontaneity and candor. The witness on the stand is likely to concern himself lest he render an opinion that will be viewed as unintelligent or egregious by his audience or one that he will not be able to defend against carping cross-examination. Those engaged in opinion research have not found the duplication of courtroom techniques conducive to accurate probing of the public mind. I, of course, intend no reflection on either technique when used for its proper purpose. Presence in court, awareness of the penalties of perjury, and cross-examination may help a witness's memory or prove its fallibility when he testifies as to the events of a particular evening; whereas they may aid not at all when the witness is asked for a frank and voluntary expression of his attitude or his opinion as a member of the public on a particular matter.[11]

Yet there are important areas of law where it is necessary for the court to ascertain what the opinion of a sizeable portion of the

[11] In Cleo Syrup Corp. *v.* Coca-Cola Co., 139 F.2d 416 (C.A. 8th 1943), *cert. denied*, 321 U.S. 781 (1944), plaintiff introduced testimony by numerous housewives indicating that they thought defendant's product was made by plaintiff. ". . . on cross-examination, many of them indicated that their confusion had resulted from the use of the word 'Cola' in the defendant's trade name. They admitted the obvious distinction between the words 'Cleo' and 'Coca,' and none testified that they had actually been deceived into purchasing Cleo-Cola for Coca-Cola. Nevertheless, we think that this evidence was competent and relevant." 139 F.2d at 419. When the survey seeks factual information (*i.e.*, whether the interviewee has bought Cleo-Cola intending to get Coca-Cola) rather than opinion or attitude, the greater utility of cross-examination is apparent. Cf. note 5 *supra*.

public on a particular issue is. Until within the last decade or so, the courts have had no reliable indicia of public opinion. Consequently, the question of the admissibility of evidence of what that opinion is has not been faced until recently. In the absence of any evidence, it appears that the courts have frequently relied on the doctrine of judicial notice.

Under this doctrine the court—*i.e.*, the judge—recognizes the existence of certain facts without the necessity of proof. Thus, the courts, since Magellan's voyage presumably, have taken judicial notice that the earth is round—prior thereto, I suppose, that it is flat. Sometimes the court has to consult an almanac or a dictionary or an encyclopedia before it knows some fact of which it takes judicial notice.[12] While the employment of this device for ascertaining certain facts is generally encouraged as a means of expediting trials by restricting the evidence to matters in actual dispute,[13] there is of course a danger: the judge may take judicial notice of something that is not indisputable. It may indeed be a matter for dispute whether a particular thing is disputable or not.[14] The danger of abuse must be especially apparent when the judge takes judicial notice of what the status of public opinion is on a particular matter—and without the aid of any investigation beyond his own preconceptions.

Yet that is what the courts seem to have been doing for a long time.[15] Thus the very esteemed Judge Learned Hand, now of the United States Court of Appeals for the 2nd Circuit, decided in 1925 that Bayer's invented name for acetylsalicylic acid, "aspirin," had lost its distinctiveness as the name of the Bayer product because the public no longer associated aspirin with its maker.[16] Consequently,

---

[12] 9 Wigmore, Evidence § 2568a (3d ed. 1940); *cf.* Model Code of Evidence, Rule 802(c) and comment (1942).

[13] 9 Wigmore, Evidence § 2583 (3d ed. 1940).

[14] Morgan, Judicial Notice, 57 Harv. L. Rev. 269, 274 et seq. (1944). Professor Morgan's article is a penetrating study of the function of judicial notice. He carefully discriminates between the proffer of evidence to contest the indisputability of a matter that is the subject of a request for judicial notice (such evidence being admissible) and the tender of evidence to the contrary of what has been judicially noticed by the court (which should be rejected). *Id.* at 277-87. See also Maguire, Evidence, Common Sense and Common Law 174-5 (1947).

[15] See Judge Frank, dissenting in Repouille v. United States, 165 F.2d 152, 154 (C.A.2d 1947). Not always does a court articulate the process of taking judicial notice, but many decisions are explicable only as illustrations of its unacknowledged use. Thayer, A Preliminary Treatise on the Law of Evidence at the Common Law 278-96 (1898).

[16] Bayer Co., Inc. v. United Drug Co., 272 Fed. 505 (S.D.N.Y. 1921).

Bayer was held to have lost its valuable trade mark; and on the expiration of its patent every other drug company was allowed to make and sell acetylsalicylic acid tablets as aspirin. Now the decision was probably right from a technical point of view because the burden of proof was on the plaintiff Bayer and right also undoubtedly on the merits in the light of the public policy limiting, or at least avoiding the extension of, the scope of the monopoly of a patent.[17] But Judge Hand's opinion is disturbing to read, nevertheless, in view of its reliance to a very considerable extent on what the "general consuming public" understood by the word "aspirin" when the opinion reveals no satisfactory basis for arriving at that understanding.[18]

But how was this conscientious judge to know what the public thought? He got no assistance from the parties to the dispute: they were completely contradictory of each other in their contentions as to the public reaction to "aspirin."

Today scientifically conducted research can inform the court on such an issue. And cases can be found indicating that surveys of public reaction to similar marks have been introduced in evidence and considered by the courts in trade-mark infringement and unfair competition cases.[19] An unfortunate circumstance is that frequently both parties have introduced reports of surveys indicating results not in agreement.[20] This circumstance has a tendency to cause judges to discredit surveys generally.

[17] See, e.g., Kellogg Co. v. National Biscuit Co., 305 U.S. 111 (1938); but cf. Derenberg, Trade Mark Protection and Unfair Trading § 55 (1936).

[18] In discussing how the general consuming public became familiar with "aspirin" as a "kind of drug," Judge Hand does speak of the "only reasonable inference from the evidence," which, however, is not particularized. 272 Fed. at 510. And in disposing of an aggressive effort by Bayer in 1915-17 to educate the public to the trade-mark significance of "aspirin," the judge notes that he can find no basis for a secondary meaning for the term in the record. Id. at 512. Thus Judge Learned Hand does not profess to take judicial notice of any facts but to decide on the evidence or lack of it in the record. Yet the judge throughout the opinion discourses upon public understanding with a certitude that bespeaks a personal conviction, and one that could hardly arise from mere inferences or an absence of evidence in the record.

[19] See e.g., Oneida, Ltd. v. National Silver Co., 25 N.Y.S. 2d 271 (Sup. Ct. 1940), holding evidence obtained by interview of 1,000 women concerning identity of source of product to be competent in unfair competition case; DuPont Cellophane Co. v. Waxed Products Co., 85 F. 2d 75 (C.A. 2d 1936), noting the accuracy of results of survey indicating that cellophane had become generic.

[20] Oneida, Ltd. v. National Silver Co., 25 N.Y.S. 2d 271 (Sup. Ct. 1940); Quaker Oats Co. v. General Mills, Inc., 134 F.2d 429 (C.A. 7th 1943); DuPont Cellophane Co. v. Waxed Products Co., 6 F. Supp. 859 (E.D.N.Y. 1934), modified, 85 F.2d 75 (C.A. 2d 1936); cf. Alexander Young Distilling Co. v. National D. Prod. Corp., 40 F. Supp. 748 (E.D.Pa. 1941), where both parties

Even in the trade-mark and trade-name cases, typically tried without a jury, the admissibility in evidence of surveys has not received extensive or intensive judicial consideration. However, in a couple of federal district court cases,[21] objection to the admission of evidence of surveys has been sustained on the ground that it is hearsay. In one of the opinions, written by Judge Woolsey of the Southern District of New York, the *ex-parte* nature of the evidence was also invoked as a ground for condemnation.[22]

Fortunately these decisions, one of which has never been officially published, cannot be said to represent the weight of authority.[23] In the trial of a recent case another federal district judge, when confronted with an objection to the admissibility of a survey that there was no precedent for it, replied simply, "Oh, well, we will make some new law." [24]

In a more recent case, *Campbell Soup Co. and Carnation Co.* v. *Armour & Co.*,[25] a case in which Dr. Meier was called as an expert witness in connection with some tests he performed with blank red-and-white can labels, the court gave full consideration to Judge Woolsey's opinion and the vigorous objections of Armour's counsel but ruled that Dr. Meier's testimony and the testimony of interviewers

adduced testimony by shoppers engaged by each to investigate the extent of confusion in the market place concerning their respective marks but the court thought that the plaintiff's witnesses' testimony established no confusion and rendered defendant's testimony superfluous.

[21] Radio Corp. of America v. Decca Records, Inc. (S.D.N.Y. 1943) (opinion not published); Elgin National Watch Co. v. Elgin Clock Co., 26 F.2d 374 (D. Del. 1928), rejecting an affidavit of an expert as to the public understanding of "Elgin" as applied to timepieces, because the offered evidence was based, not on the personal knowledge of the affiant, but on the unverified statements or opinions of persons not called as witnesses. *Cf.* Coca-Cola Co. v. Nehi Corp., 36 A.2d 156, 160 (Del. Sup. 1944), where the court, "passing by" the question whether the testimony of psychology professors as to the results of word association tests conducted in college classrooms was inadmissible as hearsay, approved the chancellor's giving little weight to the testimony because of the differences in the mental reactions of the student in the classroom to the word "Cola" from those of the buyer in the market place when confronted with not only the full name of the beverage but also the size and dress of the bottle or package.

[22] That the survey there involved was made after the commencement of the litigation aggravated the infirmity of the evidence. Judge Woolsey noted with approval that in the *Cellophane* case, discussed in note 38 *infra*, the survey results were filed before trial so that both sides could "ventilate" the evidence. *Cf.* Alexander Young Distilling Co. v. National D. Prod. Corp., 40 F. Supp. 748, 752 (E.D. Pa. 1941).

[23] See cases cited in notes 19, 23, and 24.

[24] Transcript of Record, p. 69, Quaker Oats Co. v. General Mills, Inc., 134 F. 2d 429 (C.A. 7th 1943).

[25] 79 U.S.P.Q. 14 (E.D.Pa. 1948).

employed by Lampa and Christophersen would be admitted. He justified the admission on the ground that the court should take advantage of any medium by which it could better inform itself on the issue being litigated, *viz.*, confusion between the Campbell and Carnation red-and-white labels on the one hand and Armour's new red-and-white label on the other.

It may nevertheless be expected that tenders of evidence of the results of surveys will be met with vigorous objections grounded on the hearsay rule and that the objections will be sustained in some instances. To minimize the bases for objection, the firm of Rogers and Woodson, eminent trade-mark counsel of Chicago, offers, not the testimony of the director of the survey who planned, tabulated, and interpreted the results, but the testimony of the interviewers who acually talked to the members of the public and recorded the answers at the scene of the interview.[26] Typically three interviewers are called in to testify as to the results of a particular survey. Thus the hearsay element is limited to the answers. This testimony is proffered on the theory that the hearsay rule does not exclude statements heard by a witness when they are offered not as proof of the matter stated but simply as proof that such a statement was made.[27] A witness may testify to what he heard as well as to what he saw, felt, smelled— when what he heard is in issue. He can be cross-examined to ascertain whether he is disclosing all the circumstances of the interview, whether he has given the full statement of the person he heard. An opinion, understanding, or attitude of the public can hardly be presented in evidence other than as it is manifested in utterances of members of the public. Thus, statements of a person's own mental or physical condition at the time of the declarations have long been the subject of an exception to the hearsay rule.[28] There is of course a

[26] When the survey is used to discover witnesses who will testify for the party sponsoring the investigation, and these witnesses are produced at the trial, there is no hearsay problem presented as to their testimony. Unless the complete results of the survey, including the unfavorable as well as the favorable responses, so far as relevant, are offered, there is no justification for admission of survey data in court. A survey conducted on large enough scale can undoubtedly produce a considerable number of witnesses "who would testify that the world is flat, that the earth is the center of the universe, and that the moon is made of green cheese." Brief for Appellees, p. 25, Quaker Oats Co. v. General Mills, Inc., 134 F.2d 429 (C.A. 7th 1943). *Accord*, Coca-Cola Co. v. Nehi Corp. 36 A.2d 156, 160 (Del. Sup. 1944).

[27] 6 Wigmore, Evidence § 1766 (3d ed. 1940).

[28] The application of this exception has been pretty much confined to four classes of declarations: (1) statements of pain or suffering; (2) statements of design, intent, motive, emotion, etc.; (3) statements by the accused in criminal

danger in the application of such a limitation or exception to the hearsay rule: All hearsay might conceivably be admitted on the pretext that the fact of the making of the statement rather than the matter stated is in issue.

Firmly established as is the hearsay rule, it has had to yield to many exceptions and limitations, as has been noted. Most of the exceptions have been justified on one of two grounds, or more usually on both grounds: (1) *necessity:* the testimony is needed by the court for the proper disposition of the litigation, and cross-examination is either impossible or extremely inconvenient; (2) *circumstantial probability of reliability:* the circumstances surrounding the making of the hearsay statement are such as to afford a reasonable assurance of reliability.[29] The exception admitting a person's contemporary statements of his mental or physical condition is thus predicated on the fair necessity for the evidence arising out of lack of other better evidence of such condition and its probable superiority in trustworthiness over what would be adduced by examination at trial when there is ample opportunity and incentive for misrepresentation and no effective way of checking of such testimony by cross-examination or otherwise.[30]

In tendering the results of a survey of public opinion to the court for admission in evidence, counsel say in effect: We are offering this evidence as the honest record of a survey conducted in good faith in accordance with approved polling methods. The methods used have been validated time after time. The results are trustworthy—indeed the only trustworthy data available to the court. What the public believes on this issue or how it reacts to these stimuli is pertinent if not determinative of this case. The inherent probability of the accuracy of the data in light of the safeguards employed in their collation, the need of the court for such information, and the total lack of any other satisfactory evidence of the public's opinion or method for obtaining it fully justify the admission of the testimony.

If the hearsay objection is thought to be too serious to overcome in getting the evidence of the poll into the record for consideration by the finder of the facts, there remains another basis for

cases; (4) statements by testators in will cases. See 6 Wigmore, Evidence c. LVIII (3d ed. 1940).

[29] 5 Wigmore, Evidence §§ 1420-3 (3d ed. 1940); *cf.* Maguire, Evidence, Common Sense and Common Law 130-40 (1947).

[30] 6 Wigmore, Evidence § 1714 (3d ed. 1940).

bringing the poll results to the attention of the court. I have earlier adverted to the fact that in the absence of any evidence of what public opinion or reaction is respecting a particular matter, courts have been inclined to assume the prerogative of knowing the matter in issue as a matter of judicial notice without the necessity of proof. Then why not offer the poll results as an aid to the court in taking judicial notice? Materials thus submitted need not conform to the technical rules of evidence.[31]

To obtain admission of polls on this basis, the court must be completely satisfied as to the reliability of the poll offered.[32] It would not be realistic to fail to realize that notwithstanding the narrowness of the error in the predictions by the national political polls as to the outcome of the last election—an error which would be negligible and insignificant in most cases coming before the courts—nevertheless, skepticism on the part of many courts as to the reliability of polls on all subjects will be justified by reference to the mistaken forecasts. Another factor militating against the acceptability of polls on the basis suggested is the offer by adverse parties of polls purporting to prove inconsistent propositions of fact.[33] Now of course the experts present here today might be able to explain away inconsistencies as apparent rather than real or to discredit one of the polls. But experts may not be available. Or worse, they may be present to undermine each other's poll. When two apparently qualified poll analysts disagree vigorously as to the superiority of the quota system or the area system,[34] the court is understandably reluctant to take judicial notice of the indisputability of poll results. And that is the touchstone of the doctrine of judicial notice: indisputability of the facts noticed.[35]

---

[31] Morgan, Judicial Notice, 57 Harv. L. Rev. 269, 286-7 (1944) ; Model Code of Evidence, Rule 804 (2) (1942).

[32] Morgan, Judicial Notice, 57 Harv. L. Rev. 269, 273-4, 286-7 (1944) ; *but cf.* Thayer, A Preliminary Treatise on Evidence at the Common Law 308-9 (1898).

[33] As in the cases cited in note 20 *supra.*

[34] As in the trial of Campbell Soup Co. and Carnation Co. v. Armour & Co. 79 U.S.P.Q. 14 (E.D.Pa. 1948), Transcript of Record, pp. 1730-82.

[35] The doctrine does not necessarily require, however, that the figures obtained by survey methodology shall not be subject to any error. Typically, the court will not need to recognize that any particular percentage of the population thinks or reacts in a certain way but rather that a substantial majority or a significant number thinks or reacts that way. *Cf.* American Brake Shoe & F. Co. v. Alltex Products Corp. 117 F.2d 983, 984 (C.A. 2d 1941), *cert. denied,* 314 U.S. 631 (1941). The availability and use of research data will require the courts to refine their notions about what constitutes public opinion or understanding for particular purposes. *Cf.* Maguire, Evidence, Common Sense and

Of course what is disputable today oft becomes indisputable tomorrow.[36] That is well illustrated by a South Dakota case [37] wherein a lower court denied a request of a defendent in a rape case to order the taking of blood grouping tests to determine the possibility or impossibility of paternity of the fruit of the alleged illicit intercourse. The court on appeal in 1933 affirmed the denial of the request on the ground that the reliability of the tests had not been established as a matter of unquestioned scientific fact accepted among medical men. Rehearing was granted in the case three years later—a rather unusual procedure. By that time the tests had been validated to the complete satisfaction of the appellate court, and it acknowledged that if the question should now come up, the lower court would be required to take judicial notice of the reliability of these tests. It nevertheless refused to vacate the order previously made in the case because in the state of judicial knowledge then existing, the lower court could not be said to have erred.[38]

What is therefore needed is the validation of polling and survey techniques so that the results cannot be successfully challenged. The experts—you here—must attempt as early as possible to remove the doubt and disagreements respecting appropriate methodology, the adequacy of the sample, etc.[39] This conference is surely a most significant step in that direction.

Common Law 172-4 (1947), suggesting the propriety of taking judicial notice of statistics and data the absolute verity of which may not be provable, where recognition of general trends is all that is required to render a decision. Thus, courts have generally taken judicial notice of federal census reports when the population of a community or an area is relevant, although such reports are of course subject to minor error. 9 Wigmore, Evidence 567 (3d ed. 1940).

[36] 9 Wigmore, Evidence 572 (3d ed. 1940). And what is indisputable today may become disputable tomorrow. Cf. Sieberts v. Spangler, 140 Iowa 236, 118 N.W. 292 (1908), where the court took judicial notice that the "football season" "begins with the first frost, and ends very appropriately with the day of general thanksgiving." Id. at 239, 118 N.W. at 293.

[37] State v. Damm, 62 S.D. 123, 252 N.W. 7 (1933).

[38] 64 S.D. 309, 266 N.W. 667 (1936).

[39] For cases criticizing the sample used in a survey, see Oneida, Ltd. v. National Silver Co., 25 N.Y.S. 2d 271, 286 (Sup. Ct. 1940), where plaintiff conducted a survey in a community near its manufacturing plant and defendant conducted a survey in an area where plaintiff's competitors were located; Lerner Stores Corp. v. Lerner, 162 F.2d 160, 162 (C.A. 9th 1947), where plaintiff's interviewers stopped passers-by in front of one of its own stores in San Francisco to inquire as to their understanding of "Lerner Shops."

Several cases have suggested that the conditions under which the survey, designed to elicit expressions of opinion or understanding, was conducted differ significantly from those in which members of the public will *act* on their opinion or understanding. See Oneida, Ltd. v. National Silver Co., *supra*, suggesting that the interviewee's inspection of the defendant's product must have been more casual than in the case of an ordinary purchase (25 N.Y.S. 2d

The courts need the assistance of those engaged in opinion research. In numerous areas the public opinion on a particular issue may be crucial to the disposition of the case. The possibilities have been indicated most clearly in trade-mark and unfair-competition cases where the value of surveys has appeared in boldest outline and where the stakes have been high enough for litigants to finance the conducting of polls. But there are other areas where polls would be extremely useful. Only recently Judge Learned Hand lamented in a case [40] before the United States Court of Appeals for the Second Circuit that the courts have no Gallup poll to aid them in discovering the meaning of "good moral character" required of any applicant for naturalization.[41] This statutory term is regarded by the courts

at 286); Quaker Oats Co. v. General Mills, Inc., 134 F.2d 429, 433 (C.A. 7th 1943), where the court said, "Purchases of merchandise are not made in a vacuum with Professor Quiz in charge." Radio Corp. of America v. Decca Records, Inc., 51 F. Supp. 493, 496 (S.D.N.Y. 1943), labeling evidence of plaintiff's investigators "highly artificial"; cf. Coca-Cola Co. v. Nehi Corp., 36 A. 2d 156, 160 (Del. Sup. 1944), discussed supra note 21.

The Cellophane case offers an interesting illustration of the operation of the judicial process in the treatment accorded by different courts to surveys conducted by both parties. The plaintiff, DuPont Cellophane Co., had conducted a survey through a mail advertising house, asking 17,000 subscribers of four nationally circulated magazines whether Cellophane inter alia was a trade-mark. 72% of the 4,000 replies checked Cellophane as a trade-mark. Four items not trade-marks had been checked in 10-17% of the replies, and five other items which were trade-marks were checked in 52-95% of the replies. Defendant had conducted a survey through interviewers who asked "hundreds of people" (1) what Cellophane meant and (2) whether any other name was known for that kind of material. The 94% who knew something of the product apparently referred to its uses in their replies to the defendant's first question, and in reply to the second 88% knew no other name for the product. The trial court, which granted an injunction against use by the defendant of Cellophane in connection with any but plaintiff's product, thought the defendant's test not fair because it asked leading questions and the answers were not subject to cross-examination. While the plaintiff's survey data might likewise be incompetent and immaterial, still the court thought the question was fairly presented by plaintiff and, if admissible, showed an overwhelming number of answers for plaintiff. The trial court disavowed any consideration of the surveys, however, but allowed the evidence as to them to remain in the record. 6 F. Supp. at 885. On appeal, the Court of Appeals, which materially modified the injunction, referred approvingly to the accuracy of the answers obtained to defendant's second question and emphasized the 28% on plaintiff's survey to whom Cellophane indicated no origin. Moreover, the appellate court discounted plaintiff's survey because flattering letters from the magazines and prize offers for prompt replies "might well have stimulated a search for a registered trade-mark that theretofore had been unknown." 85 F.2d at 80.

[40] Repouille v. United States, 165 F.2d 152, 153 (C.A. 2d 1947).

[41] As a matter of fact, the American Institute of Public Opinion has conducted several polls to discover the public attitude toward euthanasia, which had been practiced by the applicant on his son in the case discussed in the text. These and other polls have found between 36% and 46% of the general populace favorable to euthanasia, between 50% and 55% opposed. See Note, 16 U. of Chi. L. Rev. 138, 141 n. 11 (1948).

as imposing a standard of conformity to the generally accepted moral conventions current at the time.[42] What are they? How does the court find out? The question in the case was whether the petitioner, who had administered euthanasia by deliberately putting to death by chloroform his own son who was an idiot and a physical monstrosity from birth, possessed the requisite good moral character. A diversity of opinion among members of the public was recognized in the opinion. The majority of the court, conceding and indeed stressing the lack of means of verifying their conclusion, decided tentatively that only a minority of virtuous persons would deem the practice morally justifiable while in private hands. Judge Jerome Frank recoiled from resorting to "unchecked surmises." He was for returning the case to the lower court to give the opposing parties opportunity to present there, reliable information as to the present-day public reactions to such conduct.[43]

[42] United States v. Francioso, 164 F.2d 163 (C.A. 2d 1947), affirming an order admitting petitioner to citizenship although he had lived with his wife, who was his niece, during the five years prior to the filing of his petition; cf. United States ex rel. Iorio v. Day, 34 F.2d 920 (C.A. 2d 1929), where Judge Learned Hand, in ordering the discharge of an alien from custody under an order of deportation, observed: "There are probably many persons in the United States who would . . . [regard as shamefully immoral] either the possession or sale of liquor; but the question is whether it is so by common conscience, a nebulous matter at best. While we must not, indeed, substitute our personal notions as the standard, it is impossible to decide at all without some estimate, necessarily based on conjecture, as to what people generally feel. We cannot say that among the commonly accepted mores the sale or possession of liquor as yet occupies so grave a place; nor can we close our eyes to the fact that large numbers of persons, otherwise reputable, do not think it so, rightly or wrongly." Id. at 921. In United States ex rel. Berlandi v. Reimer, 113 F.2d 429 (C.A. 2d 1940), Judge Learned Hand disagreed with Judge Augustus Hand and Judge Patterson, who found an alien guilty of moral turpitude, not because he was an acknowledged "moonshiner," but because he was a persistent violator of revenue laws. Judge Hand thought that ". . . people who in private affairs are altogether right-minded, see nothing more than a venial peccadillo in smuggling, or in escaping excises on liquor." Id. at 431. The dissenter feared that the court was substituting the moral repugnance of the ideal citizen for that of the ordinary man toward such conduct. The fears expressed by Judge Hand do not concern the writer of a note on Judicial Determination of Moral Conduct in Citizenship Hearings in 16 U. of Chi. L. Rev. 138 (1948). After expressing a preference for use of the jury rather than a general poll to determine what constitutes "good moral character," the note suggests that a poll of a few ethical leaders might be still more satisfactory but apparently concludes finally that any dependence by the judge on a standard outside himself in determining such a question is probably "unwise when not altogether futile." Id. at 143.

[43] Judge Frank would apparently regard such data furnished by the parties not as evidence but as information on the basis of which the court could take judicial notice but which could be supplemented by informal inquiries by the court or in any other appropriate way. All data so obtained would be put on

This case serves to raise an important problem respecting the utility of the polls in the courts. That is the matter of financing the survey.[44] In the case referred to, the petitioner, who had the burden of proving satisfaction of the "good moral character" requirement, probably could not afford to have a poll conducted to substantiate his case.[45] It is one thing for Campbell's Soup Co. or Coca-Cola or MGM to sponsor investigations of public opinions—another for a petitioner for naturalization or even a small enterpriser seeking to protect his trade mark.[46]

A judge himself has suggested the possibility of deputizing a peripatetic commissioner or examiner who would conduct surveys as an agent of the court.[47] The sponsorship or supervision of the survey by the court would eliminate the charge often leveled against surveys that they are self-serving in that they are planned, con-

the record, however, so that, in the event of appeal, it could inform the appellate court as well. 165 F.2d at 154-5. Earlier in his dissent, Judge Frank opines that were the matter *res nova* he would be guided by the attitude of ethical leaders rather than "contemporary public opinion about which, cloistered as judges are, we have but vague notions," and refers to Gibbon's remark that usually "the opinion of the world at large" is no more than that of "the few people with whom I happened to converse." *Id.* at 154. Consider Judge Frank's technique used to discover public understanding in preparing his dissent in LaTouraine Coffee Co. v. Lorraine Coffee Co., 157 F.2d 115, 119 (C.A. 2d 1946), *cert. denied*, 329 U.S. 771 (1946): "I have asked a dozen American men and women, selected at random, what Touraine means; their invariable reply was 'a part of France.'" 157 F.2d at 120. I have tried the same question on members of several of my classes in Trade Regulation and have not yet obtained the reply Judge Frank invariably received.

[44] The money available for the survey of course has a very direct bearing on the reliability that can be expected from the results. See Wilson, *The Measurement of Public Opinion*, 250 Annals 121, 122 (Mar. 1947).

[45] *Cf.* Note, 61 Harv. L. Rev. 692, 698 (1948), pointing out that the cost of producing evidence of social facts may be greater than the value of a favorable finding with respect to such facts.

[46] The services of Audience Research, Inc., are reported to be so expensive that even breakfast food and automobile manufacturers may not become its clients. "Its potential clients, therefore, are limited to companies which constantly bring out new products—and, further, have a large financial investment in each new production." "Market Research is Main Job," *Business Week*, June 19, 1948, pp. 44, 48.

[47] Judge Woolsey in Radio Corporation of America v. Decca Records, Inc. (S.D.N.Y. 1943) (opinion not published). Jurists have frequently voiced a need for a judiciary equipped with machinery to discover facts beyond those developed by the adversary system of trial. See, *e.g.*, Pound, Legislation as a Social Function, 7 Pub. Am. Soc. Soc'y 148, 161 (1913): "It is not one of the least problems of the sociological jurist to discover a rational mode of advising the court of facts of which it is supposed to take judicial notice." See also Frankfurter, Hours of Labor and Realism in Constitutional Law, 29 Harv. L. Rev. 353, 372 (1916); *cf.* Judge Learned Hand in Parke-Davis & Co. v. H. K. Mulford Co., 189 Fed. 95, 115 (C.C.S.D.N.Y. 1911).

ducted, and interpreted by a party to litigation for the purpose of proving his case.[48] Making such investigations a judicial function, at least in certain classes of cases, might be a partial answer to the expense problem where it is critical.[49] Of course there are numerous other practical difficulties presented by such an alternative, and they may be insuperable. The judge's suggestion before mentioned embraced the possibility of cross-examination on the spot by counsel of persons interviewed by the court's investigator. Social scientists might find the addition of this feature self-defeating.[50]

Once the admissibility of poll results in evidence comes to be taken for granted, as eventually I am satisfied it will, there will be numerous areas where their value will appear.[51] They may be used to aid the courts in determining what is defamatory in actions for damages for libel or slander.[52] *E.g.*, does a false reference to one as a Communist or a fellow traveler harm the reputation of the object of the

[48] See note 22 *supra.*

[49] On the other hand perhaps the cost is the primary reason why judicial fact-discovering machinery of the type referred to in note 46 *supra* has never been set up.

[50] See text accompanied by note 11 *supra.*

[51] A discussion of the treatment accorded polls in the courts should at least give footnote recognition to the potential liability of pollsters or the sponsors of polls to persons claiming injury from publication of poll results. In Advance Music Corp. v. American Tobacco Co., 296 N.Y. 79, 70 N.E. 2d 401 (1946), the plaintiff, a song publisher, sought recovery of damages resulting from the defendants' alleged misrepresentation on a radio program of the relative popularity of songs. The order of popularity was reportedly "based upon an extensive and accurate survey conducted throughout the nation." The plaintiff alleged that the defendants, a tobacco company and an advertising concern, acted "wantonly and without good faith" in their selections, to the injury of the defendant. The court of last resort in New York held that a cause of action was stated in the plaintiff's pleadings and remanded the case for trial. The burden on the plaintiff to prove his case in this kind of suit has been well nigh insuperable. *Cf.* 45 Col. L. Rev. 473 (1945). A commentator, arguing for the imposition of liability in "poll cases," suggests that ". . . there is no limit to the malign uses to which polls can be put, whether rating the chances of a political candidate, the sentiments towards proposed legislation, or the popularity of a song." Comment, 19 So. Calif. L. Rev. 45, 51 (1945).

[52] An instance—sardonic in retrospect—of the recognition of public opinion on an issue by exercise of judicial notice is provided by a Lousiana libel case, denying a claim of a Puerto Rican student for damages allegedly resulting from a story in defendant's newspaper which falsely attributed authorship of a letter to the plaintiff. The letter, published in 1938 in the L.S.U. student weekly, assailed the spirit of pacifism in youths of the United States. In finding nothing defamatory in the newspaper's story, the court said, "It is a matter of common knowledge that a vast majority of the people of the United States are opposed to this country's engaging in a war on foreign soil." The court then cited a speech of an unnamed but "very prominent United States senator" in support of its finding. Santana v. Item Co., 192 La. 819, 830-1, 189 So. 442, 445 (1939).

appellation or lower him in the estimation of the community? [53]
The public attitude toward such epithets is of obvious relevance in
this kind of case.

The same kind of issue may arise—indeed, has arisen—in a con-
tracts case, brought by one of the contemptuous ten of Hollywood.[54]
He had been discharged for violation of the standard "morals
clause" in his employment contract. That authorizes discharge when
the employee brings himself into "public hatred, contempt, scorn or
ridicule," or when his activities "shock, insult, or offend the community" or tend so to do. Does refusal to answer a question of a
Congressional committee relative to one's political affiliation have
such an effect? Would not a survey be helpful in determining whether
the contract had been violated?

The ascertainment of such crucial facts in the past has sometimes
been a matter of uninformed judicial notice, more often the drawing
of inferences from the examination of inadequate data.

The courts' machinery and processes for discovering truth are
time-tested but they are not perfect. And most of our judges recognize the value of availing themselves of all modern scientific aids
in their search for truth as soon as their reliability can be established.
If the application of opinion-research methodology can contribute
to the discovery of truth in the courts of justice, it can serve no
worthier purpose.

(Meeting adjourned.)

[53] See, *e.g.*, Spanel v. Pegler, 160 F.2d 619 (C.A. 2d 1947), 22 N.Y.U.L.Q.
513 (1947), holding that ". . . the label of 'Communist' today in the minds
of many average and respectable persons places the accused beyond the pale of
respectability and makes him a symbol of public hatred. . . ."
[54] See *N. Y. Times*, Dec. 18, 1948, p. 1, col. 2.

Part Three

THE DETERMINANTS OF
PUBLIC OPINION

10

THE DETERMINANTS OF
PUBLIC OPINION

J. W. Albig, Presiding

MR. ALBIG: Ladies and gentlemen, in addition to presiding this evening I was asked to make a few introductory remarks.

A few days ago, I perused idly in our small city evening paper a column by that eminent doctor of medicine, social philosopher, advisor of the physically and psychologically bedeviled, Dr. Frank Crane, M.D. Dr. Crane was advising a young man whose pulse rate and blood pressure had risen under the excitement, the mental strain, and worry attendant upon public speaking. He advised the young man to throw himself into many speaking situations, to become habituated to such actions, in order to diminish his tension for, said the doctor: "Familiarity breeds contempt."

Now, so far as I can tell by self-diagnosis, my blood pressure isn't up, even in the company of this distinguished assemblage of many of the most eminent practitioners of the arts of public opinion, of the academic analysis of public opinion, and of what we hope is becoming at least a partial science of public opinion. And yet, as for familiarity, how can one become accustomed to what is really the unique experience of this unusual assemblage? There are audiences and audiences.

If Dr. Crane's analysis were complete and accurate I'd be on the horns of a dilemma, with the alternative of high blood pressure or contempt for the audience. Fortunately, there are other alternatives of possible attitudes and their expression on this occasion.

But—I'm led on to a question—does blood pressure reflect attitudes and thereby express opinions? Of course it does, or rather, reflects attitudes, as do many other aspects of the functioning of our organisms.

I have heard of a famous New York dramatic critic who, upon being awakened after the third act of a play and told that he could have no significant opinion of Acts II and III as he had been sleeping through them, replied: "Sir, sleep is an opinion."

In a group where one is usually voluble, silence may be an opinion, and vice versa.

Of course we express opinions and attitudes not only by the words we speak but by many aspects of our behavior. And a growing and increasingly complex science or, more accurately stated, partial science of public opinion will need to use many, many indexes of behavior in addition to the words which we speak. Perhaps our pollster friends here would have modified their percentages after getting verbal responses to the words "Dewey," "Truman," "Thurmond" and "Wallace," if they'd have had blood pressure records of their subjects, or been able better to interpret that glint in the subject's eye, his increased heart beat, a chemical analysis of his sweating palms—the Judas! Why, there's a great future for polling; there are lots of things to do yet!

I have defined *opinion* as any type of expression about controversial subjects. And I have defined a *public* as any kind of group within which interaction on controversial subjects has occurred. Then public opinion is the expression by members of publics on controversial subjects. However, this is not a definition on which all political scientists, journalists, and sociologists would agree. And, in any case, such definitions are theoretical attempts to clarify concepts and to attempt to achieve consistency in their use.

This conference is primarily devoted to problems of measurement of attitudes and opinions. How do those who are measuring and recording conceive of public opinion? Twenty years ago we considered it to be very smart, very noncommittal and verbally intriguing, to quote a Columbia professor in saying, "The intelligence tests test what the intelligence tests test." Latterly, we refer to "operational definitions." I do not wish to play with words, but it appears to me to be evidently true that public opinion for the pollsters is those aspects and characteristics of the publics and those expressions of opinion which are elicited from the sample of individuals used. Public opinions for the pollsters are the publics and the opinions which the pollsters poll.

As Professor F. S. Chapin has stated: "In the trend toward quantitative description or measurement in social psychology and sociology, we strive to define each concept in terms of the measurements upon it. Scales to measure public opinion are constructed and tested for validity. We say of a scale that has been standardized to measure public opinion, 'Public opinion is what this scale measures.' This is then the operational definition of the concept public opinion. Does this statement of operationalism make meaningless or false the basic question of validity, which is 'Does this scale measure that which it is designed to measure, namely, public opinion?' This apparent dilemma appears at first glance to be destructive of the very basis of operationalism, because the proposition appears to beg the question by assuming the conclusion which is to be proved and making it part of the premises used to prove it. In reality, however, the dilemma is not a real one, because the assertion, 'Public opinion is what this scale measures,' is made only after the scale has been standardized. The process of standardization, if done thoroughly, disposes of the question of validity, so that the assertion of the operational form of the definition of public opinion does not beg the question."

Now as to the meaning of "group" or "public," the theorists may define a group or public as "any collection of social beings who enter into distinctive social relations with one another," or "a group involving reciprocity among its members." Or they may say, "It implies nothing as to size, form, permanence or cohesive principle. It is any number of people with such relations between or among them as to make it possible to think of them as a whole." "The public is any group that achieves corporate unity through critical interaction. The public is not a formal organization but an area of communication, critical discussion, and consensus arrived at through the clash and modification of opinions." And so on.

Now it is the pollster in the field who is defining "distinctive social relations" and who spells out what he considers to be the "size, form, permanence or cohesive principles" and the "critical interaction" which characterizes a public. He also defines the significant opinions in terms of the list of topics on which he polls.

But polling and recording are essentially a freezing of process, and inadequate excursions into the processes of public opinion are obviously responsible for failures to assess adequately the meaning and significance of current opinion statements. The exigency of failures to assess adequately the meaning of the statements at any given polling or other record drives us at once to examinations in depth, to explore the opinion process, the media of opinion diffusion, and the mind-life of the subjects. As this occurs, a new operation is added and a new definition emerges.

As Charles Horton Cooley wrote: "Public opinion, if we wish to see it as it is, should be regarded as an organic process, and not merely as a state of agreement about some question of the day. For practical uses as well as for adequate thinking this conception is better than the idea of public opinion as agreement. It aims to see the real thing, the developing thought of men, in its genesis and tendencies and with a view to its probable operation."

What are the components of public opinion when we view public opinion as process? I am not of the Lasswellian school of who, when, what, wherefore, analysis; but if I should alliterate the components of public opinion, the areas would be persons, publics, processes, and products.

The effective analyst of public opinion must explore the mind-life of his subjects, especially those attitudes, stereotypes, and values common to the persons who compose the publics. The second component is the public, which he must delimit, define, and delineate. Publics in the United States are numbered by the thousand, and their differential importance to their constituent members would probably need to be recorded on a scale from zero to one thousand. The third component is the communication process which must be explored, from the divergent symbolization of small publics to the mass media. Thus far, the significant and often subtle relationships between communication content and process and mind-life and opinion are but inadequately limned. And finally, there are the products, the expressions of opinion, the recording of which is the subject of this conference.

Our speakers tonight will concern themselves with several facets of this multi-sided phenomenon.

Our first speaker is chairman of the Department of Sociology at the University of Kansas. Professor Carroll Clark will speak on *Social and Cultural Factors* as determinants of public opinion.

11

SOCIAL AND CULTURAL FACTORS IN PUBLIC OPINION

Carroll Clark

MR. CLARK: That question of what public opinion is, is one that was thrown at me years ago when I first began studying the newspaper relations of the public opinion processes under Dr. Robert E. Park, who had a way of haranguing his students about the central object of their investigation. "What is this thing?" Again and again he would ask, "What is this thing, the public? What is this thing, public opinion?"

And my remarks tonight will be addressed principally to some simple, but I hope useful, ways of thinking about this thing, the public.

Those students of public opinion who have centered their efforts on attitude and opinion polling have come under attack by Herbert Blumer and others for their failure to identify and define the object of their study, or to adapt their techniques to the functional nature of the processes of public opinion as these operate in our society. Blumer states: [1]

"What I note is the inability of public opinion polling to isolate 'public opinion' as an abstract or generic concept which could thereby become the focal point of the formation of a system of propositions. . . . In an avowed scientific enterprise seeking to study a class of empirical items and to develop a series of generalizations about that class it is necessary to identify the class. Such identification enables discrimination between the instances which fall within the class and those which do not. In this manner, the generic

[1] "Public Opinion and Public Opinion Polling," *American Sociological Review* (October, 1948).

character of the object of study becomes delineated . . . and it becomes possible to focus study on that object and thus to learn progressively more about [it]."

In his discussion of this article by Blumer, Theodore Newcomb directs criticisms against the lack of selectivity in Blumer's aim, his failure to get down to cases in his attack on inadequate sampling procedures, and, what is most relevant for our purpose, his methodological position in first "isolating the generic object" before forming propositions that can be tested by empirical observations, whether by sampling opinions or other tests. There is some validity to Newcomb's criticisms—in places Blumer may make it appear that he is issuing a call for *a priori* theorizing in advance of, and perhaps unrelated to, concrete empirical observations.

The central issue, however, really concerns the realistic position defended by Blumer, versus the nominalist position assumed by most public opinion polling. Even though the salvo fired by Blumer may not be sufficiently centered on a specific target, his main thesis is essentially correct: Public opinion polling has not sufficiently defined the major object of its study, and is altogether too prone to treat society as an aggregation of discrete individuals.

Some years ago, the writer engaged in correspondence with his teacher, the late Dr. Robert E. Park, concerning the nature of the public and public opinion as conceived from the standpoint of the sociologist in contradistinction to the traditional conceptions of political scientists and historians. The following quotation from a personal letter received from Dr. Park suggests the basis for an approach that is realistic and nomothetic, and may be of interest in the present discussion:

"Why does the question what the public is dog the steps of the political scientist? Because political science, like history, philosophy and law, deals with events rather than things. It seeks to bring these events under normative concepts in order to decide whether they conform to a rule or norm. As soon as the public and public opinion are regarded as things that have a nature of their own and have therefore a natural history, one's whole attitude toward them is quite different from that of the original attitude of the political scientist. The reason, therefore, that this question what the public is dogs the steps of the political scientist is that the political scientist is now trying to think of his objects, including public opinion, as a sociologist would look at them. He is seeking to describe them in naturalistic terms.

"This attempt to deal with the public and public opinion as a thing which changes in some more or less regular way but still preserves its existence during the process of change, involves the analysis of public opinion and the public into smaller elements which interact and cooperate to maintain the integrity of the thing, that is, the public or public opinion. This involves the political scientist and the sociologist in that fundamental problem of all science, namely, the problem of the one and the many, how a thing can consist of parts and still have some sort of unity, what are the units that constitute the public, what are the limits of the public, how do the elements that constitute the public interact to maintain that living equilibrium we call the public? That is the fundamental question."

In the view of the present writer, public opinion studies, in order to yield dependable scientific generalizations, in contradistinction to mere discursive information, must proceed to:

(1) Construct a tentative but coherent and systematic frame of reference appropriate to its investigational tasks.

(2) Develop its inquiries and procedures in terms of that frame of reference, reorganizing the latter as dictated by the demands of the ongoing process of inquiry.

(3) Integrate the frame of reference and investigational procedures employed by public opinion polling with cognate sociological concepts and established social theory.

Spelling out these points a bit more specifically, the writer holds that, in order to make public opinion research dependable and maximally effective, we must

(1) Set forth explicitly the assumptions upon which the investigational problems and theoretical formulations of public opinion polling rest. These assumptions will involve postulates concerning the nature of society and the relation of the individual thereto; the relation of nonlogical behavior to logical behavior; the relation of the sociological area of inquiry and of sociological categories to psychological, political, economic and other special areas and the categories employed in them. Such assumptions are *starting points* and should be explicit rather than tacit or unconsciously maintained. All such postulates, needless to say, should be as far as possible consistent with what is empirically known in the fields concerned.

(2) Devise rough but workable definitions of *public, opinion, public opinion,* and such other categories as serve to denote the central object of investigation on which polling and other public opinion studies are directed.

(3) Tie in these assumptions and concepts with cognate concepts in such systematic fashion as to provide a *first approximation* of schematic theoretical representation of the field of inquiry. Such a schematic representation, comprised of interrelated postulates and conceptual categories, even though highly tentative and fraught with hypothetical elements of low-order probability, will do service in setting up a generic framework in terms of which concrete problems may be formulated and investigated with decisive results. These results should yield generalizations of a higher order of validity as research moves forward, which will react back upon the theoretical framework, thus enabling public opinion researchers to formulate better hypotheses amenable to testing by still more adequate factual data, and so on in a progressive refinement and systematization of the investigational process. It is in some such manner that scientific progress has been made in all fields of science.

(4) These remarks do not mean that every pollster must become a theoretician, though he must, perforce, become to some extent a methodologist. Scientific investigation is a collaborative enterprise that involves a complex division of labor. Sharply defined, highly specialized researches such as the polling of definite strata or segments of the population constituting a public will continue to be necessary. However, the pollster so engaged will need to define his problem, set up his sampling procedure and questionnaire, and analyze his results in a context that embraces the broader theoretical considerations discussed above. To do so adequately, he must be methodologically conscious, and alert to the implications of the broader aspects of the total frame of reference orienting the field.

In several previous articles, the writer has sketched what he considers to be preliminary and tentative basic definitions of categories vital to the theoretical framework essential to inquiry in the field of public opinion.

To the end of establishing key categories in the sort of theoretical framework argued for above, these points are advanced:

(A) The ideal-type constructs of *sacred society* and *secular society* as employed by many writers are potentially useful as starting points.

(1) The theoretical standpoint underlying this dichotomy is organic, configurational, and realistic.

(2) Use of these constructs in analysis aids in marking off publics from other social phenomena differing therefrom, and will sharpen the characterization of public opinion as distinct from other processes of collective behavior.

(B) *Nature of the Public.* The standpoint here suggested views the category *public* as a distant-contact group whose attention has been attracted by a common stimulus. It is a product of a secularized society possessed of mass-communicational media, a complex social and economic division of labor, and a consensus that places a high valuation on freedom of the individual. In addition, in order to function in political action, a public must exhibit these characteristics:

(1) Underlying common interests and sentiments strong enough to over-ride sharply opposed interests and sentiments.

(2) Divergent interests and attitudes serving to divide the group as to the course of action to be taken on certain problems.

(3) A common universe of discourse in terms of which an exchange of views may be effected, and some modicum of agreement reached as to essential facts and "rules of the game."

(4) Access through communicational media to the news or "current events" bearing on the problem at hand.

(5) Sufficient tolerance of opposing views or opponents to be willing to talk out rather than fight out the issue.

(6) Informal social mechanisms or formal political machinery for reaching a collective decision and implementing it in some kind of collective action.

(C) *Distinction between General Public and Special Publics.* Observation and analysis disclose that there are numerous types of publics. The community-at-large when its attention is captured by an issue that disturbs its equilibrium and arouses community-wide discussion is a *general public.* Since the only universe of discourse that exists in such a public is that of "common sense" and the colloquialisms of the man-in-the-street, and since its definitions of situations are couched in terms of the most pervasive and widely shared sentiments, no issues that are complex, recondite, and abstract can be dealt with by a general public unless or until they are factored into relatively simple and concrete forms of vocabulary, thought, and feeling. It possesses no special knowledge, only "common sense."

The special public, as distinct from the general public, springs up in some field of functional activity in the social division of labor. Its spearhead consists of organized interest groups, professional or quasi-professional bodies, and other "experts" or leadership elements possessed of special knowledge and experience, or at least of more than a lay understanding of the activity concerned. These are the "insiders" whose strategic role in public opinion has been forcefully described by Walter Lippmann. Closely allied to these spearhead elements are "voluntary associations" and other lay groups which have a practical interest in the programs and undertakings of the former and are equipped with some special information about these activities. Still other lay participants may rally behind this vanguard when their private interests or sense of public responsibility involve them in a current issue. Special publics, because they are concerned with activities in some degree specialized, make use of a universe of discourse that is more or less technical and not readily comprehensible to the uninitiated. Within its own circumscribed field of activity, issues dividing the group tend to be presented and discussed in the technical jargon.

(D) *The Processes of Social Opinion, Standing Opinion, and Public Opinion.* Group expression of views based solely on sentiments, and inspired by concrete personal situations or deviations of behavior that do not divide the group with respect to the validity of the sentiments, should be sharply distinguished from public opinion. Most gossip is social opinion but not public opinion even though it often has a wide "public" vogue. Social opinion invokes the existing mores or widely shared group sentiments and applies them to individual items of conduct or personal behavior, or to the behavior of deviant groups. It seeks, as a process, to fit the social rules to individual cases without calling into question the rules themselves. In this way, social control is exercised through the sway of mores or group sentiments, and existing codes are brought to bear on novel but classifiable cases. The kidnaping and murder of the Lindbergh baby aroused social opinion in the United States that was virtually community-wide, long before public opinion led to the passage of federal legislation against kidnaping. Through social opinion a group unconsciously seeks to maintain a moral order. In the sacred society of the old Polish community, Thomas and Znaniecki described under the term "social opinion" the operation of group-binding values that maintained the solidarity of the community-as-a-whole.

In a somewhat similar fashion, but with a difference, James Bryce in *The American Commonwealth* described and categorized under the term *standing opinion* those sentiments that crystallize and continue in force following the settlement of a conflict. Whereas public opinion is a process of active discussion or collective deliberation on an issue, standing opinion is the evocation of whatever sentiments people hold on the matter after the collective decision has been reached. Obviously, in decisions involving majority rule, standing opinion will differ among majority and minority components. Public opinion deals with "live" issues demanding an exigent group adjustment; standing opinion continues to be expressed and to exert a control over the behavior of group components after an issue is "dead."

A public of the deliberative type functions only with reference to an issue. An issue may be defined as a situation that destroys a previous routine, provokes a crisis, upsets the group equilibrium, and stimulates talk and action directed at finding an adjustment. For purposes of public opinion study, an issue exists when the group is divided on a problematic situation, but not so far divided as to make impossible a controversy in terms of symbols rather than by more violent weapons.

(E) *Public Opinion as a Process.* These conceptual distinctions thus enable us to mark off public opinion as a generic entity or thing. It is a thing that is derived from the repetitive aspects of events recurring in a characteristic fashion, that is to say, in a process that may be abstracted out of the flux of social phenomena. Public opinion is the process that is set in motion when a group having the characteristics of a public confronts a problematic situation or issue, proceeds to engage in active discussion or a controversy of symbols, and eventually arrives at a collective deliberative adjustment. Like the process of deliberative thinking in the individual, as analyzed by John Dewey, facts are weighed and alternative lines of tenable action are considered and debated before a decision is made. This means that public opinion is in some degree a rational process since facts are weighed and logical persuasion exerted by the discussants in their appraisal of the situation. But emotional responses such as yielding to propagandistic appeals and other reactions of nonlogical behavior also play a part as the group strives to reach a collective adjustment. The process is one of interaction in which the logical appeal to facts vies with non-rational pressures and conversional techniques. Such an interactive process cannot be reduced to disparate individual elements or described in terms of the rational faculties of the separate actors in the social drama.

Social and Cultural Factors as Public Opinion Determinants

Just what are the determinants of public opinion, and just how should they be defined and grappled with? The answers should emerge from the ongoing process of public opinion research conducted along the lines previously indicated. According to the views of this writer, we cannot at this stage announce a definitive and conclusive inventory or itemized list of public opinion determinants, and assign them specific weights or relative importance in public opinion formation. To undertake to do so would imply that we know the answers in advance. All that we shall attempt here is to suggest some of the kinds of things that analytical scrutiny and past empirical studies have shown to play an important part in the public opinion process, and hence to be worth focusing on in further investigation. The points to be made here are merely suggestive, and are limited to certain more obvious social and cultural factors.

(1) *Needs, Purposes, and Interests of Groups in Relation to Social Organization.* The forms of group life in any society emerge as established activity patterns in response to the needs, purposes, and interests of the collectivity concerned. Group action thus arising and functionally directed to group-defined ends, tends to develop an action structure. We need to study the interests of groups in relation to their organization, which defines the roles of individual members, orients their attitudes toward in-group and out-group, and regulates behavior in conformity with group definitions of situations bearing on the conception of group purposes or interests. Keen observers like Charles H. Cooley have described the emergence of new social forms which arise to meet new needs and are tested experimentally by being tried out in meeting the demands of new situations, as "a tentative process . . . not necessarily conscious." While the process is never wholly voluntary, in a secular society with a highly developed division of labor and effective means of communication, the emergence and exploitation of group interests is marked by conscious efforts to clarify aims and a critical discussion of issues in

terms of the data of current events whenever those interests are blocked or opposed.

(2) *Individual Attitude Formation and Ego-involvement.* Group organization as discussed above in connection with group purposes and interests establishes a set of norms or standards which serve to shape and modify, though do not wholly determine, the attitudes and behavior of the component members. The entire process of individual attitude formation in relation to the social interactions occurring in concrete situations where the individual participates should be regarded as a fundamental and highly relevant subject of inquiry for those who seek to understand the formation of public opinion. We need to ascertain how far, on the one hand, the individual attitude is swayed by short-cut fiats or arbitrary value dictums issued by group spokesmen or propagandists, and how far, on the other hand, his attitude is crystallized or made rigid by his devious ego-involvements. Contributions made by ego-involvement studies in the last eight or ten years appear to have important implications for public opinion investigation. Some of these contributions throw light on the selectivity of memory concerning controversial material as a result of ego-involvement, the skewing of judgment of problematic situations in which one's ego is highly involved, and the effect of the degree of personal identification of the individual with the group's codes and interests.

(3) *Institutional Creeds, Myths, and Doctrines.* Every social institution of group organization tends to project social images in the form of creeds, doctrines, or myths which serve to rationalize (in the psychoanalytic sense) the purposes and interests of the group and confirm its underlying sentiments. When a venerable and long-established institution is sharply challenged by a new and rival form, a proliferation of creeds results. Propaganda efforts are couched largely in terms of these creeds, but may misrepresent in considerable measure the basic growth trend of changing sentiments. Study is needed of the relation of creeds to basic action patterns and group dynamics.

12

PRESSURE GROUPS
AND THE PRESS

Ralph D. Casey

MR. ALBIG: Our next speaker always appears relaxed, sensible and well-balanced, and so practically informed about the world of the newspaper: Ralph Casey, Director of the School of Journalism at the University of Minnesota. His topic is *Pressure Groups and the Press.*

MR. CASEY: The objective of a pressure group is to win support for a program it favors. It campaigns for interests or ideals its members hold in common; it lobbies for legislative or administrative approval; it defends itself against "inimical" public policy. It uses persuasion and may resort to intimidation and coercion. If it is well organized and financed, it usually calls into its service experts skilled in the techniques of molding and controlling attitudes.

The communication channels must expect to feel the "push" of pressure groups. An aggressive pressure organization usually wants, and often demands, affirmative support on the printed page or over the air, and it seeks when it can to influence the editorial tone or the news policy, or both, of a popular medium. Since many of the aims of a group involve sharp controversy in legislative halls or in the arena of public opinion, a communication agency has three options when a struggle is on: editorially, it may support or oppose a group's program or stand aloof in a neutral corner. In any event, it can hardly ignore in news columns or radio newscasts the group's activities when a hot and interesting fight wages.

But the communication medium faces another pressure which is more evasive and less articulate than the highly-organized campaign of a vigorous pressure group. This can be characterized as the pressure of a given community's individual culture—its traditions, basic beliefs and ways of looking at things. The mores of a village, city, or region may be more powerful as the source of influence on the communication channel than the pressure of a zealous minority group in pursuit of its objectives.

The study of cultural pressure on the press is a challenge to those equipped with the tools of research and a knowledge of the pragmatic problem of operating a newspaper or popular periodical successfully. The social climate conditions the individual daily or weekly or other general-circulation periodical. Newspapermen and journalism teachers are constantly amazed at the lay generalizations that are made about *the press,* suppositions that appear to be based on the belief that all newspapers are standardized in outlook and policy, uniform products from the same mold.[1] Few persons stop to think of the basic social adjustments that a newspaper makes to its particular environment. The editor in Butte, Montana, has many a problem different from those of his opposite number in Memphis. Because of basic cultural and economic differences in the communities, a Salt Lake City daily is not subject to exactly similar forces confronting the newspapers in Detroit or Boston. Pasadena is not Paducah.

The cultural influences that bind individual newspapers to their special settings have never been adequately measured. For several years a limited number of seniors in the University of Minnesota School of Journalism each studied individually one Minnesota newspaper in its social environment. First they traced the historical and social development of the town and analyzed its present-day cultural pattern.[2] Then followed a rather intensive examination of the news and editorial behavior of the newspaper to determine how news coverage and editorial policy conformed with the town and regional environment. Each inquiry sought also to reveal departures from and accommodations to social norms, as well as to identify

[1] The journalist's view of popular attitudes of this sort is expressed by James S. Pope, managing editor of the Louisville *Courier-Journal:* "By nearly all its critics, the newspaper has been taken for granted as a fairly uniform organism, responding properly to the same stimuli and quickened by the same motives. That assumption is nonsense." In an endorsement of proposals for a scientific evaluation of the press, Mr. Pope commented: "Apply yourself to individual newspapers and avoid that elusive phantom known as 'the press.'" See his article, "On Understanding the Press," *Nieman Reports,* April, 1948 (Vol. 2, pp. 7, 9).

[2] In preparation for the project, students read widely in volumes on urban sociology. Some of the writers consulted were R. D. McKenzie, S. A. Queen and L. F. Thomas, E. L. Thorndike, E. W. Burgess, the Lynds, A. M. Schlesinger, H. B. Woolston, Lewis Mumford, Philip Klein, Albert Blumenthal, Warner and Lunt, and others.

certain individuals and groups possessed of power in the community and to trace their influence on newspaper policy.

These projects were exploratory and were designed to train instructors as well as students in teasing out leads which might develop methods of research in this field. No systematic pulling together of student findings has been accomplished as yet. The real challenge is to undertake a similar project with a corps of well-qualified graduate students.

Among the findings of such individual studies might come conclusions as to the techniques, methods, successes and failures of pressure groups in their attempts to influence the press. Such groups are only one segment within a social milieu. We need also to discover the degree to which the social history and cultural configurations of an entire community shape its press. Broad cultural influences difficult of measurement sway the newspaper in varying degrees and determine some of the criteria of the selective process exerted on editorial material and the treatment given to the finished product.

Every editor knows that if he alienates his public, his newspaper will cease to operate. Since circulation keeps it solvent, a paper must hold its patronage, a fact that shackles it more than any other influence. What a public wants to hear varies in greater or less degree from place to place. Unhappily, in too many communities, a public does not relish the truth,[3] and even if the editor explains that the truth is given for good motives, readers may not be satisfied.

A few social scientists and a handful of magazine writers have given us excellent pictures of the inner life of a number of American

---

[3] *A Free and Responsible Press*, the Report of the Commission on Freedom of the Press, stresses this point (pp. 57-58):

"People seldom want to read or hear what does not please them; they seldom want others to read or hear what disagrees with their convictions or what presents an unfavorable picture of groups they belong to. When such groups are organized, they let the press know their objections to remarks concerning them. The press is therefore caught between its desire to please and extend its audience and its desire to give a picture of events and people as they really are. . . .

"Every branch of the communications industry is subject to the same sort of pressure. Publishers who stick to their guns have suffered for it. The managing editor of one of the principal papers of the country testified before the Commission that in his opinion his publication took a drop of more than 50,000 in circulation because of a policy displeasing to a well-organized pressure group."

The Commission adds: "It would be a mistake to assume that pressure is always bad just because it is pressure. Testimony before the Commission reveals that pressure groups often correct unconscious bias or mistakes and bring into view neglected areas of discussion. . . ."

towns.[4] In some cases the analysts have generalized on the extent to which cultural forces operate on the press. There are some data to show how community restraints are placed on editors, limiting the newspaper as a force for social control. But the studies are few and they usually fail to see the problem of publishing through the eyes of the publisher and editor, as well as from the social idealist's point of view. As for the direct impact of organized pressure groups on the press, much of the published material usually either cries out that "leading advertisers control the press" and then lets the subject drop at that point, or the problem of pressure is dealt with largely at the national level,[5] never getting down to the individual group and the single newspaper. A detailed picture of state-wide and city-wide operations of pressure groups would be useful in providing an understanding of influences that carry on pressure and propaganda to develop public attitudes at the community level, and would provide some basis for attempting studies of pressures exerted on communication agencies as individual enterprises.[6]

Three years ago I attempted to learn what precisely were the pressure groups that editors themselves believed make the most vigorous attempts to control news and editorial policy. This inquiry was part of a much larger survey,[7] and I regard the pressure-group section as only a small sampling of attitudes. The stress placed on

[4] See as examples the Lynds, *Middletown* and *Middletown in Transition* (Muncie, Indiana); William Warner and Paul S. Lunt, *The Social Life of a Modern Community* (Newburyport, Massachusetts); Albert Blumenthal, *Small Town Stuff* (Philipsburg, Montana); Charles Rumford Walker, *American City* (Minneapolis); the articles by George R. Leighton in *Harper's*, vols. 177 and 178.

[5] Belle Zeller usefully summarizes pressure techniques at the state level in *Pressure Politics in New York: A Study of Group Representation Before the Legislature.*

[6] For generalized discussions of pressure group attempts on the press, see George L. Bird and Frederic E. Merwin, *The Newspaper and Society*, chapter 24; A. Gayle Waldrop, *Editor and Editorial Writer*, pp. 414-422, and Curtis D. MacDougall, *Newsroom Problems and Politics*, pp. 235-239. A number of cases of pressures exerted by economic groups on newspapers are cited by Roscoe B. Ellard, "How to Read Editorials" (especially pp. 64-70) in Elmer Ellis, ed., *Education Against Propaganda*, seventh yearbook of the National Council for the Social Studies, 1937.

[7] The inquiry was undertaken by the writer on assignment from Dr. Robert D. Leigh, director of the Commission on Freedom of the Press. It involved questioning editors in ten cities, including competitive and non-competitive communities, on a fairly large number of editorial problems. Pressure group activity was only one of several. This article includes some recent interviews not connected with the Commission assignment. In all, seventeen editors were interviewed.

The interview technique was on an easy and informal basis. No detailed questionnaire was used as a uniform guide to the questions put to the editors.

certain types of pressures by almost all of the editors is significant, however, and I think some of the examples of pressure are illuminating.

Dr. V. O. Key, Jr., professor of political science, Johns Hopkins University, stresses Business, Labor, and Agriculture as the "Big Three" in his realistic analysis of political power.[8] The editors whom I interviewed say, however, that in their opinion the most vigorous and persistent pressures directed at their journals and themselves came from nationality and religious groups. Some of the groups were of the hyphenate type. Others were composed of persons native to America but intent upon espousing an American foreign policy which seemed most favorable to the nationalities of their forebears.

The fact that editors placed nationality and religious groups at the top of the list in pressure drive, with business, labor, and agriculture on a secondary level, raises a number of questions. Have the communication agencies so adjusted their relations with these influences that it did not occur to many of my respondents to emphasize these pressures? Did they accept them in the day's work and take their demands for granted, or since business, labor, and agriculture are long-standing action groups, were the editors impressed currently with the increasing power of other organizations which now flex their muscles in the social scene? Dr. Key quotes Gaus and Wolcott as noting the "moral importance" of farmers in American society as a whole and consequently "their rightful claim upon that society for their fair share of its production, power, and prestige." [9] Is farm-group pressure one of the "acceptable" pressures? Can we raise a similar question in the case of business, or should we rephrase it to read "the prevailing economic order," without dwelling on the trade associations which speak intermittently on behalf of a given segment of business? What about the adjustments of communications to labor groups? More was said by the editors on labor's pressures than those of business and agriculture.

As to nationality and religious groups, mentioned often by my respondents, it is apparent that their attempts to dictate newspaper policy depend not only on local situations but on the character of events in the outside world which give rise to an overt expression of their beliefs, prejudices, and dissatisfactions. World War II aroused

[8] See *Politics, Parties, and Pressure Groups* (2nd edition).
[9] *Ibid.*, p. 18.

their emotions. During the war and immediately thereafter, the Poles were especially aggressive in their demands that the press line up with versions of the news palatable to them and with editorial expressions supporting a foreign policy in tune with their ideas of a Polish nationhood. I gathered this from interviews with editors in the autumn of 1945. This reaction of a group conscious of its "nationalistic entity" is not surprising. In World War I, during our period of neutrality, the efforts of German-language groups to sway American opinion through the press, even to the secret purchase by German agents of the New York *Evening Mail,* is a well-known story.[10] The Irish swayed the Hearst newspapers among others in the early twenties, although Hearst's political and circulation ambitions were involved. Other racial groups at various times in the recent past have demanded newspaper support of their causes.

The Polish problem was on the minds of some of the editors at the time of my interviews, as the following from a leading Canadian editor in a prairie province will reveal:

"The Poles work closely with the Polish consul. Our editorial policy was not friendly to the London committee at the time the Lublin Poles were at cross purposes with the exiled group in the British capital. This provoked the consul, supported by his followers, to 'move in' on us. I should add that this pressure was exerted even though we had always given the arguments of the London committee in our news columns.

"After intermittent pressures from Polish and other nationality sources, the greatest trouble occurred following our newspaper's report of the results in our province of the 1942 Dominion plebiscite on conscription. Poles and Ukrainians are fairly solidly grouped in certain areas of city and province. Our paper was able to analyze the result of this 'Yes' and 'No' ballot by polling districts, and we pointed out that the two racial groups cast their votes principally in the negative. Sizable delegations of Poles and Ukrainians immediately invaded our office, expressing their indignation in most vigorous terms. While their leaders admitted that the newspaper's account of the voting was an accurate one, they were angry nevertheless. The paper had an immediate drop of 1500 subscribers in the Polish and Ukrainian districts.

[10] Language, literary, and institutional kinship with the British made overt pressures on the press by English sympathizers not so necessary as in the case of German-American groups.

"Our policy has been to permit readers to express their untrammeled opinions in the letters column of the paper. At times Polish residents have bombarded the editorial office with their written views. We let them 'run wild' in the letters column."

Other editors had similar experiences with this and other nationality groups, but I shall not recite the details here. Recently Slavic groups in and around a Middle Western steel-producing city have protested the writings of a well-known foreign correspondent who has written frankly on Yugoslavian policies. Pressure on a newspaper carrying this journalist's dispatches was only mitigated when the publisher over his own signature praised and approved in his paper's columns the work of this correspondent.

A Chicago editor believes that "religious and nationality groups have more potential power to exercise pressure on newspapers than either economic or labor organizations." They can enforce harmful reader boycotts in the effort either to punish a newspaper for a given editorial or news policy, or to swerve it from given policies. It is for this reason, the editor says, that in some metropolitan communities newspapers may deliberately refrain from offending a powerful ethnic or religious segment of the population, even though it may be a minority group.

"An editor in one community may be acutely aware of a strong Polish group; in another city an Irish or Italian group, and so on," the editor added. "In still another city he may be conscious of the unity of the Catholics or Jews, or again, of the Protestants. In the South there are settled convictions on the status Negroes should occupy. Fearless newspapers at some time or another may have to combat one of the minority or majority groups, knowing that when the issue is joined, the response will be immediate and probably unpleasant for the editors and possibly damaging to the newspaper."

When I discussed pressure influences in an important Pacific Northwest metropolis, one editor asserted that his community was "unusually free from highly organized pressure groups." The locals of the American Federation of Labor were the most persistent in their demands on the press, but the problem of pressure "was in no wise important." The editor of the competing newspaper attributed "the lack of racial, nationality or religious pressures" to the "homogeneous character of the city's population." In the last years of the war, however, the editors realized they had a racial, if not a pressure-group, problem of some dimensions with which they had to deal. With the development of ship building adjacent to the city area, Negroes were drawn to the yards as workers. Racial tensions developed, culminating in a murder case in which the city police played an ignoble part. This required the press to take note of a situation having explosive possibilities and to suggest remedies to relieve community tensions and to call the offending peace officers to time.

One of the Northwest's cities, Portland, has had socio-religious pressures that affected the press. In the early twenties, a strong Ku Klux Klan movement developed in Oregon with Portland and the Willamette Valley as the focal point. The Klan and its supporters were able to elect a governor and other state officials. The movement unquestionably was backed by certain Protestant sects. The Klan's power was fully understood by the newspapers. The editors of the two leading Portland dailies agreed to avoid direct attacks on the Klan and to "play down" its activities, although they took account of the state political developments that grew out of the movement. The third paper, a daily with the smallest circulation of the Portland trio, vigorously attacked the Klan. It suffered heavy inroads in circulation and eventually collapsed (although other causes also contributed to its downfall).

When I recalled this era of Klan activity to an Oregon editor during my round of interviews, he remarked: "You can't reason with people on religion. Why attempt it? We didn't." [11]

For the record, all Oregon newspapers outside of Portland did not conform to the policy of the leading metropolitan journals.[12] Robert W. Ruhl, editor of the Medford *Mail Tribune,* went after the Klan hammer and tongs. A few years later this crusading editor won the

[11] Since the Klan movement in Oregon did capitalize on religious and racial prejudice and since it got its support from those affiliated with certain Protestant sects and drew some members from non-sectarian orders with religious coloration, the editors of the leading Portland papers preferred to think of it as a religious movement. The fact that other psychological drives besides religious emotion accounted for the Klan's roster of members apparently was not regarded as significant.

[12] Newspapers varied in their policies toward the Klan. William Allen White of the Emporia *Gazette* fought the Klan in Kansas with extraordinary vigor. (See Walter Johnson, *William Allen White's America.*) In later years White was on the affirmative side of a pressure campaign when he served as chairman of the Committee to Defend America by Aiding the Allies. The New York *World* carried on a merciless campaign against the Klan.

Pulitzer prize in recognition of his newspaper's leadership in a civic campaign.

Strong religious and nationalistic currents run through many international issues which come to the focus of attention of American readers. The Civil War in Spain, which created deep "ideological" divisions in the Iberian nation, also affected opinion in this country. Heavy pressure was brought to bear on the metropolitan press to take sides in this struggle. The experience of the late Thomas J. Dillon, for years managing editor of the Minneapolis *Tribune*, is no doubt similar to that of many other editors who were besieged by pressure groups while the war was on.

"The war in Spain was productive of intense group pressure," said Mr. Dillon, "and, I am certain, resulted in a loss of faith in the fairness and honesty of newspapers on the part of many, many persons. In the last months of the war I was practically bombarded with complaints from various organizations, none of which had any particular connection with Spain. To some of these organizations the Spanish war was a battle for liberalism and democracy; to others it was a battle against Communism and for the preservation of religion.

"The so-called Loyalists had flooded the country with propaganda and certain religious forces had their counter propaganda. To the protagonists of one side, there could be no doubt but that the other side was 100 percent in the wrong, and the newspaper that failed to make this clear was obviously partisan and dishonest; thus the newspaper was regarded as either the tool of the Communist party or the Catholic church. A newspaper that chronicled the events of the battlefields was stigmatized with the responsibility for the events." [13]

A good many editors coped with a serious problem only recently when two groups, both part of the same racial and religious amalgam, but with differing political views, approached the newspapers with appeals for support of their respective programs. I refer to the Zionist movement, which espoused a Jewish national state, and the American Council for Judaism, which opposed it.[14]

[13] From "Pressure Groups and the Editor," an unpublished manuscript read at the Fourth Annual Daily Newspapermen's Conference, University of Minnesota, May 20, 1939.

[14] The Zionists appear to have been the more aggressive of the two.
In the mobilizing of public opinion, editorial advertising played a significant role.

There is no question that the controversy between the two movements raised serious problems in cities like New York, where the Jewish population is large, and in other types of communities as well. New York editorial comment ranged from mild to positive on such questions as partition, the Jewish-Arab armed conflict, the Bernadotte and Bunche plans, the attitude of the British foreign secretary, Israel's petition for membership in the UN, and so on. Above and beyond the factional argument, newspaper publishers and editors have had to decide on editorial policies concerning Palestine in relation to American over-all foreign policy. Some day a research student may be able to report on the forces involved in the Palestinian disputes. Scholarly studies of both the Spanish and Palestinian controversies would throw light on pressure influence as it seeks to affect national policy.

Periodicals as well as newspapers meet with religious and racial pressures. The public becomes widely aware of these when a controversy breaks into the open.

In June, 1948, the *Nation* was barred from the list of publications that could be purchased for circulation in the libraries of the public high schools of New York. The *Nation's* editors assert the belief that this action apparently was taken because of criticisms in the *Nation* of the Catholic church or Catholic hierarchy for stands and policies with respect to a number of problems. A number of prominent Americans rushed to the *Nation's* defense. They appealed to the New York Board of Superintendents to revoke the order barring the *Nation* from the New York schools.[15]

A prominent Middle Western editor believes that a newspaper can demonstrate over a long period that it will not be intimidated by pressure groups and thus convince them it is useless to make the attempt. The groups come to understand that, although they have every right to present their cases to the editor, the newspaper must be free to make its own independent decision on policy.

"It takes a newspaper twenty years to demonstrate permanently and finally to such groups that they cannot force either news or views

[15] Pressure on the press from organized religious groups is hardly noticed unless a church appears in the field of temporal power and seeks to influence decisions on important political questions of a highly controversial nature. Publicity methods of religious organizations get little public attention and are not usually discussed in the press. Edwin F. Dakin's *Mrs. Eddy: The Biography of a Virginal Mind* describes the work of the Committee on Publications of the Christian Science Church. See Bird and Merwin, *op. cit.*, pp. 500-503.

into the paper or censor its content," said this editor in my interview with him. He presides over the editorial pages of two strong dailies in a farm belt area. "The people of our community have come to understand our policy in this matter."

A Far Western editor in a city of 30,000, who won the Public Service Award of the press association of his state, is not convinced "the problem of dealing with pressure groups gets any easier as time goes on." He has just completed twenty-one years at the helm of his newspaper. When he first took over news and editorial responsibility, he gave notice to pressure-group leaders that he was prepared to oppose them when their programs conflicted with what he regarded as the public interest. His first skirmish came with the followers of a powerful fundamentalist clergyman. The editor launched a campaign against so-called "blue-nose" restrictions in the community and ran head-on into the churchman, characterized by the editor as the "Protestant Pope of my town." The newspaper had aroused opposition by campaigning to open the motion picture theaters on Sunday. It won the fight only when the newspaper's public opinion poll revealed that the large majority of residents were against Sunday restrictions. On another occasion, the Townsend clubs in the county attempted an organized boycott of the newspaper. The circumstances were these:

In the middle thirties the clubs presented a petition to the state legislature signed by thousands of old people in the county demanding the passage of a Townsend-written old-age-pension bill. A county member of the House of Representatives voted against the measure. The newspaper opposed the bill also, arguing that the proposed pension benefits would bankrupt the state. County Townsendites organized a recall drive against the offending legislator. Then through the nine-week recall campaign, the editor campaigned in his editorial column against the attempt to unseat the House member. At every Townsend meeting, in town, village, and hamlet, the recall leaders urged auditors to boycott the newspaper, and throughout this campaign, the editor in question was faced with the editorial opposition of the town's other daily, which supported the Townsend plan.

The end of the story: The legislator was recalled, but the newspaper opposing the oldsters' pension bill suffered no loss in circulation.

"I think the reason we survived this attempt to weaken or ruin us," said the editor when I interviewed him, "was that the people in the county were fair. They knew we had printed the news of Townsend activities before and during the recall fight. In fact, old people in Townsend audiences said so to their speakers when these leaders of the movement urged a boycott of my newspaper."

I asked all editors: "Are pressures always annoying and troublesome?" The uniform answer was that no paper wished to forego contacts with the groups, despite the frequent difficulties arising in dealing with them. The editors' answer may be summed up in the statement that "it is the business of pressure groups to exert pressure, but the business of the editor is to resist pressure when it is improper." Pressure groups are frequently helpful in making an editor aware of the grievances and desires of a large block of readers. One editor remarked a pressure group "affords the lone individual an effective means by which he can articulate his views." Some editors find that a telephone canvass of pressure-group spokesmen on a given issue is helpful. Pressure groups are often a source of news.

Since so many pressure groups are advocating causes that are worthy, with a leadership that is sincere, the problem in such cases is usually one of newspaper space. This can become a serious problem. The greater the difficulty the group encounters in arriving at success, the more likely it is to demand that the newspaper turn over its columns to the advocacy of the cause. There is no reasonable possibility of satisfying the proponents of all these pressure programs. The OWI was compelled during the war to "ration" federal radio programs and news releases because of impossible demands for news space and radio time and to require that a scrap drive should not be timed coincidentally with a "blood bank" campaign, and so on.

Professor Ellard has suggested that there are two types of pressure more difficult for an editor to combat than racial-religious, business, labor, and other influences. "One is the sincere class-consciousness of either the publisher or of stockholders of authority," he reports. "The other an apathy on the part of readers toward important issues over which they cannot get excited." [16]

It is difficult to generalize on the socio-economic orientation of the publishers and editors of 1781 daily newspapers, quite aside

[16] *Op. cit.*, p. 68.

from the owners of thousands of weeklies, and while this article does not attempt to discuss the "internal pressures" that operate within a newspaper,[17] the remarks of two editors on the possible effect on their views of their status and role in the social order are pertinent:

Said one, epigrammatically: "The most persistent and powerful pressures are those the editor never hears about. By that I mean the pressures that are exerted silently and inferentially by groups of which you see yourself a part."

Another editor remarked: "The most subtle pressure, but one which is the most difficult of measurement and which is perhaps the most persuasive, is the pressure of association which inevitably throws publishers, editors and even most of the staff writers into contact with persons of a predominant economic point of view and a privileged social level."

In an effort to guard against pressure through staff affiliations with outside groups, one newspaper in a Middle Western city of 600,000 requires that no staff member enter organizations as member or officer. So strictly is this policy enforced that men on the editorial and news side do not even accept invitations to join service organizations and luncheon clubs. Phil H. Parrish, editorial-page editor of the Portland *Oregonian,* derides this policy as one that smacks of "military methods." [18]

There is much to be attempted on the scientific level before a rounded treatise can be written on the problems of cultural and group pressures on the press. Case studies of special situations are needed. The struggle over the Truman civil-rights program, especially as it affects attitudes in the Deep South, is a case in point. The factors influencing Southern editorial behavior are variable and no generalization can be made on editorial policy on civil rights. Valid judgments must flow from studies of individual communities and specific newspapers. These variables include the family and geographic background of publisher and editor, the economic and social level of white groups, the percentage of Negroes resident in the circulation and trade area of the newspaper, and the proximity of the town to areas where northern troops carried on a "scorched-earth" policy during the Civil War.

[17] For a discussion of publisher-editor relations, see the writer's "Professional Freedom and Responsibility in the Press," in *Communications in Modern Society,* Wilbur Schramm, ed.

[18] *The Bulletin of the American Society of Newspaper Editors,* June 1, 1947, p. 2.

What are the techniques used by pressure groups in their efforts to influence the press? Many procedures are similar to those employed in seeking to influence legislators and administrative officers in governmental capacities. Once a program is agreed upon, the group will organize its propaganda and seek to identify the interests of the group with that of a city, state, or the nation.[19] It is then up to the editor to inquire "whose honor, prestige, security or interest is actually at stake." The group sometimes organizes mass demonstrations in the hope of bringing organized pressure on the public and the communications agencies. It creates news by shaping events or conditions in the expectation that such events will become so newsworthy that the press cannot ignore them. It may seek temporary alliances with other power groups to make its influence felt. If it can gain an alliance with a political party to which a newspaper may be committed, this may be a net gain.

Any one or all of these influences may have effect. My own conclusion is that the types of pressure used most *directly* on the press, are: lobbying tactics against publishers and editors; letters and telephone calls to the newspaper proprietor, his editor, and, in some cases, his departmental subordinates arguing the group's case; articles in the group's own periodical applauding or taking issue with the newspaper's policy; and the use of rumor and gossip to undermine an editorial point of view.[20]

If an editor offends a powerful pressure group, a frequent technique is to make a call on the publisher. The group wants to abolish or throttle down adverse editorial utterances or, affirmatively, to "sell" the publisher with the group's program. This is sometimes

[19] Editor Dillon remarked: "Within the last few years, definitely since the period of the depression, every conceivable ideology has organized itself with a president, secretary, treasurer, and the inevitable press committee. The result in a nutshell is that practically every man and woman in the land has become a member of some sort of organization and has become intensely and cleverly publicity minded, and is demanding of the newspapers that their particular beliefs and desires must be given publicity and editorial support." *Op. cit.*

[20] Editor Dillon expressed the fear that the unsatisfied demands of various pressure groups was creating in the minds of the people the belief that the press is not serving their interests. He remarked:

"The existence of these pressure groups, and the existence of hostility toward the press, may of course be coincidental in time, and without causative relation to each other, but I suspect there is a relationship. Many of these groups have propaganda papers of their own, and these propaganda journals are not sparing in their criticism of the newspapers. They tell their followers how to bring pressure to bear on the press and at the same time tell them that any lack of newspaper support is due to unworthy motives." *Op. cit.*

an insidious technique as far as the public is concerned, since if a publisher or editor who has opposed the group decides to retreat, the public at large is not always aware of what caused the shift in policy. In extreme cases when groups are "mad" at the editor, they may request that the publisher abate this editorial "nuisance" by firing him. Group leaders may make such frequent and persistent demands that the publisher may finally decide not to be bothered and annoyed any longer. In such an instance, he will rationalize his decision by deciding that the issue is not sufficiently important to merit a continuation of the editorial policy.

The group may organize a letter-writing campaign. It may commend the newspaper in a flood of letters, if it approves of its policy. If offended, it will either prove unsparing in denouncing the policy or explain ever so carefully how greatly in error the newspaper is. Often an editor can detect a similar style running through a dozen such letters, indicating clearly the genesis of such communications. Another technique is to use the group's own periodical to make positive charges that an editorial writer or foreign correspondent is biased or uninformed or guilty of outright distortion in editorials or dispatches. This can be damaging to a newspaper if the group's specialized publication has a devoted following, which it probably possesses. To defend its writers from such attacks, a newspaper is unlikely to engage in a brawl in its own columns with the editor of the group's journal. Again, group leaders in their face-to-face contacts with their own members can reinforce antagonisms of followers against a defiant newspaper by claims of editorial bias. Gossip of this sort can stir doubts of a paper's integrity among other social groups in which the pressure forces move.

The outright organization of an advertisers' or readers' boycott against an offending newspaper is sometimes threatened and sometimes carried out. In certain cases, private news distributors not on the payroll of a newspaper can occasionally cause trouble by the device of burying on a newsstand the paper which has offended the group prejudices of a number of such dealers. Since the right to distribute is as essential as the right to print, the newspaper comes up against the danger to free expression through this technique. In extreme cases, groups may attempt to induce legislatures to pass laws crippling the freedom of the press, and sometimes the apparent sincerity of the group's motive may prevent the public at large from appreciating that press freedom can be nibbled away by such isolated efforts.[21] Huey Long no doubt felt he had the support of the people in the back parishes when he imposed his newspaper tax aimed at opposing newspapers in New Orleans.

How to deal with pressure groups? The editor occupies an uneasy chair when he finds himself under a pressure which his common sense or his moral conscience impels him to resist. William M. Tugman, editor of the Eugene, Oregon, *Register-Guard,* remarks: "In general, I have found that it is a wise policy never to straddle in dealing with pressure groups. If we do, we pay for it through the nose later on."

The interplay of pressure groups and the communication agencies requires the gathering of a good many case studies before adequate interpretation of the relationship can be made. The techniques and practices of such groups in given instances when they are seeking to sway the press requires more analysis than research men in the schools of journalism and the social science departments have given to the subject. The success or failure of group action in dealing with the communication channels has not been documented adequately. The long-range effects of newspaper campaigns and crusades against specific pressure groups requires study. Some editors say "crusading" is either a lost art or that in today's society the long-range dispassionate education of readers through well-balanced treatment of news and editorials is the better technique in the attainment of a program. Is that really true?

We can obtain real light on the effect of society and its constituent parts on the press only by systematic study of individual communities and the newspapers operating within these individual environments. Systematic investigation "at the grass roots" will also provide sound generalizations on the effects of the press on society. Individual studies will answer questions on other problems relating to the communication channels. At any rate the conclusions reached will prove more valid than the many unprecise assertions that are current at present concerning the newspaper.

[21] Legislation aimed at restricting the right to publish news of crime is a case in point.

13

COMMUNICATIONS AND PUBLIC OPINION

Wilbur Schramm

MR. ALBIG: The next paper was prepared by Wilbur Schramm, Assistant to the President, Director of the University Press, and Director of the Institute of Communications at the University of Illinois. His topic is *Communications and Public Opinion*. Professor Saunders will read the paper, as Professor Schramm is unable to be here.

MR. SAUNDERS (FOR MR. SCHRAMM): Let me say, first, how very sorry I am not to be in Iowa City to read this paper. The prospect of revisiting Iowa is always pleasant, and the thought of coming back to a meeting in Old Capitol especially tempting; for Iowa in general, and Old Capitol in particular, have a way of writing themselves into the hearts and memories of Iowa men.

In the second place, let me hasten to say that what we *know* about the relation of communications and public opinion is considerably less impressive than what we do *not* know. Last year a distinguished lecturer created some consternation among University of Illinois students by summing up a brilliant discussion of this subject as follows: "Some kind of communication on some kinds of issues, brought to the attention of some kinds of people under some kinds of conditions, have some kind of effects!" I judge that this gentleman would be the first to agree with me that we are not yet prepared to develop a scientific theory of the relation of communications to public opinion. In the year since the lecture I have been talking about, two members of this conference, Dr. Berelson and Dr. Lazarsfeld, have published excellent and thoughtful essays on the subject, Mr. Louis H. Bean has published a provocative book, and we have had an election which, I am reliably informed, has been educational. But I am afraid we are still in the stage of observation and hypotheses.

140

Therefore my intention in this paper is to set down a few notes toward a theory. They are in the form of ten rather broad hypotheses, some of which I have developed more than others, and none of which, in the next twenty or twenty-five minutes, I can develop enough.

(1) *The relation between communications and public opinion is an INTER relation.*

The influence works both ways. Communications affect public opinion by means we shall explore later in this paper. Public opinion, operating through the "daily re-election of the editor," the daily referendum on the radio program, powerfully affects communications. The true complexity of this interrelationship is just beginning to emerge from our descriptive and experimental data, but I judge that the hypothesis is generally accepted. Let us pass on to another point.

(2) *The pipelines of influence are extremely tenuous.*

Any form of social control or public utility necessarily fractionates and dilutes as it gets farther from the source and nearer the individual. In mass communications, however, this is carried to an extreme. There is nothing like the rigid pipelines of law or the direct pathways of physical force. In fact, so tenuous are the pipelines that the nature of the communication may actually be changed en route.

No aspect of mass communications is more striking then the tenuousness of the connection between communicator and commicatee. At both ends of the process there are very respectable flurries of nervous and mental activity. In the communicator we observe preverbal tensions, symbol formation, finally the choice of a sign. Electrical impulses pass between nerve cells, several million neurons light up, and in one way or other the whole state of the communicator's organism and all his stored and clustered experience stand ready to help in the process. In the communicatee, there is the same impressive process—arrival of the stimulus, nerve currents, preverbal tensions, symbol formation, choice of a sign. Both these centerings of activity are out of all proportion to the quality of the mechanism which connects them. For when the sign is chosen, it has to be committed to a spot of ink, or a shadow on celluloid, or a succession of condensations and rarefactions in air.

As a writer, I can testify to the feeling of helplessness when once a sign has been turned loose as writing. It is as though a coach had trained his team and then told it to go out alone and undirected and win some football games. There is no schedule; they find their own opponents. What will the boys do? Will they find anybody to play them? Will they find an opponent in their own class? Will they play as a team or disintegrate? Will they find the going too hard, and come storming back to take revenge on the coach?

I don't want to labor the point, and there is hardly time to develop it fully. But I want to point out that there is nothing like a one-to-one relationship between what is put into the channels of mass communications with the supposed intention of influencing people, and what issues forth from those channels. At best we have a slender and unreliable pipeline. At worst—for example, when we communicate across cultural boundaries—as Dr. Margaret Mead has shown, we may have an effect far different from the predicted effect. The pipelines of communication have been enormously extended, but they are the same old slender pipelines.

(3) *The tools of effect are rapidly changing the conditions of effect.*

Thanks to the work of such scholars as Dr. Gordon Allport, Dr. Hadley Cantril, and Dr. Lazarsfeld, we can distinguish fairly systematically between the uses of the time and the space arts, and the relative strengths of communication by print, picture, and sound. Likewise, we have been able to distinguish the historical functions of the chief printed media in society. The newspaper has stood out on the horizon of experience, reporting on new developments. The magazine and the editorial columns have focused society's reaction to these developments. The book has caught up the distilled wisdom of social experience and passed it on.

But those relationships are rapidly changing, thanks to motion pictures, radio, and television. Radio, now more than newspaper, stands out to watch the horizon and bring the news flashes. The newspaper has been forced partly into the magazine's territory, and radio programs like America's Town Meeting and the Chicago Round Table have found themselves in the same area. The magazines are publishing books, motion pictures have moved into the area of culture transmittal, and the book is under serious attack as a teaching device. Television is combining the space and time arts in a new and effective way; and facsimile, in one dramatic demonstration at the rate of nearly one million words a minute, has speeded the book up faster than the newspaper.

With boundaries blurring and new forms appearing, the media are therefore in an extremely fluid situation which must be considered in trying to describe their effectiveness. Not only are the media different, but these differences themselves are changing. Perhaps the most important questions in this area today concern television: what it is doing to the learning patterns and information levels of its audiences, what functions of other media it is taking over, and what new and effective combinations of media it is creating.

(4) *Cues are the key to what reaches the audience.*

If you will permit me to take a simile out of my summer troutfishing (my wife has suggested that I should be permitted to take at least one simile out of it, inasmuch as I seem to take out very few fish), I shall say that the process of mass communication is rather like a fisherman casting his most likely fly in the most likely place hoping that the most likely fish will strike. The communicator casts his best cues in the best channels, hoping for a response from the best audience. In the newspaper he casts headlines, which enable the reader easily to select the one-sixth to one-third of the news content he reads. A similar process of selection operates in listening to radio news. We have been studying that process at Illinois this year. Certain words or phrases seem to serve as cues. The newscast seems to present itself to the listener, not as a continuous stream of information, but as clusters of sound indexed by these cue words or phrases. When one of these cues is selected by the listener, then the related sounds are perceived as signs, and process of symbol formation and retention goes ahead.

The nature of this selective process is important to a theory of communication and public opinion for a reason of which I scarcely have to remind this audience: that the media present every individual with far more material than he can handle. Therefore it is important to know why he selects what he perceives and remembers, and hence what enters into his opinion and action patterns. Momentary needs and wants, and mental sets, are, of course, determinants of choice. So, in a more basic way, are the qualities of personality. Even with an instrument so relatively blunt for this purpose as the Allport-Vernon test of personal values, we have been able to get quite close correlations between value patterns and facts remembered from a newscast or a newspaper. The principles of learning seem to apply to the treatment of cues, as they do in many other communicative situations. By carefully placing a cue, we have been able to predict what part of a news item a listener would remember.

By overplaying a cue we have secured partial extinction of a drive. By carefully fitting cue to material, we have been able to secure reinforcement of a drive.

(5) *The nature of mass communications makes for inertia in public opinion.*

When I speak to you, I can frame my communication individually, and check it by responses. When I speak by mass media, however, I must strike some middle ground which will be as widely attractive as possible. My audience will differ widely in interests, background, and tastes. Furthermore, it will tend to resist opinions to which it is not predisposed. It tends to buy the papers, tune in the programs, select the speakers, columnists, commentators, and editorials with which it is likely to agree. Therefore, I shall avoid content that deviates from accepted opinion and therefore would alienate part of the mass audience, and the audience will cooperate with me by turning me off if I begin to express opinions that might change the listener's mind.

To a man from Mars, it must look like a conspiracy between communicator and audience to avoid any social change or opinion change whatsoever. Yet this situation seems to be inherent in the nature of the system. We might mention other factors that contribute to it. We expose our audiences to a series of contradictory opinions and competitive selling, which is desirable, but which certainly raises the threshold of acceptance. We encourage passivity and wish-fulfillment in fantasy, by providing a great abundance of entertainment and escape material. By developing communications into big business, we have encouraged them to conserve the conditions under which change will not threaten business.

This tendency of mass communications to preserve the status quo is certainly an influence of the greatest importance.

(6) *Communications affect public opinion more readily by creating a climate of information than by direct efforts to change opinion.*

In the Roosevelt campaigns, the editorials and commentators were overwhelmingly on the losing side. But although the editorials were Republican, the news was Democratic. I do not mean that the news was slanted, merely that for four years between campaigns the news columns had told the social plans and measures of the New Deal, the victorious battle with a depression, the promise of greater security for the individual, and toward the end the darkening of war clouds and the need of an experienced leader. These were very practical things; the voter could measure their meaning to him and compare it with the more abstract arguments of the editorials. And while none of us, in view of the results, can claim to be experts on the 1948 campaign, I think the same principle must have applied there: the Republican dominance of the editorial columns and the radio time had to contend with what the news columns told the farmer of high farm prices, the laboring man of the Taft-Hartley law, and everyone of the 80th Congress. Because of this climate of fact, reinforced by the homely fighting words of President Truman and by certain other conditions which the other sessions of this conference will certainly develop, the polished abstractions of Governor Dewey were, to put it mildly, less effective than they might have been.

In this connection let me say that the concept of deutero-learning set forth by Gregory Bateson is exceedingly important for an understanding of how communications contribute to the climate of information. What a reader or listener absorbs secondarily and behind the symbol or idea which he may consciously reject is of great significance at a time like this when the pipelines are overcrowded and the level of conscious rejection is high.

(7) *Communications contribute to the climate of opinion by creating culture heroes and myths.*

As the community has expanded, society has moved from the fireside story to the Fireside Chat; from Robin Hood in the legend to Babe Ruth on the sports pages and Johnny Lujack on the radio; from Venus in the poems to Rita Hayworth on the screen; from Merlin to the atomic scientist; from the epic poet and troubador to the daytime serial and magazine feature. These heroes, of course, enter into our value patterns, and therefore into our opinions.

I am inclined to agree with Dr. Berelson that, in America, "personality" arguments are more effective than "issue" arguments. We like to have heroes, and to talk in terms of men and stories.

(8) *Communications contribute to the climate of opinion by conferring status and enforcing norms.*

This hypothesis is so well accepted that I shall not develop it here. It is chiefly a taking over by the mass media of functions that, in the smaller community, were carried out by direct experience. The citizen used to know the norms and the leaders because he saw them in action. Now the mass media have the power, by describing norms of social action, to suggest that any deviation from them is abnormal and antisocial. By mentioning names, the media have the power of lifting citizens from anonymity; by quoting or giving radio voice to individuals, they have the power to lend a certain kind of authority to what these chosen people say. Thus they create in the community certain points of authority, and help to give weight to certain opinions over others.

(9) *Monopoly of the media makes for greater effect.*

It is a reasonable hypothesis that if the media agree, they are more likely to create a parallel climate of opinion. This is the reason why minority groups fear communications monopoly. Fortunately in this country we have little expectation of government control and resultant monopoly, and the present system of multiple and overlapping media leaves little chance for monopoly through ownership. We do have certain bottlenecks in a free flow of information. Some are in the gathering and transmission of foreign and other distant news; some are in the distribution of mass communication material.

(10) *Communications make community.*

Finally, let us record what seems to be obvious, but perhaps so obvious as usually to be neglected in discussions of this topic. At the point in human relations where face-to-face contacts become diffused, mass communications take over and extend the understandings and adjustments that make one feel at home in a large group. Some of the accomplishments of mass communications in this area are spectacular. For example, the sports reporters have managed to create a loyal and enthusiastic chapter of synthetic Notre Dame alumni wherever press and radio have carried the story of the Irish team. Less spectacular but more important is the record of the last thirty years in breaking down provincial loyalties and extending horizons.

It may be well to close on this hopeful note. Ever since the first World War, most considerations of communications and public opinion have been in terms of propaganda: how the channels of communication could be controlled to reproduce the will of the communicators in the actions of the audience, and, in the most studied cases, to set men against men and nation against nation. Now let it be recorded that mass communications can also make it possible for large groups of people to understand each other, and thus to create a climate of public opinion which will relax social tensions.

In fact, I should say that is a more natural use than the other. And if we permit our communications to be used for a contrary purpose, we shall be going not only against our best interests but also against ten thousand years of social history during which the communication process has helped ever-expanding communities to live together in mutual understanding and cooperation.

14

EVENTS AS AN INFLUENCE UPON OPINION

Bernard Berelson

MR. ALBIG: Dean Bernard Berelson, our next speaker, was an analyst of foreign short-wave propaganda for the Federal Communications Commission from 1941 to 1944, was afterwards with the Bureau of Applied Social Research at Columbia, and in 1946 returned to Chicago. His topic is *Events as an Influence upon Opinion.*

MR. BERELSON: In any symposium on the determinants of public opinion, attention must be given to the role of "events" as an influence upon opinion change. Publicists and scholars both agree that "real happenings" are often more influential in changing people's minds than "mere words."

Although several writers have discussed the role of events in opinion formation, not all of them have made it precisely clear how broad or narrow a definition was given to the term. In certain scientific vocabularies the term "event" is given an extremely wide definition, almost synonymous with "thing." In other vocabularies, the term refers only to the kinds of activities ordinarily reported on the front pages of the newspapers. Even here, however, the distinction between "events" and "words" is not easy. "Is a major speech by the President of the United States an 'event' or just 'propaganda'? Or a report issued by a pressure group? Or an investigation by a Congressional committee?" [1]

For purposes of this discussion, a relatively narrow meaning will be applied to the term, referring to "real happenings" in the external world. Although the definitional problem will not be considered here, the suggestion might be made that the distinction between "events" and "propaganda" can best be made in terms of the degree

[1] Bernard Berelson, "Communications and Public Opinion" in *Communications in Modern Society,* edited by Wilbur Schramm (University of Illinois Press, 1948), p. 175.

148

of control exercised by influential parties. Thus activities in which a unilateral exercise of power is effective, such as the delivery of a speech or the issuance of a statement, might not be considered as "events." That term would be reserved for those acts determined by at least a bilateral exercise of influence, as in the passage of legislation or the calling of a strike or the outcome of a war. This criterion involving the basis on which the act is effectively determined may provide a key to the definitional problem.

It may be useful to distinguish between different types of events which may influence public opinion. In the first place we may distinguish between remote events and immediate events. Remote events are those which occur outside our sphere of primary contacts and are brought to our attention typically by the mass media of communication; immediate events are those which people experience themselves at first hand. Another distinction can be made between public events, which happen simultaneously to all the members of a group (or to a large proportion of them), and private events, which happen to an individual or to a small intimate group.

There have been several studies documenting the effectiveness of events in the formation of public opinion.[2] Such studies indicate that events tend to crystallize and solidify opinion changes and suggest that events are often more powerful than "propaganda" in changing opinions.

Such studies sometimes overlook what ought to be kept very clearly in the foreground of attention, namely, that most events are neutral, i.e., capable of various and even contradictory "meanings," and that it takes interpretation to make events meaningful. Events always occur against some sort of predispositional background, or else they would have no significance for people. The interpretation of their meaning ought not to be confused with the objective event itself; often contradictory meanings are assigned to the same objective event. This paper was originally delivered at the height of concern over the Mindzenty case, an objective event which was given one interpretation in one half of the world and a quite different interpretation in the other half; and this paper is being revised when public attention is focused upon the Atlantic Pact, an objective event which also receives differing interpretations depending upon the predispositions of the interpreter. Various public events

[2] See for example Hadley Cantril, "The Use of Trends," in *Gauging Public Opinion*, edited by Cantril (Princeton University Press, 1944).

are susceptible to the same sort of multiplicity of interpretations. Take, for example, the welfare acts of the Roosevelt New Deal; they are a series of benevolent and humanitarian acts to one person and a series of oppressive and despotic acts to another. In short, an event, however objectively it can be described, is ordinarily capable of several subjective interpretations deriving from the differing predispositions of the observer. Because many important world events are given only a single interpretation in most of our mass media, we sometimes tend to forget that a monolithic interpretation can masquerade as no interpretation at all. Events are ordinarily neutral, a *tabula rasa* on which predispositions write meanings.

It is generally agreed that events are an important determinant of public opinion. One reason for this is that events secure a good deal of public attention because they are often dramatic and always "real." Any good propagandist knows that he makes his case increasingly effective if he can tie it to some event which supports it, or rather seems to support it. The event helps to carry the argument. Another reason for the relative effectiveness of events as an influence upon opinion is the strong tendency for people to view events as real and propaganda as manipulated. To some extent, of course, this derives from people's fear of being taken in by various propagandas. People have not yet recognized that certain powerful individuals can manipulate events quite effectively and almost as easily as they can manipulate symbols.

If, then, one accepts the proposition that events are effective in influencing opinion, the next step is to ask *how* they are effective. In what ways do they exercise their influence? What are the types of conditions under which they are influential? In the rest of this paper I shall mention only seven ways in which events affect opinion. Some of these are applicable to other influences upon public opinion as well; that seems to be all to the good since they may present a typology of conditions for opinion change, whatever the determinant. Thus a wide range of influences upon opinion may be analyzed in terms of the following schemes.

(1) Events affect opinion by *changing the social and economic position of the subjects*. Here the obvious example is the economic depression of the early thirties. A series of events affected the socio-economic position of a large part of the population and thereby modified or changed a whole set of political opinions. Since we know that opinion is to a large extent a function of self-interest, any events

which affect the economic or status position of people is bound to have repercussions upon their opinion patterns. Thus, for example, changes in rent control or price control can similarly affect opinions of those directly involved.

(2) Events affect opinion by *changing the individual's value structure*, on the basis of which his opinions are formed. In 1940, for example, world events led people in this country to attach a greater value to experience in foreign affairs as against domestic affairs as a requirement for presidential candidates, and votes in the presidential election of that year were influenced by that shift in values. During the depression, too, certain events made people value security above liberty, and they changed their political opinions accordingly. In some cases, the events can contribute to changing the definitions of basic symbols given a key position in the individual's value pattern. During the 1920s, the common definition of the symbol of freedom probably centered upon the concept of nonintervention by government. However, with the New Deal some people began to give a different definition to freedom, oriented upon the opportunity of the common man to realize his best potentialities. Here a series of events provided an attitudinal environment within which people could accept a different definition of a key symbol while continuing to give basic allegiance to it.

(3) Events affect opinion by *changing the individual's evaluation of external conditions* without changing basic objectives or values. Take, for example, the "purge trials" in the U.S.S.R. during the 1930s. Many people who had been sympathetic to the Russian regime were forced by the trials to re-evaluate the political conditions existing in that country. Such people continued to give their loyalty to the central (i.e., socialist) values involved, but this series of events caused them to evaluate downward the political program of this particular country.

(4) Events affect opinion by *changing the individual's conception of the means* for realizing basic objectives. For many Americans, the fall of France in 1940 changed their ideas about the most appropriate means for insuring the defeat of Germany. It greatly increased the proportion of people who believed that American power would have to be brought to bear against Germany if the Nazis were to be defeated. Or, again, the aftermath of the Munich agreement illustrates the way in which a series of events can lead to changes

in people's evaluation of the means by which they can realize objectives, and thus change their opinions.

(5) Events affect opinion by *changing the individual's level of information* about an issue. Here we can take an illustration from the category of personal events. In states which have Fair Employment Practices laws promoting occupational contacts among various groups, there is some evidence to suggest that people have changed their minds about minority racial groups as a result of increased contact with and knowledge of their members. To some extent, the same thing has happened in public housing projects which have brought members of different races together in the same community. Thus a series of personal contacts with individual members of a minority group have exposed the typical stereotypes and thus led to a change in ethnic attitudes.

(6) Events affect opinion by *crystallizing latent opinion* by "forcing" decisions. Thus a series of events related to international affairs occurring over a relatively short time period stimulate people to bring their opinions on such matters to the level of visibility and expression. Indecision falls away under the impact of external events. Again, events sometime have this effect by facilitating or "legitimating" the expression of opinion through the exercise of prestige factors. Many Jewish people in this country were more likely to take a strong pro-Jewish stand on certain issues in view of the vigor and courage and efficiency with which the Palestinian Jews were fighting for their own state. This series of events brought many American Jews to a fuller recognition of their own ancestry and probably facilitated the expression of attitudes associated with their religious position.

(7) Finally, events affect opinion by *providing a rationale or rationalization for justifying previously held opinions*. Events are among the most effective agents for justifying opinions people want to hold for whatever reasons. Illustrations of this condition are numerous. Take, for example, the case of strikes: by those favorable to labor, they are used to justify their opinion of management as an antisocial force; by those sympathetic to management, they are used to justify their opinion of labor as an antisocial force. Such simultaneous reinforcement of diverse opinions is a striking phenomenon in the relationship of events to public opinion. Or, as a minor example, take all the propaganda which the motion picture industry distributes to convince people of the purity of Hollywood life; it

avails very little against a few specific instances like the Mitchum case or another Lana Turner wedding or a Charlie Chaplin trial! People who feel that Hollywood rivals certain Biblical cities in the depth and intensity of its sinfulness are only confirmed by such isolated events.

To sum up, then, events do have an influence upon public opinion; they do so not simply because of their very occurrence, but because certain interpretations and meanings are attached to them; they are particularly effective because of the attention and evaluation given them as compared with "propaganda"; and they are effective in various ways. The important thing is to elaborate and refine the particular conditions under which events and other determinants are effective in changing public opinion.

DISCUSSION—Paul F. Lazarsfeld

MR. ALBIG: I want to thank our speakers at this time—Mr. Clark and Mr. Casey, Mr. Saunders for reading Wilbur Schramm's paper, and Mr. Berelson.

Our discussant is Paul Lazarsfeld, Director of the Bureau of Applied Social Research at Columbia. We all esteem Paul, and have learned very much from the results of his fruitful research. I was going to say I wouldn't indicate what he was likely to say tonight— you can never tell. Last year at Illinois I introduced him to an evening meeting, present at which were a handful of top research men from the mass communications media and half a dozen from the universities. I wished to indicate that—as this was such a new field— both groups were tolerant of one another and quite given to well received mutual criticism, and I said so. Dr. Lazarsfeld rose. His first sentence was, "If there is one institutional disease to which the media of mass communication seems particularly subject, it is nervous reaction to criticism."

MR. LAZARSFELD: Well, it isn't seriously possible to discuss four so thoughtful papers in a few minutes. Maybe the only useful thing to do is to point out the common atmosphere behind the speakers and I suppose it was the same all during this conference, although I wasn't here. I know the opinions of some of the men who talked. The obvious effort of this whole meeting here is to show that public opinion research has become part of the social sciences in general, that there are still some difficulties of integration, and that the most important thing is mutual exchange of ideas to help along this development of public opinion work from an accidental freak to a very legitimate and well-organized part of the social sciences in general.

It seems to me that tonight three different ways to do that were indicated. One was remarked by the chairman, and then emphasized especially by Professor Clark. After all, we didn't invent public opinion in 1935 when the first poll was published in the newspapers. There were a few thousand years before when people thought about those matters, and there is the tremendous tradition in thinking about public opinion in social philosophy and political science and so on, so that the young technique of polling in empirical research is really an outstanding task.

It so happens that for our meeting on Saturday morning I also have collected a number of examples on the same topic, and just as it happens that I disagree somewhat with Professor Clark, it will be very interesting to see how one man who is more inclined as a philosopher and the other one who is more inclined as a door-to-door bell pusher look at the same topic. And as I myself have only a very few ideas on one topic, and I don't want to spoil the little show I have for a later session, so, Mr. Chairman, I ask your permission to come back then to your and Professor Clark's comments.

The second way of trying to get out of a fragmentary approach to public opinion is efforts to take empiric knowledge and to generalize it in a number of propositions, and it is very interesting that Schramm's paper and Berelson's paper had exactly the same purpose, in different parts of the field, to get to a few generalizations. I think we should be tremendously thankful to people who do such kinds of work because the literature has become so large and there are so many little things in this magazine and in that speech that one gets quite nervous thinking, "What have I missed?" and, "Is this a contradiction to what I found the other day, or does it corroborate it?" and so on. And I think that papers like Berelson's and Schramm's provide a really important contribution. It is impossible for us just to listen once and to say whether one agrees or disagrees with Schramm or Berelson, but the effort to do such things is most important and presents a second direction in this field of integration to which I think this conference is given.

The third approach with the same aim seems to me given in the paper we heard from Ralph Casey. As I understand him, he wanted to point out not only that we should study pressure groups, which we all do since he has in a way pioneered the field and maintained our interest in it, but also that we should look at the pressure-group studies not just as a little isolated business but as something which is a necessary part of communications research and really a necessary part of social science work.

Now, the way I listened to Casey, he brought out, for instance, that this pressure-group business is only a special indication of what has become quite fashionable in many studies now, and that is this study of the decision-making process. It has become of great importance in many types of research. When we study democracy we want to know, How does a government make up its mind? How does a big corporation make up its mind? The making up of the mind of an institution has become very important. Also, how does a newspaper make up its mind about what it puts in an article? This is an essential part of the social science of communication and pressure groups, since the effect of the pressure group on the editor, it seems to me, is one element in the decision-making process.

Just as we are in sympathy now with the poor editor who has trouble with the pressure group, I am also inclined to think a little bit in sympathy with the pressure group which has so much trouble with the editor. And that brings me to a part of social science which I hope in my old age to see developed in the end as super communications research, and it is what I like to call "social acoustics." The science of How do people get hearings? and How do people listen to each other? and Under what conditions is an editor listened to and under what conditions not? When does a pressure group get vocal and get access to the newspaper and when not? When is an editor getting along with the publisher, and when not? The whole idea of social acoustics seems to me very important and if you look at it this way, Casey, I would suggest that you add to your study the reverse process: Why do the newspapers make the pressure groups so nervous? (*laughter*).

And I borrow from Schramm and suggest a proposition: the less able a newspaper is to explain the position it is bound to take, the more will it create these irrational pressure groups. It is partly the irrationality of the newspaper which creates the irrationality of the pressure group, and it is not the fact that the newspaper takes a position which creates pressure groups, but that the newspaper takes a position without giving the necessary background to the reader to understand the position. The newspaper takes a position as if it were playing red or black in roulette, and does not give the feeling that its position is based on facts.

I would like to give you an example which has so fascinated me in the last few days that I think it would be a good end for tonight. The *London Economist* has just published two weeks ago a report on this genetics case in Russia, where Mr. Stalin decided which biologist should be right or not. I read those biology stories of Russia with horror because it seemed to me to show an abyss of the human mind in the twentieth century, until the *Economist* pointed out that the newspapers completely misunderstood the situation, that what happened in Russia was this: Stalin and his crowd need wheat which can grow in Siberia. They have for twenty years poured billions of dollars into experiments to get it. Mr. Roosevelt poured two billion dollars into atomic fission without knowing anything about atomic fission. He guessed right. Poor Mr. Stalin guessed wrong. He poured millions of dollars into genetic theory which, for some reason he didn't understand, didn't deliver him the wheat (*laughter*). He therefore has decided that he now will gamble on another crowd of genetic theorists who also claim they can grow wheat in Siberia but in a different way. Mr. Stalin doesn't understand the one side or the other side, but after he has spent so much money on the one side without getting the wheat, he gambles on the other side. If Mr. Roosevelt hadn't gotten an atomic bomb in three or four years he would also have gambled on another crowd of physicists.

There was no word in the whole press of America that would have helped me to understand what was going on in Moscow. If they had explained to me what it was all about I would have had a more reasonable reaction. The irrationality of the newspapers and the irrationality of groups who clamor for hearing should be the topic of a more integrated science of social acoustics.

(*Meeting adjourned.*)

PUBLIC OPINION POLLS
AND ELECTIONS

15

CAUSES OF THE DISPARITY BETWEEN POLL FINDINGS AND ELECTION RETURNS

Dewey B. Stuit, Presiding

Archibald M. Crossley

Stuart C. Dodd

J. E. Bachelder

George H. Gallup

Henry J. Kroeger

Mr. Stuit: The program will consist of presentations by the members of the symposium, followed by discussions by the two persons whose names appear on the program. We hope that there will be time available for questions from the floor.

Ever since early November there has been a great deal of speculation as to the causes of disparity between poll findings and election results. Newspaper editors, radio commentators, college professors, and I suppose the man in the street, have all had their say at diagnosing the causes of the disparity. And I suppose most of us in this room have at some time or another offered an opinion on the subject. We are very fortunate this morning in having with us a group of people who have made a serious study of the subject and who will give us the benefit of their analyses.

Since most of the speakers were introduced yesterday and since our program this morning is rather full, I am not going to take a great deal of time to introduce them individually. Our first speaker is Mr. Crossley of Crossley, Incorporated.

Mr. Crossley: Mr. Chairman, ladies and gentlemen, we are not allowed to quote the President, as the press well knows, so I can't vouch for the truth of this story, but the story is going around that on the third of November, on Wednesday morning, an old friend of the President's telephoned him and said, "Harry, you have been going up and down the land saying that you were absolutely sure you were going to be elected. Now, you don't have to kid me. Just tell me frankly, how do you feel on this Wednesday morning?" And, according to the story, President Truman is reported to have said, "Well, I feel like Father O'Malley in the story of the Irishman who was known for his profanity." And he said, "You may not know that story, so I'll tell it to you. This man Finnegan had the job of trying to pry loose a manhole cover, and he was having a great deal of difficulty doing it. He was using lots of expletives; he was out there with asterisks and exclamation points and all sorts of things, and the manhole cover wouldn't come off. Finally Father O'Malley came along and after watching the proceedings and listening to Finnegan for a bit, he said, 'My good man, you shouldn't use language like that.' He said, 'Let me show you how to get that manhole cover off. You must have faith. You must believe that you can do it.' And he talked to Finnegan for a while, and finally convinced him that if he believed he could get the manhole cover off it would come off. And about that minute there was a blast from somewhere up the line, and a big explosion, and the manhole cover flew up into the air, and Father O'Malley said, 'Well, I'll be asterisk damned!' "

We are not here to praise the polls, but *certainly* not to bury them.

Polling may need a shot in the arm, but it certainly does not rate a shot in the back. The *snipers* on all sides are having a field day. I think that it is time they were searched out and brought into the open. We respect the honest critics, and we have a high regard for the painstaking and penetrating studies of the Social Science Research Council Committee on Election Polls and Forecasts. These studies, though necessarily limited by time and other factors, have made a major contribution and pointed the way to further advancement.

We have taken our medicine. We have demonstrated our willingness to lay all of our cards on the table—face up. We have not, and do not intend to, hide behind any *alibis* whatever! We did make *some* errors in judgment, and to those we are willing to admit in clear, unmistakable language. But in equally unmistakable language we should question the sincerity and the purpose of much of today's widespread invective and unbridled criticism.

We are not charlatans, as some would have you believe. Our skirts are clean and have been found so by those to whom we have voluntarily opened up all of our records for careful and intensive study. Neither are we quite so stupid as some of the new crop of Monday-morning quarterbacks proclaim.

I present to you as a very serious problem, for all marketing and public opinion research, today's ratio of *quarterbacks* to *total-line players*. If we are to advance the ball, I believe very sincerely that we need some good old-fashioned line-plunging, and most of all the very maximum of team play.

Does this sound to you like crying "Hold! Enough!"? I have hesitated to say these things because I can well understand that they might be misconstrued. I say them now because they must be said and this seems to me a most appropriate time and place. If anyone thinks they are just personally defensive, let me say that my organization carries on no continuing polls, and that the total income from all the newspaper polls we have ever conducted since 1936 is very definitely less than the present income from one client, whose job, by the way, started after November 2nd and will be completed in the early spring. We have therefore no concern with poll sales. We are not operating any now and have no plans for political polls in the future. But we have a very considerable interest in the application of polling techniques to marketing research. To that end I propose to examine freely and frankly here and now what we know so far about the reasons for the differences between the polls and the elections, and what these reasons mean in terms of the common interests of all of us.

I shall start with the facts, and relate them to our own poll as one example.

Our poll, based upon field interviewing three weeks before the election combined with earlier interviewing, showed Truman with 44.8 percent of the total expected voters, and called attention to a slowly rising trend. He received 49.5 percent of those who cast a ballot for president.

1.4 percent of those who voted did not vote for anyone for president.

We showed Wallace with 3.3 percent and declining. His final vote was 2.4 percent. The Thurmond figure by election time was 2.4, an increase over our 1.6 in mid-October.

We estimated a total vote about the same as the Associated Press estimates from election boards throughout the country—a little over 51 millions. The actual vote, including those who chose to vote for others but not for president, was 49.4 millions.

The disparity between our Truman percentage of decided voters and the Truman percentage of actual voters for president was 4.7 percentage points.

The problems before us today are these two:

(1) How much of those 4.7 points were error?

(2) What was the cause of that error?

The distributed report of the Social Science Research Council Committee makes this statement.

"Looking at all the evidence now available, the Committee tentatively concludes that in the last two weeks there was a net shift to Truman of 2 or 3 percentage points, probably varying quite a bit from state to state. The complexity of the problem of allowing for all the kinds of errors of interpretation is such that it is possible that the shift at the end of the campaign was even greater than these figures suggest."

Subtracting 2 to 3 points from 4.7, we are therefore dealing with a possible error of 1.7 to perhaps 2.7, three weeks before the election. The Committee indicates that it may be less, and confines its findings to the shift in the last fortnight. I think I am justified therefore in taking the likely error at about 1.7.

As to the cause of this error the SSRC Committee implies several possibilities:

(1) Our assumption that any of the undecided who voted would vote in substantially the same way as the decided. Polltakers are criticized for failure to assess future behavior, and told that this factor may be the cause of anything up to 1.5 points of the disparity. I do not know today how the factor could be properly measured in advance. And if the Committee's staff report is published in the next few weeks as originally written, I feel that the polltakers' side of this story will be given very understanding treatment.

(2) Perhaps partly the way the questions were asked. The evi-

dence does not show how much or in what way we may have erred in this respect.

(3) Perhaps partly the manner of covering the rural vote. This may be a valid criticism upon which I for one would like to see more evidence.

(4) Mostly, I think, the Committee feels that we did not get far enough down the income scale perhaps because we chose not to use an alternative sampling method. As nearly as I can compute what the Committee believes the error to be in this respect, it would seem to be about 1.5 percentage points, perhaps more.

Adding all this up, we find that the sum total of all our believed errors at the time of our last poll, in the Committee's judgment, may exceed the 1.7 or thereabouts which we have to account for.

Now, this word "error" in the public mind has an extremely bad connotation. It has been grossly misused throughout the United States, and in a number of other countries, in connection with the polls. But in statistics, the word is not necessarily bad. We speak of "allowable error," "error that is not significant," "probable error of tenths of a point," etc.

I think that most statisticians would agree that a disparity of two percentage points, and perhaps more, between sample results and known facts for the same universe at the same time would be considered "allowable error." Any careful study of the SSRC report would therefore indicate some confirmation of my original belief that *at the time of our last poll* we were not a long way off the beam. If that sounds like blustering, it is farthest from my intention. It is a deep and very sincere conviction. It is most certainly *not* said for personal gain, but rather to question vigorously for all polling some of the loose comments that are being made in many quarters about polls in general.

In my opinion, it is high time to remove the smear and to obtain the true facts as to whether the polls were as bad as they were painted. If they were, let's admit it frankly. If they were not, let's insist upon the truth.

Very properly, the SSRC Committee examined two angles of the polltakers' work: (1) sampling and interviewing, (2) forecasting. As to the latter, I think we ought to take what's coming to us.

The Committee finds that: "The pollsters over-reached the capabilities of the public opinion poll as a predicting device in attempting to pick, without qualification, the winner of the 1948 election. . . . The election was close. Dewey could have won by carrying Ohio, California and Illinois, which he lost by less than 1 per cent. In such a close election no polls, no advance information of any kind, could have predicted a Truman or Dewey victory with confidence. The failure of the polls was due to neglecting the possibility of a close election and the necessity of measuring preferences very accurately just before the election."

The election was actually so close that slightly over 29,000 voters —not enough to fill one side of a large football stadium—could have elected Dewey: about 3000 in Ohio where something like 100,000 votes were invalidated, about 9000 in California and 17,000 in Illinois. Or looked at another way, a small further shift to Truman could have given him much more than 303 electoral votes.

I agree with the Committee's findings as to our straining the capabilities of any poll in making a prediction and plead guilty to the error of attempting a forecast based upon interviewing several weeks before the election. For that I have no excuse. The forecast was made for two reasons: (a) we were told on all sides that the worst sin of poll reporting was hedging, (b) in previous polls there had been little change in late weeks. And while we knew Truman's popularity was on the increase, the speed of rise in mid-October seemed far too slow to swing states like Iowa, for example.

The actual fact is that we did not catch the late Truman upsurge because we assumed campaigns do not change many votes and stopped polling too early. We did not foresee a rapidly-rising labor movement or major late events in farming areas.

We were not justified in making forecasts in mid-October, if ever. I doubt now if we ever are because in so many elections so many electoral votes are decided by such an extremely small percentage of the voters that calling results in those states involves a considerable factor of chance.

Now as to sampling and interviewing, aside from informed criticism, there have been throughout this country and in other countries many irresponsible statements. I think that we should take some action to prevent their continuation and further that we should locate the evidence which does not now exist as to whether our sampling and interviewing were good or bad. Again, if evidence is found to prove that they were bad, let's admit it. But let's insist upon the facts.

It is a fact that there has been a tendency toward overestimation of the Republican vote on the part of some of us for a long time. That is a problem which we have known well, and studied carefully. What could we have done about it?

Well, first, we might have made an arbitrary adjustment for such disparity based upon past history. It is my opinion that such an adjustment, being purely speculative as to current conditions, could not possibly be justified. I would like to see that submitted to discussion and to a vote.

Second, there are various possible other adjustments. In general, the SSRC Committee defends the use of adjustments as a principle, calling it a desirable procedure under certain conditions. One of the adjustments which they seem to favor is a mathematical allowance for distortion in the findings as to education. I have already advised the Committee of the incorrectness of the statement that "all the major polling organizations interviewed more people with college education than the actual proportion in the adult population over 21 and too few people with grade school education only. . . . Crossley did not make adjustments [for education distortion], although the procedure would have improved the accuracy of [his] forecasts."

This is only assumption. Based upon our own past experience with respondents' exaggerated statements as to education, we chose not even to ask the question. It is therefore not known whether or not we achieved the right proportions or would have improved our forecast with an adjustment. If such adjustment were based upon inaccurate information from the respondents or inadequate base information on education, it *could* have introduced an error itself. And if we merely cancel errors by an adjustment, I would feel that we do ourselves no good in the long run.

Third, we might have used a different sampling method to get farther down the income scale. This idea is very popular generally. The word "quota" is anathema, the word "probability" is sacrosanct. I really think that most salesmen will now have to operate on "sales probabilities" instead of "sales quotas." In our own marketing research, we do a considerable amount of probability, block and various forms of area sampling, as well as stratified sampling, and have done so for years. So I have no greater interest in one form than in another. There are, however, some pretty important questions in this matter of sampling upon which I think this conference should deliberate:

(1) If we are to assume that only probability will work satisfactorily, then we should face squarely, and do something about, what that means:

(a) Today because probability is both expensive and time-consuming, and at the same time popular, a great many sins are being committed in its name. We are being asked on all sides to cut corners on both time and cost, which means a bastardized form of probability, and we seriously suspect that some organizations are cutting those corners. If you don't do a careful job of probability, you are apt to come up with extremely unreliable figures.

(b) As between a *poor* probability sample and a well-designed and -operated stratified sample, there can be little question.

(2) Is there a tendency to jump too fast to the conclusion that whatever the points of our actual error may be, they are due principally to our decision not to use probability sampling?

I personally do not believe that we have enough evidence yet to prove that sampling was consistently and positively the cause of substantial error, nor that we are quite so stupid in this respect as is being bandied about sometimes for competitive gain. It *is* entirely possible that evidence *can* be found to prove that our sampling was inadequate, but unless and until that evidence is conclusive it seems to me that its restricted nature should be made known. In my opinion, a careful study of the first draft of the SSRC staff report shows very clearly the need for further information. I am all for obtaining reliable information on this point, and suggest that this conference should publicly observe its need.

Now, what else could there be but sampling to bring about some tendency toward Republican overestimation in the past? Is the only possible explanation the assumption that nobody's interviewers could get far enough down the income scale without predesignated homes and large numbers of call-backs? Or could there be some other factor?

In my opinion, any such assumption waves aside the greatest problem of polling. That is, how do we know who will vote? That is where we really are experimenting, and that is where we need the maximum of team play.

Some of us introduced this year a cross-section reporting of what would happen *if everybody voted*. We showed back in August that *under such conditions* of 100 percent vote, Truman and Dewey would tie, and that if some of the Wallace vote shifted, Truman would tip the scales to win!

In simple terms, this indicates also that if, for example, only half the potential voters actually voted *and voted in the same proportions*, then also a Wallace decline would elect Truman. But if the proportions changed and Republicans stayed home much more than Democrats, Truman would win. If vice-versa, Dewey would win. Is it possible that these proportions of voting intention at one point were weak on the Truman side and then were changed by rising Truman turnout interest and/or declining Dewey turnout interest?

It is a very curious situation that the election results with allowance only for a late switch from Wallace-ites to Truman were not very far from what we found in August would be the case if everyone voted. So it may be that the actual ratio of Democrats to Republicans in the election was just about what it would have been if everyone voted. In mid-October, our questions to try to find out who would vote indicated that the Republican turnout ratio would be greater than the Democratic ratio. There is some evidence to indicate that there was a considerable change in this situation after mid-October.

If you will grant that this total potential voters' poll may have been reasonably well conducted, then our problem became one of measuring stay-at-homes. For this purpose we polltakers had different methods, and I think that some polltakers had none. My own organization used a new technique which consisted of a scoring system based on a series of filter questions to find out who would really vote. Others used a system of sample weights to allow for an expected vote heavier in some income levels than in others.

My frank opinion is that if we neglect the solution of this problem we are wasting valuable time. There is an extremely important job to be done here and this conference *should get it started*.

Most of us in the past have attempted to measure voters by one or more of these methods: (a) a question as to how you would vote today, (b) an attitude scale, (c) a weighting system of some kind usually based upon past vote. How do we know that these methods have not of themselves tipped the poll balance in favor of the Republicans? The answer is that we do not. How do we know that political or labor organizations have not influenced turnout at the end of the campaign? We believe they have but we do not know how much. These and other similar problems of vast importance in the analysis of poll performance are begging for solution. What are we going to do about them? The most difficult job in polling is to find out who will vote, especially in a year when nearly 700,000 did not vote for President while they were in the voting booths.

Again I refer you to the SSRC staff report. If its final form follows its original draft, it will present some preliminary information along this line.

We already know some things about this turnout and stay-at-home phenomenon, and there are many statistics at our disposal for adequate analysis. There is some evidence to indicate from the polls themselves that the intention to vote among Truman followers was increasing late in the campaign, and that this was not true of the Dewey followers. There is some evidence to indicate that far fewer people voted than intended to vote at registration time.

It is not an error on the part of the polltakers that they have not yet found out how to correct their cross-sections for last-minute voting behavior. It is a challenge. And somehow I do not think that challenge is being flung across a deathbed.

MR. STUIT: We will hear next from Mr. Stuart C. Dodd, Director of the Washington Public Opinion Laboratory, and from the Co-director of the Washington Public Opinion Laboratory, Mr. J. E. Bachelder. We will hear first from Mr. Dodd, who will then introduce Mr. Bachelder.

MR. DODD: In telling you our contribution to the whole situation and particularly the experiments we made in the Washington Public Opinion Laboratory, we are dividing our time and letting Mr. Bachelder tell you of those experiments as he was in charge of them, and executed them, and has them much more at his finger tips than I do. I shall take only a minute or two to make one or two pleas for particular types of research ahead that I think we should follow up as the result of the election situation. We all know the various factors that were at work. What we do not know is just how important each factor was in the particular local situation or national situation. We know there were such factors as differences in the techniques of polling, possibly differences in methods of sampling, possibly differences in methods of controlling interviews or phrasing questions, and all the other sampling or surveying sorts of errors which may have been at fault to unknown degrees.

We know that on the other side, as far as the phenomena we are trying to measure are concerned, there were factors in the public—shifts in the voting intentions from the "don't-know" category, from the Wallace and Dewey categories to the Truman category—that occurred at different periods with apparently an acceleration very sharply at the end. We know there were differential intensities of opinion, resulting possibly in different turnout at different times and different places. These and many other factors—we must go on sub-dividing them and get at the details more analytically—we know or believe existed. But what we don't know is the share that factor contributed. And at present we have only a very crude technique for determining the excellence of our net prediction with whatever factors we take into account, such as determining the average percentage points of discrepancy between a given poll's prediction for the several candidates and the actual vote for those candidates.

That is a rather crude summarizing measure but it is about the best we have at present for determining how accurate the polls were. And we know that in general, as Mr. Gallup's study showed for 512 election polls in many nations by many agencies over the last dozen or more years, that four percentage points of discrepancy is about a normal figure to expect. That is about the average degree of accuracy, shall we say, to expect of polls. Possibly we have erred in not educating the public to expect inaccuracy to that extent, or to put it the other way, to expect no more than 96 percent of accuracy from the polls. And when an election is close and hinges on a fraction of a percentage point or so, then the prediction should be made, qualified with plus or minus points of percentage.

Now to get at the relative shares: Couldn't we have someone (possibly an SSRC Committee continued) try to work out for us a multiple regression equation that would take into account all the different factors that are likely to come up or have come up in previous elections, and provide a pattern which different polling agencies could apply, and determine from their data what those regression coefficients were, thus giving due weight to each factor? Ogburn did this in one form back in 1929 in the Al Smith presidential election, giving the relative size of the factors of Catholicism, wetness, traditional allegiance to the Democratic party, and so forth. Each had a certain assignable percentage share of the net result, and they

added up to something like fifty or sixty percent of the total outcome, the rest being unmeasured factors. Now, that was for one
particular kind of analysis using electoral precincts and so forth. But
I wish we could have this kind of a tool for us to use in the next
election. We need to develop a skeleton regression equation that
would take into account all the factors. Then the different polling
agencies could report in parallel terms and in comparable units,
under specified conditions, just what their degree of accuracy was
and what share they found for each particular factor in the whole
situation. Then we would get on with knowing what the different
factors contributed, how changeable they are under local conditions
or different elections, and so forth, and be able to increase the
accuracy of our total prediction and know the reasons why each
error may have occurred. I wish the SSRC Committee would set
a competent mathematical statistician to work on this regression
equation. If we do that, I think we could go a little further and
ask the Committee to suggest from the post-mortem analysis they
have been making—what are recommended principles for the next
election polls. I would like some sort of a clearinghouse for the
phrasing of questions so that we could pool our experience and find
out what were the most successful questions in getting at the factors
we want to know. For instance, it is very easy to ask a question on
getting at the probable turnout, "Do you plan to vote?" We asked
that, and it was a complete dud. It didn't show anything. Everybody
planned to. Another agency asked, "Do you expect to vote?" and
got very successful results with it. Just a slight difference in phrasing of that kind may make a tremendous difference in the percentage
splits and the correlation with the actual turnout later. At present
we just don't know what phrasings are successful and what phrasings
are not successful in predicting the probable turnout.

One other group—I hope Don Cahalan will tell us about it later—
has been working out a scale for predicting probable turnout, and
reports rather promising results with that. The rest of us should
know that and be able to use that scale.

We found one question was quite successful in determining the
trend of the "Don't know's," and how they would split, so that instead of splitting them in traditional fashion in proportion to the
"Do know's" they could be split in proportion to the shifting trend
that was going on in that particular election campaign. Another
useful question can take the place of a series of polls at different

dates. It is a simple retroactive question at one poll, namely, "When did you make up your mind?" and that question analyzed by the length of time back at which different groups had made up their minds would show those who were "Don't know's" on successive monthly dates, what percentage of them went for each candidate, and therefore what the trend was. We found, for instance, of those in the State of Washington who didn't know on September first, 70 percent in the next month decided for Truman; of those who still did not know on October first, 70 percent of them decided during October for Truman. We found that out in a poll in the week before election and thereby were able to plot a little curve of the trend of the "Don't know's" from one question on one survey date.

Well, doubtless other people have had experience turning up rather successful questions or phrasings of them that we should all know about and be able to use in the next election to make the whole thing more accurate. So my plea is that the SSRC Committee should not end up merely with a diagnosis of what happened in the last election. It should go on to make very definite recommendations for the next election. It might be asked by this conference to continue in business and carry the job a little further to specialize on how to do the job more accurately in the future.

I think for the actual data our experiment turned up I will turn the discussion over to Mr. Bachelder.

MR. BACHELDER: The topic this morning, "Causes of the Disparity Between Poll Findings and Election Returns," is not one upon which I would like to speak. Frankly, I am a little tired of the criticism of polls. For one reason, it is still the most miraculous thing in the field of social science that by interviewing a few thousand people you can come within even four to five percent of what forty-nine million people will do. The other reason is that we should be talking on "How, for heaven's sake, do we come as close as we do?" and not talking on how we get as far away as we do.

About a year ago I had the fortunate and unfortunate task of preparing a paper on the topic of the "Unexplored Hypotheses and Problems in the Field of Public Opinion Polling." After driving myself to examine the field I decided to investigate the price of dark glasses, some pencils and a tin cup, and look for another profession.

The disparity of polling results and known results I feel is not the fault of the pollsters, and I would like to go on record with that, but it is largely due to the other social sciences and what they have failed to give us. Polling is a type of cooperative research requiring help from all the other social sciences. I would like, before going into what we did in the Washington Public Opinion Laboratory, to run over just a few of the unexplored hypotheses awaiting solution by the other social sciences before we can get close, or closer, to other known data. These may sound naive but I'd like to give you the complete list—there is never a complete list, but a partial list.

First of all, we are dealing with an attitude, and the psychologists and socio-psychologists can tell us very little about what an attitude is at the present time. Oh, yes, it is a predisposition to react in a certain way, in a given situation, with a given stimulus, and so on. That tells nothing to us in the applied field. We are dealing with opinions, and opinions are verbal responses to verbal or visual stimuli. Fine. What controlled laboratory experiments do we have in the field of socio-psychology, psychology, et cetera, to help us with the exact measurement of an opinion? Attitude scales? Fine. Playing around with whether gradations on a thermometer shall be this far, or that far, et cetera, but with the actual relationship of a verbal response to a verbal stimulus in relation to known behavior, actual behavior, we have very little experimental work to help.

Then we come to the area of sampling. Sampling is based, with the exception of one type perhaps, upon an old sociological concept of the stereotype, which we of social science have bandied around for several years without even knowing what it is. We assume the farmer will vote differently than the person in the city. Why? Because he is a farmer. How do we know it? We haven't anything but, oh, a few little studies here and there, a few frequency tables saying he is different. Is it because he is a farmer? Is it because of his age, education, economic level, or what? We need a considerable amount of factor analysis before we know whether this stereotyping process in sampling is of any use to us. Yet we go merrily on our way—sadly, let us say, not merrily. If nothing else, the sociologist should tell us what we mean by stereotype. Is there such a thing, and what is the relationship of stereotype to actual known behavior at a later date?

Then there are the laws of chance. The mathematicians need to help us. We have had very little help from them, excepting through esoteric formula—formulas which we use to cover up the inaccuracy of our data which we gather in the field (*laughter*).

But seriously, we are using a law of chance which is based upon a dichotomy, the flipping of a penny—or five pennies; five makes it more accurate than one. And yet can the psychologists tell us whether an attitude is dichotomous or whether it is continuous, whether there is such a thing as an attitude for or against, or can we apply these laws of chance? It is perfectly possible mathematically to devise a law of chance not based on dichotomy but based on infinite numbers, or infinity minus one—such as the chances of a ball, which I might flip on this table, coming down on any number of points—infinity minus one. Perhaps we need a new law of chance; we are using an outmoded one—not outmoded perhaps but all we have available today from the mathematicians.

I will just mention and then not touch the problem of semantics and words—that is a whole Pandora's box of problems. What we need from the linguist is an atlas of cultural areas of the United States. What do words, verbal symbols, and the rest mean? When you say "Truman" in one place, does it mean the same as "Truman" in another? What help can the linguists give us on this? Very little as far as experimental work; a lot of opinion, but not experimentally defined work.

Passing on to the social relationship of the interview, has the sociologist contributed a great deal for us to use? An interview is a social relationship. What effect does an interviewer with brown eyes have upon a respondent with green eyes? We don't know. Interviewers fall into a pretty well-known category: a good interviewer, one, likes people; two, likes to interview; and three, probably needs the money (*laughter*). We should know then that we do not have a non-stimulus situation where we have a colorless, mouse-like individual giving a minimum of stimuli to the respondent. We know practically nothing about the social relationships involved, and yet that is the field of sociology. They give us very little, and psychology gives us little. We know little about the interview itself.

Well, we will move on to another problem. That is the coding of responses, and here is where some of us in the field of polling should take down what hair we have left (*laughter*). Actually we get triple coding of open-end answers and responses. In the first place, you ask a question. The respondent codes his answer because he can't talk for half an hour. So he codes and gives a very short answer. There isn't room on the ballot, or time for the interviewer to write down all of that, so he codes it. It comes in to the laboratory and we only have twelve places on the IBM card, so we get it down to eleven plus a miscellaneous. Triple coding. What does that do in the process? Well, that is one of our problems.

And then we come to the statistics of manipulation. I will just mention this and, as a gentleman, not go on (*laughter*).

We come to the publication and analysis of results. We discuss age, sex—as I will in just a moment—and education of the respondent. Let me explain that in some polls—I'll speak of the one with which I am most familiar, our own—we have eighty columns punched in an IBM card. You take the possible combinations, but not the permutations—just combinations. You have over 144,000 separate combinations. You begin taking it by the entire sample, multiply it by your sample, then take the permutations, and you can see the number of possible relationships within one study. But what do we do? In our wisdom we take certain ones and relate those to certain other data and publish that. The point has been brought out beautifully by one of the men in England, in discussing the type of publication that is done, the analysis given.

Finally I would like to just mention this problem of polling. The most common rationalizations in our culture today perhaps can be classified under: First, "They say"—that great horde of people passing across the mountain in the dim distance. "They say" proves things. Secondly, if it's "in numbers" it proves things. Third, "I saw it in a book, I saw it in print," proves things. Fourth, "It's psychology"—that proves things (*laughter*). And unfortunately polling falls into all those four categories: "They say—it's gossip—it's what the man in the street says"; "It's in numbers"; "It's in print"; and "It sounds psychological."

Briefly, what we did in the Washington Public Opinion Laboratory was to make a technical study with no idea of predicting the election. Our combined boards said, "Yes, go ahead and find out how good our sample is, how close we come to known data." We ran, briefly, an area sample, which is the interdomal type of area controlled down to the respondent within the household. At the same time we ran a quota sample. The poll was run the week prior to the election. It was run by interviewers not well trained in the quota system; their training had been in the area sample.

They interviewed up until forty-eight hours before the election. All ballots were mailed before midnight; they were in the mail to us at the time of the election. Wednesday morning I got into my office by taking the signs off, "Office for rent," and so on, and we started tabulating the report. We ran the quota first, and the data on this I tried to distribute to as many of you as possible. The IBM machine tabulator came up with the figures for the quota sample findings, and there it was. We were off on quota. We ran the area sample next and it came up just the reverse of the quota—it was correct. With one adjustment on the basis of the trend of the election in the last month, in which we found 70 percent of the people who were undecided thirty days before the election were making up their minds for Truman, we did even better. Adjusting it on that basis we are too close statistically, with the errors less than one-half of one percent, in estimating the election in the state of Washington. You have that data in front of you.

Then, for the Social Science Research Council we made a study following the election, in which we reinterviewed the respondents in the area sample. We not only reinterviewed those people, asking them how they voted, did they vote, for what reasons did they vote; we also went to the local courthouses and places of record to find out which respondents actually did vote, so we have the information on whether they actually did vote.

To what extent we were lucky—I won't go into that at the present time. For every question you might ask, I could ask another question. What I'd like to confine my remarks to briefly, are some of our preliminary studies of the relationship between the quota sample and the area sample studied. Whether the differences are luck on the area sample we don't know and the answer to this will not be available for a year. We will have our first publication on that in about two weeks. But with the 150,000 combinations to make, I am not sure.

I'd like to run over very briefly just a few differences between the area and quota systems. You will probably be most interested in the so-called "important" ones.

Income distribution between area and quota: The data I will give you as a comparison between quota, area, and those who actually voted, and not a comparison with the known data of the state. Just the three. I will give the percentages to you later. The quota sample got more people in the lower-income brackets than the area sample. It also got more people in the higher-income brackets.

It compares on high and low income with those who actually voted better than the area does. There isn't very much there until we start running lengthy analyses with the statisticians' help.

On density of population, the rural vote: Did we get the rural vote? The quota got more of the rural vote than did the area sample, but in the state of Washington the rural vote is largely Republican. That doesn't help much.

Age distribution: The difference between the quota, the area, and the known vote is very little. We haven't run the highly refined statistical analysis, but at present it doesn't seem that there is much difference.

Sex: On sex, a slight shift. And it might be that on this point we have one answer. We have an error in the area sample that we haven't been able to avoid as yet. We get too many women. The reason for that is that when our interviewers must substitute, they must substitute the opposite sex. They miss more males than females, even after three recalls, so they interview the opposite sex and get too many women. The quota sample gave us a better distribution of males and females in the state of Washington than the area sample, but the females in the state of Washington were more heavily for Truman than the males. Therefore a distortion we were trying to avoid is perhaps the answer to the problem of the percentage of the area sample (*laughter*).

Education: On education the difference is very little between area, quota, and the known data. However, as with most education questions, it doesn't mean very much, because all it shows is that Washington is the best-educated state in the United States (*laughter*). And so on through.

We have available all of this material— Oh, on *the foreign-born:* There is no appreciable difference. I would like just to give you an example of what I mean by no appreciable difference. I would like to read figures for the foreign-born for the total area, registered area, total quota, registered quota, and finally those who actually voted: 11.9, 10.7, 10.1, 9.0, and 11.3. As far as getting the actual number of people who voted, the registration—we were in the known percentages in both quota and area on registered voters. We don't know. That's the answer.

It's going to take a long time, but I would like to say this in conclusion. The area sample in the state of Washington hit the election practically on the nose. We showed a shift from a Republican Governor, to a Democratic Lieutenant Governor, in which the vote showed less than one percent difference between them. We got that. On down the line it was uncanny, how close it comes. We get such things as hitting practically on the nose the number of widowed males in the state of Washington, the number of widowed males over the age of sixty-five. It's uncanny. I don't know why.[1]

MR. STUIT: Our next speaker is an alumnus of this university, who is known to many of you personally, and to all of you as the person associated with the Gallup Poll. It is a great pleasure therefore to have as our next speaker Mr. George H. Gallup, Director of the American Institute of Public Opinion.

MR. GALLUP: The performance of sampling or cross-section polls in the 1948 election should be viewed against the background of poll performance recorded in the years since 1935 when polls were first established on a continuing basis.

During this period a total of 512 election forecasts were made by some twenty polling organizations operating in twelve democracies of the world. In this country alone a total of 446 forecasts have been made in this fourteen-year period.

The average error in these forecasts—including those made in the presidential election of 1948—is approximately four percentage points. In short, poll predictions, based upon the vote for all parties, have on the average varied from absolute accuracy by this average degree in elections dealing not only with candidates but those dealing with issues as well, referenda issues. The winners have been predicted correctly in more than eight out of ten elections.

This is a record of which we can all be proud. Probably, as one of the earlier speakers said, in no other field has human behavior been predicted with such a high degree of accuracy.

The mistakes made by polling organizations in the 1948 presidential election, in my opinion, were what I would describe as mistakes in judgment and not in basic procedures. They were mistakes which can be laid, in part at least, to lack of experience in this new field.

---

[1] Editor's note: A comparative study using the two methods is reported in Part Five under "Technical Problems: Methodology as Related to the Requirements of Public Opinion Measurement," pages 241 ff. Discussion of this aspect of sampling will be found in that section.

We in the polling business have been justifiably criticized on one point, however. We permitted the public to get the impression that polls had reached a stage of absolute perfection. As someone said, we led the people to believe that we could walk on water. But we were not wholly unaware of this fact, and we did try to correct this situation, albeit without too much success.

In April of last year I prepared a paper for the New Haven Chapter of the American Statistical Association which described in detail the accuracy of polls throughout the years. This same paper went on to detail the limitations of polls and the special problems which had to be met in this country in making predictions. In this paper I said: "There is always the danger that the public will begin to attribute a degree of accuracy to poll predictions which polling organizations cannot maintain, and do not claim." This paper was later published in pamphlet form and copies were sent during the campaign to every member of Congress, to every political writer and radio commentator, and to every member of the American Association for Public Opinion Research.

In an article which I wrote for the August issue of *Cosmopolitan Magazine,* entitled "How Accurate Are the Polls?", I repeated many of these same statements. Elaborating on this whole theory of infallibility, I said, and I quote: "Oddly enough, one of our problems is that people think that polls are more accurate than they really are. We expect to be pretty close in forecasting the outcome in November, but we don't expect to score a bull's-eye. Accuracy within three or four percent would be well within the range of good performance."

Now if you will examine our predictions and those of Mr. Crossley and others you will make the surprising discovery that on an all-party basis—on the same basis used for making this statement before the election—the polls performed in 1948 according to expectancy.

I quite agree with you in admitting that an average margin of error of four percentage points is not good enough to pick with certainty the winner in many close elections. In fact, to have predicted with certainty the election of Mr. Truman last fall would have required methods with an average error of far less than one percentage point! That is too much to ask of polling research at this stage of its development.

The problem which we in the field of public opinion research face can be stated simply. It is the problem of how to reduce this present average error of four percentage points to three percentage points. After we have reached that goal we can try to reduce the average error to two. But I do not believe that anyone who is familiar with polling problems would seriously suggest that polling accuracy can be reduced below this point—at least not in this country where problems of turnout and of party efficiency represent variables that are hard to control and measure.

To get a true perspective on the problems presented by the 1948 campaign it is necessary to go back a year to November, 1947. I recall that shortly after the off-year elections held during that month, we sent a report to our newspapers in which we said that the Congressional by-elections indicated that the Democratic party was still the dominant party of the country.

In January of 1948, in trial heats which we ran with Truman as the prospective Democratic candidate, Dewey the Republican, and Wallace the third-party candidate, Mr. Truman won handily over Mr. Dewey despite the fact that Mr. Wallace at that time received 7 percent of all votes cast in our sample. Mr. Truman remained ahead for the next couple of months, at which time he began to lose popularity and voting strength. He continued to drop until his nomination by the Democrats at Philadelphia. You will recall that shortly before the Democratic convention virtually all the party bosses in the Democratic party said that Mr. Truman didn't have a chance, and most of them were ready to drop him for almost any other candidate.

But the important thing to remember is that all during this period, and in fact throughout the campaign, the Democratic *party* continued to be the dominant party in the country. In every poll that we conducted we found that more persons called themselves Democrats than Republicans.

Mr. Truman's fighting campaign had the effect of winning back the Democrats who had strayed from the fold. All the evidence that I have seen shows that relatively few persons who voted for Dewey in 1944 shifted to Mr. Truman in 1948. Mr. Truman won by mustering most of the Democratic vote of the country.

When our special corps of interviewers went into the field early in September, they reported a general lack of interest in the campaign as compared with 1944. I suppose that this was natural because there was really no great and burning issue, and neither candidate had a very fanatic following.

As a consequence of this situation we found more persons in the "undecided" group than in any previous election. This in turn indicated that more persons held lightly to their preferences than in previous elections in which Roosevelt had been a candidate.

This should have been a warning signal to us, because in similar situations we and other polling organizations have found last-minute shifts of considerable proportions. The fact, however, that opinions during the last of September and the early part of October remained fairly constant lulled us into the belief that no change was likely in the last days of the campaign. Moreover, in the two previous elections evidence indicated that not much change had occurred in the final days.

The biggest error which we and other polls made was in not taking a last-minute poll. I wonder what the Washington state poll would have shown if they had conducted their poll not the last week but two weeks before? A good many polls—at least two or three I happen to know about—were conducted during the last few days of the campaign and all of them, so far as I know, did show a fairly dramatic shift downward and away from Dewey to Truman. Or maybe I should say "upward" (*laughter*).

Post-election studies have indicated that many voters—mostly persons who had voted for Roosevelt in 1944, and who had reported that they preferred Dewey as of the middle of October—were lured back into the Democratic fold. Likewise many persons who were Democrats but who said, as of the middle of October, that they planned to vote for Wallace, returned to Truman and the Democratic party.

The second major mistake which we made was in assuming that so few of the persons who reported that they were "undecided" in our last survey would actually get to the polls, that this group could be ignored and eliminated from the sample.

We knew from New York registration figures, and from Sidney Goldish's studies of Minneapolis registration, that the national turnout in this election would be extremely low. A normal turnout for 1948 would have been in the neighborhood of 58,000,000. But the New York and Minneapolis figures indicated a turnout of only 47,000,000 to 50,000,000.

Since our samples normally embrace a cross-section of the entire voting population, the problem arose as to what voters should be eliminated. On all of our ballots we asked respondents to tell us whether they were registered to vote, whether they planned to vote, how certain they were of voting, and whether they were interested in the election. But even after using these filter questions we found that more voters had still to be eliminated to reduce our sample to the indicated turnout.

We decided, and I think you would have made the same decision under similar circumstances, that this group made up of the "un-decided's" was least likely to get to the polls. But post-election studies indicate that many of these persons did vote, and that most of them voted for the ticket which they had supported in previous elections—the Democratic party.

I believe that these two errors in judgment—the failure to take a last-minute poll, and the decision to eliminate the "undecided" voters in our sample—account for most of the error in our 1948 predictions. Obviously other factors entered into our error. They enter into every election prediction. But I believe that all the evidence which has been studied to date indicates that they were relatively minor in importance in 1948.

Some of our critics have said that our sample was at fault, that we did not interview enough persons of low income. While this statement was undoubtedly true in earlier elections, I am reasonably sure that this was not the case in 1948.

Our pin-point surveys which represent a modified form of area sampling produced figures as much in error as our regular quota samples. Our figures, unpublished, on Congress were within a percentage point of the true figure.

The size of the samples which we used could account for only a small part of the error. Oddly enough, our smallest errors were registered in the states where our samples were smallest, but this can be accounted for largely on the basis that polls in these states were for the most part taken at a later date.

Interviewing bias was probably not important because our secret ballot results showed almost the same results as our regular inter-view ballots. Moreover, our highly trained and supervised inter-viewers brought back almost the same results as our less highly trained resident interviewers.

The problems of sample design and interviewing are far less important than the problem of identifying those persons who will vote and those who will stay at home. In the pamphlet to which I re-ferred earlier, I said this: "One of the most difficult problems confronting polling organizations in making election forecasts in the United States is the problem of turnout." (Plainly, it is a problem in the United States, because fewer persons vote in this country than in any other democracy in the world. In countries where voting is compulsory they haven't this problem of turnout. In England and France, for instance, this problem doesn't come up, because normally they can expect a turnout of around eighty-five to ninety percent.)

And again quoting: "Although the American Institute of Public Opinion and other polling organizations have tried hundreds of experiments with different types of questions and procedures to sort out the persons who will actually vote from those who will stay at home, there is still no test which can be applied which will perform this task with complete accuracy." This was said six months before the election. It is still true today.

The answer, unfortunately, is not to be found in questions measuring the intensity of voting intention for the very simple reasons that many of the persons with the lowest intensity scores actually get to the polls.

Women in the low income and education groups normally show the least interest in elections. Some of them don't even know who the candidates are. When we interview them they say, "Talk to my husband." But if pressure is put on this group of people on election day by labor unions, the Church, and party machines—if baby sitters are provided and transportation to the polls—they do get to the polls and vote.

So without a measure of the efficiency and zeal of these groups, the best filter questions in the world are not likely to work too well.

The very mechanics of voting can introduce errors of sizable degree. In at least one state there is no secret ballot; in others the ballot is made up purposely to confuse voters. There is no easy way to take these factors into account.

In some cities like Chicago, Albany, and Jersey City the machines somehow get an amazing number of persons to the polls, and these people always seem to vote just the way the machine wants them to. It may be pressure or it may be corruption. But whatever you call it, the task of a polling agency is not made easier by their efforts.

When all of these facts are taken into account I, for one, marvel that elections in this country can be forecast with an average error of only four percentage points.

When as many persons get to the polls in this country as in other democracies—when, as, and if we have compulsory voting laws—then most of our problems will vanish and it will be reasonable to expect that prediction errors can be reduced from four percentage points to two percentage points.

MR. STUIT: Our next speaker is also an alumnus of the University of Iowa, whom we are very glad to welcome back to the campus, and we welcome him as a participant in this discussion. It is my pleasure to introduce Mr. Henry J. Kroeger, Director of the Research Department, *Des Moines Register and Tribune,* and the Iowa Poll.

MR. KROEGER: As a one-time advertising man, I have some elementary sense of showmanship. If I were to follow my personal impulse in arranging a program such as that we have had this morning, it would be my first inclination to build up to a climax. However, I want to get into the record, as a service to you, an explanation that I come on at this point in the program, not as a climax, but because the program committee simply followed the alphabetical order of the names included.

I am sure that there are some people in this room who can realize that my position on this program at this particular time, and amidst these immediate surroundings, is by no means a comfortable one for obvious reasons. Also, because as I have already mentioned, I am in the uncomfortable spot of having to follow the greater satellites in the field of public opinion measurement. What I mean is that after all, the things that I do are on a rather small scale; the operation is a department in a publishing organization. Our field is a single state and by contrast and by physical limitations, that is certainly something of much less magnitude and offers much less background than that of the speakers who have preceded me. In fact, during my discomfort because of that particular situation, I have been reminded constantly of an old story. Mr. Chairman, if you have heard it before, don't stop me. I want to hear it again myself.

The old story is about a flea who was riding one day in an elephant's ear, and as the elephant ambled through the jungle the elephant crossed a bridge. The bridge was rather rickety and it teetered rather dangerously. They got across the bridge, and the flea in the elephant's ear spoke up and said, "Well, Big Boy, I and you sure shook that one!" That will give you an idea (*laughter*).

I was quite aware before this program that Mr. Crossley and Dr. Gallup and Dr. Dodd would do about as they have done, and I am certainly not in any position to contribute a very great deal to the areas which they have covered so effectively. Therefore, it seemed to me that the only thing that I might do would be to perhaps contribute a little something to your information by making a few scattered, somewhat related observations on our experiences here in Iowa.

Mr. Crossley made a statement yesterday in speaking about market surveys, something about measuring a stream before you had a log-jam farther down the stream, which later you would have to blast loose. For a long time before the 1948 election here in Iowa it was my firm belief that we were observing something, trying to measure something which certainly was in a fluid state, which certainly in some respects would measure up to the analogy of being a stream, rather than a pool in which we would try to measure certain depths at certain points. Quite early there were certain undefined cross-currents, certain indications of indecision, that later came to the surface in an unmistakable way.

Now in making these scattered comments as we go along here, they will of course relate to the cross-section. They will also relate to the polling methods and all that. I am not attempting even to indicate or infer that there was no room for improvement in those directions. But I do want just to give you as a sort of a yardstick to some of the complications in 1948, our experience on something that was less complicated.

I refer to the fact that in 1948 the Iowa voters had an opportunity to approve or disapprove a soldiers' bonus—in other words, a referendum. Now, in that instance the probabilities were of course not very many. A voter could vote or not vote, and if he voted he could vote "yes" or "no." There was no complication due to straight-ticket voting or anything like that. It was a hazardous affair for a number of reasons: for one, because of the fact that the bonus referendum was on a separate ballot. Also, because of publication requirements we were compelled to make a final survey on that issue about the tenth or eleventh of October. And it developed later that all of the publicity from veterans organizations got into the mail after that date.

Nevertheless, and in spite of those developments, when we separated those there were good indications of an actual vote on the bonus (and incidentally the vote was nearly as large as the vote for president) : we found that we had in that group 73 percent who said they would vote in favor of the bonus, 23 percent who said they would vote against it, and 3.6 percent who were undecided. Dividing that undecided in the traditional manner, in the proportions of those who expressed definite opinions, we had a projected majority of 76 percent. The actual majority when the votes were finally counted was 77.9 percent.

Now, I mention that because it is some indication that there were some things about this operation that must have been right. I don't think you can say always that something like that is a matter of sheer luck.

In line with observations by Dr. Gallup and others, here in Iowa we too saw evidence of a lower level of interest in the 1948 election. For instance, in 1944 in October, the percentage of those who said they were absolutely certain they were going to vote was about 70 percent, and later in October, somewhat higher. In that year the turnout was about 76 percent.

In early October of 1948, that group of those who classified themselves as absolutely certain to vote was in the neighborhood of 57 percent, and late in October it had risen only to about 63 percent.

There has been comment made here both yesterday and today in an area about which we in our limited way have been very much concerned and where we have tried to do some experimentation— namely, this all-important matter of measuring intention to vote on a firmer basis than self-appraisal. Therefore as an experiment we tried in the primary election last June, and in the general election in the fall, a somewhat indirect approach. This I realize probably has serious inadequacies and in the long run may not prove to have any degree of utility whatsoever. Dr. Dodd mentioned yesterday attempting to accumulate various measurements of action as validating criteria, something which in me struck a responsive note. In that area, the approach which we used as an experiment, because it did have some universality and because it was on somewhat of a behavior basis, was the very simple question of asking people whether or not they had talked about the election within the last week, or something like that.

Now here is the performance of that measurement. In September there were only 46 percent of the group interviewed who said they had had any conversation about the election. In early October it went up to 55 percent, and in late October it had risen to 68 percent. I invite your attention to one thing which may or may not be significant, which may be somewhat accidental, but to me it does have some significance. It is one of these things which because of a lack of experience you cannot use in a forecast. Taking those two figures, those that were absolutely certain to vote and the other one, those talking about the election, you come out with percentages very close to the actual turnout in the 1948 election here in Iowa.

Another phase of the political situation in Iowa about which we were tremendously concerned was the behavior of the labor group. We were concerned about that because of certain history in connection with the primary election last June. Realizing that the turnout might be light, and that if this group were to be motivated enough to turn out in a very substantial way, the election result would be greatly influenced, we devoted special attention to the attitudes of labor people.

Now here is something that to me is of more than passing interest. As was done with all other respondents, we asked the union people whether or not they had talked about the election. We found that in the final survey 77 percent of the members of the labor unions in our sample said they had been carrying on some conversation about the election. And that related to certain activity of which we were aware.

Now you will note that that percentage is greatly higher than the percentage for the entire cross-section. We also found among the labor union members and the members of their immediate families that the intention to vote was a great deal higher than the average for the entire sample. As a somewhat crude attempt to measure that particular indication of voting behavior, we separated those in the sample on the basis of grade-school, high-school, and college education. Obviously many of the people found in labor unions would be found in the first two educational brackets. It was seen that among the grade-school people, for instance, only 59 percent said they were absolutely certain they would vote as against the 77 percent labor union members.

Thus you see that we had an indication of something that was not only rather volatile, but that was bound to be rather influential, as it ultimately proved to be.

Another circumstance in our Iowa election which was surely a complicating factor and surely difficult to measure, and at the same time one of the facts of life, was the expectancy of "scratching."

I will not go into all of the history of the 1948 election in Iowa. That would probably not serve too useful a purpose, but suffice it to say that there were certain groups that were crossing over; there were groups that would customarily vote Democratic, who were expecting to vote for the Republican candidate for Governor. We also had of course the fact that the Democratic candidate for United States Senator had a long record of ability to get votes, to win the independent voter, and so on. Therefore, realizing that as a practical political proposition that would affect more than one candidate, we gave a rather intensive study to that.

To sum it up: we took our final survey and made a special tabulation in which we put in one group those who named all three Republican candidates—for President, for Governor, for United States Senator. We put in another group those who in like manner had named the candidates on the Democratic ticket for those offices. The remaining group would be those who had, in being interviewed, named candidates on more than one ticket. It was found that 41 percent of that sample had you might say "scratched" in the manner in which they had named their preferences.

Now I submit to you that when you have that large a group whose intentions are to cross political lines when it comes to the final act of voting, you have on your hands a group which is certainly more than even gelatinous in my view. It approaches being rather fluid, for the very good reason that it is recognized as a matter of practical political behavior that a great many people have well-founded intentions of voting for candidates on more than one party ticket, but when they find themselves inside the booth and see the number of levers that they have got to pull—down in Des Moines for instance—on the voting machines, and the number of crosses they have to make on the printed ballot, a significant percentage of them become discouraged at that moment and immediately decide to vote it straight.

And there we come to something which was, at least so far as Iowa is concerned, an important phenomenon in the 1948 election. In my view there is no doubt that Senator Gillette on the Democratic ticket, through this influence which I have mentioned, created a tremendous number of votes for President Truman at the head of the Democratic ticket. I have wondered sometimes if in the discussion of the 1948 election, there shouldn't be more attention given to that particular phase of the whole affair. After all, Iowa was not unique. There were innumerable other situations where there was what you might call a "coat-tail" influence that came from the bottom up, that exerted an influence on the head of the ticket, adversely or favorably as the case might be.

I want to comment very briefly about one candidate in the 1948 Iowa election. As I have mentioned, we had ex-Senator Gillette as the Democratic candidate, running against Senator George Wilson, the Republican incumbent. Now, in our final report we did not make too flat a prediction, because that was not indicated by the situation as of that time. We did, however, point to a Gillette victory. To that extent it was a tribute to the sensitivity of modern polling, because the expectation in many quarters was that Senator Wilson, the incumbent on the Republican ticket, would pull through by "straight-ticket" voting's creating enough votes for him.

Now that supposition, or assumption as you choose to call it, was not altogether theoretical. It was based upon Iowa political history. It was you might say a matter of tradition, because in the last few Senatorial elections it has been only once that a Senator from the opposite party to the Governor has been elected, and that was an off-year election. In the presidential elections the two offices have always been on the same side of the political fence, by varying majorities to be sure, but nevertheless Republican or Democratic as the case might be.

Now in that connection there developed some things that were very difficult to deal with, and that were somewhat surprising—at least they were to me. In the case of Senator Gillette, back in September we came up with something somewhat unusual. As many of you know, it is usual that politically men and women are found on the same side of a political fence. They tend to name their preferences that way, and apparently to vote that way. But beginning in September we found that while we still had the men and women both Republican so far as the President and Governor were concerned, when it came to the candidate for United States Senator we found that the men had moved over to Senator Gillette's side of the fence— namely, were Democratic.

That particular development proved to be a bit troublesome for a time because there were some people who even went so far as to say, "We'd better retabulate our figures. That couldn't be." One thing that was very helpful to me was the fact that my friend Don Murphy took a survey among a group of Iowa farmers for *Wallace's Farmer* and the *Iowa Homestead*, and uncovered among the Iowa farmers the same phenomenon—namely, that the men were on the Democratic side of the fence and the women were still over on the Republican side. Well, not only did that particular situation continue to exist, but there was a gradual strengthening in preference for Senator Gillette among the men. It was only at the very last that the women interviewed were found to be over on Senator Gillette's side of the fence, only they still were not quite as far over as the male voters.

Now there is an explanation for that particular situation which is not altogether hypothetical. Because of the fact that it is somewhat of a personal nature I hesitate to describe it from this platform. However, what I have been leading up to was that here was something obviously very fluid. You had the men going one way, and the women had just begun to follow. You could assume of course that finally when they came to vote, the women would vote the way the men were leaning, but that would be an assumption which we certainly would not be warranted in making. The painful part of that situation was that if it had been possible to use as a final criterion— and I do not see how it could have been—but if it had been possible to base a prediction at the last moment upon the preferences found among the Gillette voters, it would have been within one per cent of Senator Gillette's final vote.

Now there were a great many other things that indicated there were changes going on. We found the farmers veering away from the Republican candidates. We found a certain amount of apathy among Republican voters, and so on. But I have already used up one minute more than I have been allotted and so I will drop everything and simply come to a conclusion.

I had prepared in my own mind at least what to me would have been a very satisfactory peroration but I decided I would be performing a greater service to this highly intelligent group if instead of inflicting upon you some of my own observations I would read you a few paragraphs, or sentences, from an article which I just picked up. I do this because they reflect in clearer language than my own some of my own views and also relate to some of the things that have been discussed on this platform this morning.

I refer to an article in the February 4th issue of *Printers' Ink* by W. Edwards Deming, Adviser in Sampling, Bureau of the Budget, Executive Office of the President. Mr. Deming says this and I quote: "In election forecasting, this step requires a prediction, on the basis of an inventory of opinion and with *the aid of any other relevant knowledge or judgment* how the election will turn out on Tuesday."

When you are making election forecasts on a state basis, I can assure you that you encounter some things that do not necessarily create difficulties, but that make it very difficult to know precisely how to use the findings in a situation as fluid as that which we had here in Iowa in 1948.

And now another excerpt from Mr. Deming's article. He has been speaking about the definition of the "universe" and he says this: "Given thirty million dollars and unlimited manpower for an opinion poll so that I could take a complete census of the continental United States, I should still wonder how to instruct interviewers how to recognize every eligible voter in a household. Because of the difficulty of recognizing the universe of voters, no sample of adults on Monday, not even a complete canvass, could provide the basic data representing unequivocally the intention of the voters as they look forward to the election on Tuesday."

One final statement and I shall cease to inflict myself upon you. Again I quote: "I believe that publicity emphasizing the difficulties of forecasting an election and making a clearer separation between forecasting and eliciting information on which to forecast, will go a long way toward restoring public confidence in sampling surveys, if not in opinion polling as well."

DISCUSSION—Paul F. Lazarsfeld, Norman C. Meier

MR. STUIT: Thank you, Mr. Kroeger, and all the five members of our symposium this morning, for a very objective and critical analysis of the causes of disparity between poll findings and election results.

We turn next to a discussion of these papers. At the meeting last evening, because the hour was getting rather late, the presiding officer sounded out the audience as to whether or not the last speaker should appear. The results of that opinion poll indicated overwhelmingly that the audience wanted him to speak.

It is a pleasure therefore to welcome back to this platform Dr. Paul Lazarsfeld, who will be the first discussant of the papers delivered this morning.

MR. LAZARSFELD: I suppose you all had the same feeling I had when I listened to Mr. Kroeger and to our friends from Washington State—Stuart Dodd and Dr. Bachelder. Mr. Kroeger ended with a kind of apology that the work of the state laboratories on this local and state level is a little bit more complicated and maybe less interesting for the listeners. I feel it is quite the opposite, that those contributions have again shown that there are certain things you can do on a state level which you cannot do on the national level. This comparison between two sampling procedures is almost only possible if you have special regional facilities such as those which Stuart Dodd has built up around Seattle, and you have this detailed matching of your local political knowledge with specific questions you ask in your questionnaires.

Those are the things which in my opinion will really ground the future knowledge of political behavior based on poll data, and I have listened to these three speakers with great envy and with some concern because those things escape us, and it is almost a coincidence that Mr. Kroeger is here today. I am sure someone from Minnesota or someone from Texas would also have similar stories, and if the people who organized this Conference so successfully would give some thought to the question, How could we poor New York and Washington, D. C., provincials find out what is really going on in political polls—that is to say, what people do on the state level— it would be a tremendous help. Polling work and this kind of analysis on the state level, if it is a little bit co-ordinated and communicated to the rest of us, will be a tremendous contribution, much more than we realize now. I am very glad that we had this splendid demonstration of this point this morning.

On the national level the trouble is you can only discuss a limited amount of things, and we have therefore a tendency to repeat ourselves a little bit more than you state people do. But I think at one point this morning's discussion was really helpful even on the national level, and that is, that the point of predicting turnout came out so clearly and with every speaker, and we were especially impressed by the detailed analysis which George Gallup gave us. Now at this point, I might make a suggestion which might be somewhat helpful because it really recasts what the national speakers have said with just a slight difference in terms, but a terminology which might reveal some hidden difficulties here. The words "predicting" and "prediction" have been used in two areas of the social sciences in very different ways, and the distinction and interrelation have never been brought clearly to our general attention as far as I know.

You take the classical book from which social science students learn prediction techniques—and this is a book published by the SSRC called "Predicting Success and Failure in Personal Adjustment." It was written by a colleague of Stuart Dodd's, Paul Horst, under the general supervision of our colleague, Sam Stouffer. If you go through this book, which is absolutely the classic on prediction studies, the word "polling" or any material looking in any way similar to polls, doesn't appear at all, for to Paul Horst—he is a social scientist—prediction means this: You have a couple of young people and they want to get married, and they are foolish enough to ask a marriage counselor whether they should get married, and the marriage counselor is now supposed to make a prediction whether this marriage will be successful or not. The last thing he will do is ask whether they intend to be happily married. That is to say, he will not take a poll of these people and ask them whether they intend to be happily married. That's why they want to marry; he takes that for granted. But he looks for what the social scientist calls "correlates." He looks at previous case studies and says, "People who come from very strong different religious backgrounds, that might not forecast so well; or people who have been engaged too long—or ask too many marriage counselors" (*laughter*).

This whole tradition is shown by Paul Horst in the same kind of examples he gives for predicting parole breakers. In many states the judges use prediction studies to find out whether a man is a good risk, whether he will keep parole or not. The last thing the judge asks is whether he intends to break the parole or not, because he will get a one hundred percent "No." But, for instance, people who committed certain crimes, in company or alone, and so on, are different parole risks.

So there is a social science tradition of calling "prediction" any statement on a future event; any expectation of future event you express on the basis of data correlated with phenomena you are studying, like marriage intention, but not identical with intention. Now in polling we have a kind of study where you ask a man, "How do you intend to vote?" and essentially we base our predictions on this intention. But these are two completely different notions of prediction: one predicts from intention to execution of intention; the other predicts from the antecedent correlates of the phenomena to the final phenomena.

Now the polling type of prediction also happens in a variety of fields. For instance, Stouffer in the Army had to make a study of how many people would use the veterans' schooling benefits after the war, and essentially he had to ask the soldiers, "Will you go to school after the war or not?" He made all sorts of correlations but the base had to be an intention data like you use in polling.

Now the point I am trying to make is to distinguish between those two types—the extreme types of using only intention data and only correlates, and then all sorts of transitions will help a great deal to clarify the problem. For instance, *how* people will vote, *if* they vote, can be obtained fairly safely from the intention type of prediction. If a man votes, he usually—in the great majority—votes as he had intended to do. It turns out, however, and that is what we see now so clearly, that voting itself, not what they vote for but the act of voting, cannot be predicted so well from intention predictions but has to be much more predicted from correlates.

Now you could be very extreme. You could for instance say that the best way to predict whether a woman who says she will vote will actually vote, is to count the number of children she has. Because the more children she has, the more likely she is to be busy on election day and if she also has no maid (*laughter*) she may not vote. I think that a lot of predicting whether people who say they will vote will carry out this intention can be obtained from completely objective data which has nothing to do with their intention. Some of it can be obtained, as George Gallup well pointed out, from intermediate questions where in addition to asking them, "Do you intend to vote?" you ask them, "Have you talked with someone?" or "When did you make up your mind?"—as Dodd suggests. Let us say additional psychological correlates and not objective correlates.

Then there is the case of the person who says, "I don't intend to vote," where you have to make the opposite guess. If she says, "I don't intend to vote," will she carry out her nonvoting intention? In that case, probably not even any objective data about her will help, but what you need there are correlates pertaining to the community because the nonvoter, the intended nonvoter who says, "I don't intend to vote," and who then votes, is best predicted by finding out whether there are enough community forces which are likely to bring pressure upon him or her on election day.

So we should weigh what type of prediction procedure we intend to use; this can go from what I might say is the extreme Paul Horst type of prediction by correlates and the extreme intention type of prediction, which is just predicting from the "Do-you-intend-to-vote" question, to which I don't want to attach any name of course. Where in this you really should operate is essentially the problem which most of the national speakers have been discussing this morning.

Now, to end this, I would like to pick up one remark from Arch Crossley's speech. He stressed and gave evidence how he is not moved by competitive considerations of any kind. Of course none of us is, or should be, but should Arch and I for instance feel inclined to feel competitive to great giants like George Gallup, we ought to stop it right away; it's a hopeless business. I just came back from Europe and I spent election week in Norway and election week end in Sweden, and the way things are discussed there is so: "Do you have a 'Gallup' yourself?" "Has Crossley's 'Gallup' been better than Roper's 'Gallup'?" (*laughter*). And I tried to understand what they meant by "Crossley's 'Gallup,' " and then I found out that their notion of the word "Gallup" is the American word for "polls." What I need is a "Lazarsfeld's Gallup." I have definitely lost status by claiming that I know Mr. George Gallup, who does excellent polls, because no one really believed me.

MR. STUIT: Our next speaker has spent many hours in assisting with the organization and arrangement of this Conference. Public opinion is a field of special interest and research for him, so we are very happy to have him as our next discussant. Professor Norman C. Meier, Director of the Bureau of Audience Research on the campus, and a member of the Department of Psychology.

MR. MEIER: I'd like first to review some observations that I have picked up during the course of the morning. I think we would agree that the criticisms attendant on the alleged poll failures in November have been way beyond justification. I was glad to hear one of the men from Washington, Mr. Bachelder, state that the marvel is that poll error is not greater than it is. Unfortunately, the public at large expected the polls to predict in very much the same way as picking the winner of a horse race. If you do not always pick the winner you are no good; you should just go out of business.

It should be clear that the public needs some considerable re-education in the nature of polls and in the nature of error and sampling variation. Although these items have been brought to the public's attention, apparently they are still not very well understood. There has also been of late some inclination to attribute great forecasting ability to a man who is new in the field, and ignore the fact that another man—who is in this room—has been successful in picking about eight out of ten. Because after all, Mr. Truman has only successfully predicted one election (*laughter*).

It has been observed that the New York City registration, which is held anew for each presidential election, has a very definite relationship to the turnout in the nation. I believe none of the speakers mentioned this morning that the registration indications of the New York City electorate this last year indicated a very low turnout. And that was reflected all over the nation in what seemed to be, from all poll findings, a general apathetic condition even throughout most of October. Everybody of course knew that back in June Mr. Truman's stock was very, very low, even among his own party chieftains, among all the big-city Democratic bosses; and there was almost nobody, perhaps except a very few friends, who thought he even should make the try.

That was the state of mind the public was in and the public remained in all through the summer and into the fall, and hence it was the public's own reflection which was picked up by the polls. Yet when it was found out that there was a disparity between the poll findings in mid-October and election returns in November, the public turned on the polls and said, "Here, you misled us." I can't quite see the justice of that because the polls are simply mirrors, reflectors of what is in the minds of persons and there is no question, at least in my mind, that in early summer, certainly in June, everyone (probably including Mr. Truman) thought that whoever was nominated on the Republican ticket would be elected.

It certainly seemed to us in Iowa from reports of the Iowa Poll —there were three surveys made between the fifteenth of September and the twentieth of October—that all these polls agreed that the interest was low. It did rise somewhat, as Mr. Kroeger pointed out, but it did not rise very much except on the part of interested groups —labor and the farmer. But even in the case of the farmer—I think

Don Murphy would agree with that—there was more or less only a dormant interest up to the last few weeks, which was then aroused, however, by the falling price of corn. Iowa has been traditionally —and if you will consult the *Official Register*, you will find it verified in election statistics—Iowa has been normally Republican, and the farmers as a group have been consistently Republican voters, but in late October when their granaries were filled, all their storage space was occupied, and they still had a great deal of corn standing in the fields, it had to be sold at a falling price or dumped on the lots. It was at that time, we will say about the third week in October, that the farmer began to reflect upon whether or not his future would best be served by a Republican administration.

Here I want to say that I have never personally subscribed in my teachings of political psychology and public opinion measurement to the view that campaigns do not influence elections. That is one thing I disagree about with my friend Ted Gallup, and with anyone else that holds or did hold that point of view. Certainly, it goes back at least twenty years to some pretty good authority—to Frank Kent and to the old idea of the Tides Theory.

I'd like to tie that in with a closely related matter: the alleged error in preceding past elections. There has been much comment made that the Gallup Poll for instance has shown a Republican bias through now four elections. In 1936 the error of the Gallup Poll was greater than it was in 1948 but it was in Roosevelt's direction and the Roosevelt vote was then high—the error was six percentage points. In the next election, in 1940, it was less—much less —about three points. And in 1944 it was still less, only about two points. But in all three there was an underestimation of the Democratic strength.

Whether in the four last elections there was also a post-poll upsurge, greater in 1948, will be argued; but it must be conceded that the upsurge explanation *can* explain all these events. That hypothesis is given strong support when one studies the whole picture of the discrepancies between the poll findings and the four election results. In fact, the poll indications of elections can be adequately understood only by a full understanding of the *political strategy* of the contestants in those campaigns.

During four different campaigns, this country witnessed in action one of the greatest political strategists it has ever seen, Franklin D. Roosevelt; and if one goes back over the history of the campaigning you will observe this fact: that he was a person who waited patiently each time until his opponent had had his say; then stepped in and in the last two or three weeks did the bulk of his campaigning. His main speeches, his major efforts, were made usually in the last two weeks. If you go over the history of the campaigns I believe you will find that bears me out closely.

In 1944, as you will recall, his Fala Dog speech was the first effort he made in that campaign; it was a trivial thing but a very great vote-getting speech. It showed him to have the human interest that made him a popular leader. He didn't make another speech for ten days or more after that, but later reached a climax with his Sixty Million Jobs speech in Grant Park, Chicago, and another to the great outpouring in Shibe Park, Philadelphia. And in those last ten days or last week we have the explanations for the fact that the Democratic strength has always experienced in all four of those elections a definite upsurge.

In this election it was not only different in degree, in my opinion, but the datum points were confused because in this case there was no great cleavage between a master politician, as Roosevelt was, and a candidate of lesser strength, as Hoover, Landon, Willkie, or Dewey. In this case we had a choice between two minor candidates —I mean by that, lesser candidates compared to Roosevelt in stature. They simply did not have the political appeal, the political "It," which Roosevelt always enjoyed, so that it should have been no surprise that the New York City registration indicated a low turnout in 1948.

There should have been fifty-six to fifty-eight million persons voting, to have a normal turnout compared to population. Instead there were about forty-nine million only, and it seems that fact provides one of the keys to the whole uncertainty. In fact, it is surprising that polls came as close as they did with so many things kept in an uncertain, fluid state right up to the last minute, where the choice was neither impelling nor decisive, and where there were many people who apparently did not care who was elected.

I am somewhat inclined to think there is something in Colonel McCormick's observation of having received a letter from some woman in the South who said, "Thank God, they both can't be elected!" (*laughter*). We may not agree with that observation but there is something in the fact that that does express the equivalence—the ambivalence—of the two candidate-prospects, and with

many people it would result in no decision. They simply, seven
million or more persons, just didn't bother to vote. Some even went
into the voting booth—700,000, wasn't it, Crossley?—and didn't
vote for president. They voted for other candidates but had no
choice for president. And therefore in a situation where the balance
of deciding one way or the other is so slight, a great many people
just didn't take the trouble to make that decision.

Since the election, one of my graduate students has been investigating voting behavior in several areas including one precinct in
Iowa which has been for fifty years without any deviation from the
state greater than expressed by a standard deviation of 0.4, and
while he didn't get everybody, he tried to get every voter in that
precinct. Here are some of the findings of this house-to-house survey: 3.6 percent stated that they had made up their minds *on the
day of the election;* 19.8 percent in the two or three weeks just before the election; and 14.9 percent two or three months before the
election. Somewhat similar results were found in other parts of the
state among farmers and residents of another city. While isolated
sampling studies perhaps mean nothing in themselves, yet if many
of them all come out with similar indications, as they have in quite
a number of other post-election checks that the American Institute
of Public Opinion and others has made, we have then a good indication that the disparity can be accounted for on a perfectly normal basis which is little to the discredit of the polls. And I think
the more we learn about this, the more eventually will we also
understand more about voting behavior in the United States.

One other observation I'd make is that it is a very significant
fact that almost all polls by any method—and nearly all straw-vote
collections as well—came up with practically the same indications
—in October. In other words, *they all underestimated Truman* no
matter where they were taken, except in the South. Some of the
Gallup state figures showed that the Democratic underestimates in
the South have been small, which would be expected because Democratic voting is normalized in the South, but not here or in many
other places in the country. But the thing that strikes me is that
even all the collections of straw votes underestimated Truman.

When there is a common experience like that, there can only be,
it seems to me, one common explanation—namely, that polling
methods are not important in this disparity. The important, the one
chief explanation, seems to me to be obviously the Truman upsurge

brought about by the man who did the most effective campaigning in the last few weeks, coupled with a decline of a faltering Dewey who failed to impress voters, and the withdrawal of some groups that normally should have voted for Dewey or Wallace and couldn't exactly come to the conclusion to support these candidates. And therefore all those conditions and perhaps a score or more of others, put together, tend to explain the disparity without any unnecessary and unproved assumptions as to methodology or interviewing practices, which could have been contributing factors but certainly not basic ones. Moreover, the two regional studies tend to confirm the basic hypothesis that the timing of the polls provides the chief key to the causes of disparity. The Elmira study, made in October, by area methods, shows a 6 percent error, whereas the Washington state study made late and practically right up to the election with tabulation running through and after the election was over shows a close result, even though the method departed widely from area principles, as regards many substitutions and incomplete sampling.

When all is known that can be known, impartial opinion may regard the "poll failure" like the report of Mark Twain's death, as greatly exaggerated. Hindsight now provides two certainties about which everyone seems agreed. The first is that the polls *may have been right as of the time they were made.* The second is that the poll-takers, like everyone else, *are fallible human beings* and failed to anticipate possible changes in the final weeks. Had they been in any slight degree omniscient in that respect, however, it is doubtful that much could have been done about it. In the 1948 election the interviewers would have had to continue right up to and into the voting booth. The "poll failure" is hence seen mainly to be a failure to prevent public expectation that poll results in October necessarily indicated election results in November in an election characterized by a depressed turnout with many fluid conditions operating to affect normal predictability—an election that in many respects was unique and in some respects at least unparalleled.

16

THE SSRC
COMMITTEE REPORT

Leslie G. Moeller, Presiding

Archibald M. Crossley

George H. Gallup

Paul F. Lazarsfeld

Samuel A. Stouffer

MR. MOELLER: Most of us remember a day along in early November when most of this nation was agreed upon the potential membership of one Harry Truman in what is perhaps the most exclusive club in the United States, the living ex-presidents. It was on the following day that Mr. Truman held one of the largest social events in the history of this nation, a surprise party for approximately one hundred forty million persons. There were of course varied reactions to that event. There were newspapermen who, perhaps because of a willingness to obscure their own shall-we-say "inattention to duty," were willing to look elsewhere for a reason and were on that occasion going back to a remark attributed to Adam. They were pointing a finger and saying, "The woman deceived me." There were pollsters who were saying either "What hit me?" or "I didn't know it was loaded."

If all these comments with their varying titles were to be gathered together in one volume, it might well carry the title suggested by one of our journalism students, "Rationalization Following Miscalculation."

We have for consideration today a somewhat more, shall we say, scientific study in this particular field of explanation. That is the report of the Social Science Research Council Committee. We shall proceed in our discussion this afternoon, first with a report of a brief public opinion poll which, strangely enough, resulted in "Undecided," zero; "Yes," zero; "No," one hundred, when it came to the matter of having the presiding officer read the entire report. We have compromised on a plan of summarizing very briefly the seven major points in the summary, and then proceeding to ask three participants in strict alphabetical order—Mr. Crossley, Mr. Gallup, and Mr. Lazarsfeld—to raise some points about the report. Then we will call on one of the members of the Committee which wrote the report, Sam Stouffer, to make such comments as he cares to. I trust in his own comment that he will keep in mind that while there would perhaps be a tendency on the part of the members of the Committee to defend the report as it was issued, I hope he will also give us a rather complete picture of what must have been the internal discussion of the Committee before the report was issued.

With that preliminary, I will pass on to this summary of the seven points.

"First: the pollsters overreached the capabilities of the public opinion poll as a predicting device in attempting to pick, without qualification, the winner of the 1948 presidential election.

"Second: the pollsters could have foreseen the possibility of a close contest had they looked more carefully at their data and past errors.

"Third: the over-all operation of making election predictions from pre-election polls is a complex one, involving eight major steps at each of which error may enter. It is very difficult to unscramble the total error and allocate components of it to these various steps. The evidence indicates that there were two major causes of errors, errors of sampling and interviewing, and errors of forecasting, involving failure to assess the future behavior of undecided voters and to detect shifts of voting intention near the end of the campaign.

"Fourth: these sources of error were not new, and this point summarizes briefly evidence as to some earlier occurrence of these errors.

"Fifth: to improve the accuracy of pre-election poll predictions satisfactorily it is necessary to reduce the error at every step in the over-all polling process. The error at some of the steps, notably sampling and interviewing, could be reduced by using methods now available. Reduction at other steps depends on further basic research in psychological and political behavior.

"Sixth: the manner in which the pre-election polls were analyzed, presented, and published for public consumption contributed materially to the widespread misinterpretation of the results of the poll and to the great public reaction to their failure to pick the winner.

"And finally, seventh: the public should draw no inferences from pre-election forecasts that would disparage the accuracy or usefulness of properly conducted sampling surveys in fields in which the response

does not involve expression of opinion or intention to act. There are
more appropriate methods to check the accuracy of such surveys."

Now, with that preliminary I will present as the first person to
raise questions, Mr. Crossley.

MR. CROSSLEY: There is something fundamentally wrong about
having a name at the first part of the alphabet. If I didn't have, I
could listen to what the others are saying and make my remarks
accordingly. Sam Stouffer just said to me that he hoped that if I
felt like it I would tear into the SSRC report, and I think that that
is a very swell attitude on Sam's part. I'm quite certain that if the
other members of the Committee were here they would agree with
Sam, because their attitude has been the same all the way through
in the work which we did with them day after day, answering questions, gathering data and so forth. They were most considerate and
most penetrating, most anxious to get the true answer.

So I find myself in this position, much as I like a debate and
like to start a fight and so forth, I am completely unable to tear
into the SSRC report. I think it is an excellent job; I think it is a
job which we all should be very glad that we have. I don't agree
with some of the things in it and I am not sure that all the members
of the SSRC Committee fully agree. I suppose there had to be some
compromises here and there. I do not agree with the press release.
I think the press release was unfortunate in that it did not give a
fair picture of the Committee's activities. I am not saying a fair
picture of what the poll-takers did, but the press release did not
reflect fairly on the careful work that was done by the Committee
itself.

Now I have already said this morning that the staff report when
it comes out—and I think that is going to be in a month or so, isn't
it, Sam?—will give a lot of the material upon which the Committee's
eighteen-page report was prepared. Until that comes out I would
definitely suggest that you all read this eighteen-page report, even
though you voted not to have it read here, because there is a great
deal of good material in that.

As I said this morning, I think we were distinctly in error in
making forecasts; we are not justified in making those forecasts.
You know how I feel about that. You also know how I feel about
the question of our errors, and I think that if we wanted to start
a discussion here which might go on and on and on, the best way

to do it would be to express my feeling. I think maybe some members of the Committee may agree—I don't know who they are but I have the feeling that the case against our sampling techniques has not been proved. I would like to say again that I am not in any circumstances defending the quota or stratified sample, because a very large percentage of the work which we do at Crossley is with the probability sampling. I am simply saying that while the type of sampling we did in the poll may have been in error, I do not feel that the material which has so far been released in the SSRC Committee report has definitely proved that case. And I would like to see the Committee's work extended. I'd like to see them go on and prove it one way or the other, either that sampling was very much at fault or that it wasn't quite as much at fault as some of the newspapers would like to imply.

I would like to ask Sam, if questions are in order, whether there is any possibility that the SSRC Committee could be induced to carry on and make further studies, crack this thing down and let us get these facts.

MR. MOELLER: Without further preliminary, Ted Gallup.

MR. GALLUP: Well, my first reaction to this report when I saw it a month or so ago was this, that hindsight is always twenty-twenty! I think that it is so easy to decide just a few hours after an election what went wrong.

But if you realized the hours of careful thought that go into making every decision, I think our critics would be a little less likely to condemn the pollsters for not having seen what seems to be so obvious after the election.

I want to echo what Arch Crossley has said about this particular Committee, because I have never known a group of people who approached a problem with such a sincere desire to find the right solution. I happen to know a great many of the members and I don't know of a single one who didn't approach the job in a completely objective way.

However, I think the Committee itself felt that it had to point an accusing finger at the pollsters. Now I may be unfair, but it is my impression that committees of this type believe they will be attacked by their fellow academicians as not being objective if they praise anything. There are parts of the full report which do come right out and say that we—Gallup, Crossley, or Roper—did a fine job in some respect. But I think that the over-all tenor of reports such as this is likely to be on the highly critical side.

May I examine some statements in the report. "The pollsters could have foreseen the possibility of a close contest had they looked more carfully at their data and past errors." Well, that's absolutely true. Senator McGrath sent me a long telegram which was printed in many newspapers the Friday before the election. He said, "If you will recognize your errors of the 1944 and 1940 campaigns and apply them to this campaign, you will have Mr. Truman winning." The funny part of it is, if we had taken Senator McGrath's suggestion we would have been right. He was right, but for the wrong reason.

Well now, why did we ignore Mr. McGrath? We did because we were trying to do something about that error of 1944. We would have been completely stupid if, aware of our underprediction on the Democratic side by two or three percentage points in 1944 and in 1940, we did nothing to correct these errors.

Actually, we turned heaven and earth not to repeat that error of 1944 and 1940. And that is why we ignored the suggestion of the Chairman of the Democratic campaign committee.

If we hadn't done anything, if we had followed exactly the same method that we followed in 1944, then his criticism would apply.

I have still to see any evidence to support the contention that our sampling and interviewing methods accounted for any large part of our error. I presume that this was written to generalize on polls of all three of the major organizations.

The report says: "To improve the accuracy of pre-election poll predictions satisfactorily it is necessary to reduce the error at every step in the over-all polling process." With that statement I am in complete agreement. I think we can make improvements in every single department and I want to tell you this afternoon about some of those steps that we are planning to take.

I think that the criticism that we let the public get an erroneous idea of poll accuracy is merited. I think that is a good point. As I tried to explain this morning, we did do something about it. But as I pointed out in one meeting, probably we should have employed some sound trucks to go up and down the cities of this country bleating, "The Gallup poll has an error of four percentage points. The Gallup poll has an error of four percentage points." Crossley too! (*laughter*).

The last statement in the report is a half truth: "The public should draw no inferences from pre-election forecasts that would disparage the accuracy or usefulness of properly conducted sampling surveys in fields in which the response does not involve expression of opinion or intention to act." One of the amusing sidelights of this election was the fact that everyone in the field of market research, the day after the election, was running for cover, saying, "Those pollsters use different methods. We don't know them" (*laughter*). "Don't look at us."

If we could be within ten percentage points on most market and advertising problems, we would think that we had done a very wonderful job for our clients because I don't know anyone in the business field who can maintain that degree of accuracy.

But I think on the whole, that this business has been very wholesome. You may think that I am merely a chronic optimist but I can't help feeling that this bitter experience of November, 1948, has made a lot of people examine the whole business of polling more critically, and I think that is a real gain.

MR. MOELLER: Now, Paul Lazarsfeld.

MR. LAZARSFELD: I have had so far a rather definite feeling that the committee has used me as a kind of "Yes man." Every time there were a group of four or five men who had excellent papers they put me on as a discussant so I could say I completely agree with everyone. I have two minutes now not to be in this role, because I disagree with everything that everyone has said (*laughter*). First I very much disagree with Arch Crossley and Ted Gallup in the way they look at the situation. I can understand it perfectly, and if I were in your polling business I would probably behave this way too. But they always, and still now, four months later, put as the main question, "Which are the good boys? Which are the bad boys? Which are the dumb boys?" I think the issue isn't the question of how good or bad the pollsters were. (Is it cruel to discuss it and pull their legs, or shall we come to their defense?) But that isn't the problem at all though I might feel differently if I had been a pollster.

We are simply doing ourselves a disservice if we look at the situation as we are. Here are the social scientists, and pollsters, and we all, and we are discussing whether something was badly done or not badly done. The much more important problem is to get at the whole logic of poll taking and not a discussion of it in terms of what you men did in November. No one believes you did anything other than your best, and I would very strongly suggest that we carry on this discussion today not in terms of this wrangling of what has been done but of what is the polling situation altogether. I cannot blame you for the way the discussion always comes back to "Were you right or wrong?" Because partly the report is ambiguous about that. The Committee moves back and forth from being a kind of judgment over you to being an intellectual group which is supposed to discuss a scientific procedure.

So I disagree with the way we started to discuss it and I hope we will not go on to discuss it this way. I disagree secondly with the statements that the SSRC report is good. I can see that you two men have to lean backward on this and feel that if you had eighteen blank pages of paper you would have to say, "It is a most impartial report!" But again I have to say I don't think it is a good report. I don't think it is a good report for a variety of reasons. First, in many places I don't understand it. I don't know what the report is talking about. Unfortunately, as most of the audience haven't read the report it doesn't make sense to go into detail, so what I am really doing here is sticking my neck out for the sake of the discussion and just being in a general way unpleasant (*laughter*).

I think the report is vague. I think secondly that the report is undefinitive—that is to say, in many places it doesn't even formulate the problems correctly in my opinion, and on the problem of turnout, for example, at no point in these eighteen pages do they formulate clearly what the problem of turnout is.

Furthermore, the report has a kind of empty preaching attitude. They say experiments should be done in this and this and this, but they say at no point what kind of experiments should be done, so they are not even helpful in any complete way, and I personally say that the way I did understand the report I didn't learn anything (*laughter*).

Finally—and this is the one point I think I should specify—I think the report is even dangerous in a way because of its vagueness and its non-willingness to really be creative about the whole matter, and that is one point of which I think we should all be aware. I could say that I "view with alarm" the last two paragraphs of the report, and the only consolation I have is that no one will read the darn thing so it doesn't make any difference (*laughter*).

But supposing it should be read. Then those last two paragraphs are really very bad. For instance, when the market researchers say, "But after all, we shouldn't be worried because those boys measure only attitudes and you can't measure attitudes anyhow. But when it gets down to solid facts like 'what brand of coffee do you use?'" then we are on solid grounds (*laughter*).

Now, I have in my time done service on the drinking of coffee, and I enjoy doing it. But now when a group of social scientists write those two final paragraphs as the result of some political lobbying or something in the Committee which I cannot see—"But after all, real substantial work will go on even if silly psychologists claim they can measure attitudes which of course cannot be done"— then those men have really done us a great disservice.

Now I would like to add one remark, not to be misunderstood. It is my hope—it is almost my conviction—that the staff report they promise us will very much change the picture. Knowing how hard those men worked, and knowing the quality of the people who worked on it, I hope that those few hundred pages of staff report will really teach us something and will show that my criticism in the end will not be justified.

Inasmuch as we discuss today those eighteen pages I would have to say that I have not gained much out of them, and maybe later in the discussion, if someone disagrees too strongly with me, I might be able to pick out one or two examples to justify my position.

MR. MOELLER: Now to have the last word—for the moment, that is—Sam Stouffer.

MR. STOUFFER: As I understand it, the people who arranged this program tried to get the chairman of this Committee to come to this meeting. They couldn't get the chairman of the Committee to come, so they tried other members of the Committee and they couldn't come, so finally they got Phil Hauser to agree to come, and when Phil Hauser heard about the session that was planned for today he took a plane for Rio de Janeiro (*laughter*). So I am left here to make a few pleasant remarks about the report of this Committee.

I don't agree with everything the speakers have said and particularly not with the last one. I think I understand something of his disappointment. Maybe he expected us to make a more careful analysis of the influence of a book called *The People's Choice* * and

* Editor's note: by Paul Lazarsfeld, *et al.*

the concept that elections are decided early and therefore nobody needs to look at a last-minute shift. This isn't really what the book says, if you read it carefully, and especially the preface to Volume II, but I have heard the view expressed that Mr. Truman owes his re-election to Paul Lazarsfeld! (*laughter*).

I think it's only fair to expect in a group as diverse as the membership of our Committee that different members of the Committee approached the problem with somewhat different points of view. That was a deliberate factor in the choice of the Committee by the SSRC. On this Committee were mathematical statisticians, social psychologists, historians, political scientists, sociologists, and various other people with quite diverse backgrounds.

Dr. Gallup has said that he felt that the Committee approached this job in a completely objective way. Now that isn't true. There were some members of the Committee who were pretty well convinced in advance that the answer was simple. If you'd only used probability sampling and not those sloppy quota methods, you might have been all right. There were one or two who were quite sure in advance that the further research that would be done would make it perfectly clear that much of the shift was due to not taking a count of the last-minute shift. Was that because of their faith in Paul Lazarsfeld? (*laughter*).

And there were other members of the Committee who were inclined to think that the problem was very subtle, that there were all kinds of unmeasurable issues here which required such complicated analysis that it would be impossible for anybody to really untangle them at all and you couldn't do anything about it. Some tabulations they made showed you couldn't predict elections anyway and they soon figured out, on the basis of a study of the last half-dozen elections, that because of our electoral system and because of the kind of errors that had occurred in polls, it was just impossible for any polling procedure at the present time to be right more than about half or a third of the time. And the conclusion drawn early by these people was that the Committee didn't have any task to do; that there is not much point in the Committee's doing any research; and that all we needed to do was present the facts that the pollsters were undertaking an impossible job.

Well, it was in an atmosphere of diverse expectations that the Committee went to work. I am being frank about this, and I think it is to the credit of the SSRC that they didn't go and pick people with one common point of view who would come up with a simple answer conforming to their own predilections. The Committee got a staff of young people, a very able staff, which worked awfully hard for a period of about three or four weeks with the complete cooperation of Dr. Gallup, Mr. Crossley, and Mr. Roper. They obtained information from various of the state polls and, particularly important, were aided by panel studies. The study in Elmira which Lazarsfeld helped design and the panel study in the state of Washington which we heard reported on this morning, and two or three other panel studies, were very useful. We had this information, and we worked day and night on it. We ran IBM machines and reanalyzed a great deal of data.

Now, Dr. Gallup made another mistake, I think, when he said that after the election it is easy to have twenty-twenty vision. Well, I would say that the longer the Committee worked and the more we discussed the results of our work, the more we developed a combination of astigmatism and progressive myopia. The answer to this thing becomes less simple and clear, not more clear. Those of us who had predilections that it was this, or this, or this, found ourselves facing facts which didn't prove conclusively one way or the other, that it was this or wasn't this, but which still raised doubts of too high plausibility to make a flat answer difficult. We had hoped, you see, that it might be possible, along the lines that Mr. Dodd spoke about yesterday, to allocate a certain percentage of error to this, that, and the other thing.

Mr. Crossley's paper yesterday said something about the percentages of error attributable to various causes. As he made guesses about the percentages of error attributed to this and this, I mentally added them up and they added up to double the total error. I think that one of the things that some of the people on this Committee initially didn't fully appreciate, until they started to work, was what an extremely hazardous job a poll is.

I am one of those who didn't realize how hazardous this job is in terms of forecasting an election. Let's look at it. Let's look at one of the simplest aspects. No matter whether you draw a probability sample or whether you draw a quota sample, your respondents in most cases are going to tell you what their preference is. In fact, we found that most of the polls managed to extract from most of their respondents—anywhere from 85 to 90 percent of their respondents—an expression of preference. On the one hand we have 85 to 90 percent of the respondents telling you how they are going to vote; on the other hand, only about 50 percent of them are actually going to vote. Now I want to say this, that I happen to be one of those who believed it important to have a probability sample if possible. I am on that side. I believe that probability sampling is the only method we know now by which we are going to be able to know how much error is involved, and how much is attributable to the selection of respondents by interviewers. But with the best of probability samples, if you get 85 percent of the people telling you whom they prefer, and only 50 percent are going to vote, you have a margin of error there that is positively staggering when you think of the problem of forecasting from it.

This leads to the question of how are you going to use screening questions. Let us say you do use a good probability sample. How are you going to use screening questions to decide who will vote among this 85 percent who say they are going to vote, or among the 15 percent who say they are undecided? Now I don't think that is going to be answered on a sheer empirical basis. We were particularly impressed, the Committee was, by the very ingenious screening questions devised by Mr. Crossley. But we don't know enough, and I don't know that we will know enough for a decade or more, to ask the right questions here with respect to what factors are likely to lead people to say they are going to vote when they are not going to, or to vote when they say they are not going to, and what kind of people are involved in these groups.

All right, that is a terrific hazard right there. That hazard is enough to scare one, even if there is no shift whatever. We are not talking about any shift; it's just the fact that 85 to 90 percent tell you they are going to vote, and only 50 percent will vote. We have that problem right to begin with, and it's a tough one. I think Dr. Lazarsfeld is completely right when he says the Committee in its analysis didn't analyze far enough, didn't tell constructively what ought to be done to clear up that aspect of the problem. Well, it was just too big a job to do in three weeks, Paul, and it may be just too big a job to do in two years, and it is one of the further things that the SSRC and NRC Committees are going to try to give attention to in the meeting we are having next month. But this is just one problem.

Let me take the other, let's take this shift business. I also happen to be one of the members of the Committee who believed very strongly that there was a last-minute shift. I believed that in advance—I mean, I didn't believe it in advance, I believed it the day after election (*laughter*). And I was quite prepared to find it and perhaps had too low a threshold for it, but I ran cards, thousands and thousands of punch cards, through machines on this thing. We analyzed Gallup's stuff and Roper's stuff, their pre-election polls and post-election polls and so on, and I don't think there is any doubt at all—there is no doubt in my mind—that there was a very substantial shift in the last two weeks of the campaign. In fact, if we take the post-election re-call of people and we ask them when they made up their minds, it's possible then to reconstruct, from what they said about when they made up their minds, what was the position as of two weeks before the election. We did that with Gallup's data and Roper's data with as careful analysis as we knew how, and the two checked out very well in spite of the fact that Roper had a larger educational bias than Gallup, which had to be adjusted. But once those were taken care of, Gallup and Roper checked out very well and got almost exactly the same figure. When we projected such figures back, I found that the most probable figure I could get as of two weeks before the election was a figure which was almost the figure Gallup reported. In other words, conceivably, it is possible that Gallup and Crossley—not Roper, he was a little too far off this time—but Gallup and Crossley were almost on the beam as of two weeks before the election.

However, in order to be conservative, the Committee said there may have been about a two percent shift. Actually, and you will see it in the staff report, the *prima facie* evidence is of a shift of probably five percent, but there is a danger in taking the evidence uncritically. We have got to watch it because there is a danger that respondents, after the election, tend to say that they voted for the winner and you have got to allow for that. But also there is another compensating bias, in that after the election, many Truman voters were likely to say they had been for Truman all the time when it is possible they made up their minds late in the campaign.

We had those two compensating biases to consider. We went to work on those. Paul Lazarsfeld worked all night, running the stuff from Elmira to help us on that point. In Elmira they had asked the people after the election whom they had voted for. Two weeks before the election they had asked whom they were going to vote for. And in Elmira they asked them, "Did you change your mind?" "When did you make up your mind?" So it was possible in this case to get a direct check from this sample and to check this point. Well, evidence seemed to show—unfortunately when you break it down that way, there are only a small number of cases but there is a little evidence here—that there was a tendency for people at the end to say they were for Truman all the time when in fact they were not for Truman as of two weeks before the election.

You may say, "Well, maybe they were for Truman as of two weeks before the election but didn't tell the Elmira interviewers correctly." That isn't likely either, because the fact is that they were interviewed in great detail, both before and after, on their attitudes on issues, and if they made any shifts they were asked to tell why they shifted. I don't think there was much reason to doubt the answers.

Well, nevertheless the Committee took the attitude that, on the whole, it was better to be cautious. They saw the great danger of our coming out, in the *New York Times* and so on, with a report which said flatly that the data showed that the Gallup and Crossley polls could have been correct as of two weeks before the election, because we are not sure. While the data on the surface may show that, you can make very plausible arguments against it. These arguments could include a dozen different assumptions.

Different people on the Committee used different adjustment factors. Some of them would come up and show only one or two percent shift, and others five or six percent shift, so under the circumstances it wasn't safe to come out with one flat figure. Now that's always a discouraging thing, because it's so nice to wrap everything up in a neat little package and say, "This is it." We couldn't do that. Nevertheless, I am pretty sure there was a very substantial turnover in the last days of the campaign.

Now why didn't the pollsters get that? Well, Crossley did not run a poll then and wouldn't have known it, and Gallup didn't run a last-minute poll and therefore he couldn't have caught the shift in the last week, and there are various complications, as we know, involved in running a last-minute poll. I think, Dr. Gallup, you did run one four years ago and you got a little burned by it, because there is a tendency in the hurry-up at the last minute for such a poll not to be done as accurately as it would be normally, and there is not as good a chance to check the adequacy of the sampling. However, Roper did run a poll in the last week. We analyzed that pretty carefully, and there is every reason to think his sampling was no worse on that than the others. His last-minute poll did show a shift in the direction of Truman—by no means enough to elect Truman—but quite a shift in that direction.

Well, in view of these hazards and so on, we couldn't come out and flatly say we thought that it was all attributable to sampling procedures, as some members of the Committee might have liked to show. We had the results from the Washington state study—the results which you have seen this morning—showing the difference between the probability sample and the quota sample. There were some other evidences too that suggested, at least, evidences of inadequate sampling. Certainly there was a substantial educational bias in Gallup's and Roper's samples. Gallup was publicly accused by some Senators and what-not some four years ago for jiggling figures, and now this time he jiggled his figures; he weighted them for education, which I think was the right thing to do under the circumstances. Mr. Roper very proudly said he never jiggles his figures so he left his educational bias in there, and his results were even worse. It is a very interesting thing about the kinds of compensating errors that saved Roper four years ago. We studied those. In fact, we were able to put our fingers on the compensating biases he had four years ago and know why they gave him such close results then and not now.

I agree with what Dr. Lazarsfeld has said in insisting that the concern of the Committee is not and should not be primarily with holding post-mortems or autopsies or something like that. The purpose of this Committee's report should be to suggest the kinds of things we don't know which we need to know. If this kind of an operation is going to get ahead, certainly there are two big areas here, in addition to sampling, that I feel we don't know much of anything about. I don't think the Committee has contributed much except to point out that not the pollsters alone, but all the social sciences, have a responsibility. Psychology and political science and sociology must try to analyze what are the kinds of factors that lead people to vote or not to vote, and what are the factors that lead people to change their minds and to shift, and so on.

Now the Committee tried to do what we could, even in the short time we have had, to contribute to this constructively from an analysis of the poll data, and I think that here and there there are some very interesting leads. The Committee erred, I think on the caution side, in not giving more emphasis to these leads. We do feel that further research was needed. It will take perhaps another year before the results of the Washington study, the Elmira study, and various other studies are fully analyzed and presented.

Let's don't kid ourselves that this is an easy one. It is not simple. There is an awful lot that we don't know. I may say that the more I worked on this report, the more I felt the debt that we owe to these men who have been willing to risk their own money in going out and trying to learn something about American political behavior. The pollsters have been ahead of the universities; the universities have been tagging along behind. This is no time for the universities to say, "Oh, well, this is something we don't want any part of." This is the time, it seems to me, for the universities to say that in this device, this new invention that we have, lies one of the great opportunities for developing an effective social science. And we have a responsibility, we in the universities, to do our best to help improve these techniques. With the improvement of these techniques I think we can have every confidence that we are going to improve social science, and I think we are going to help our country, because I believe in this work as an instrument of democracy.

(Meeting adjourned.)

Part Five

THE FUTURE OF
OPINION SAMPLING

17

THE FUTURE TRENDS OF OPINION SAMPLING

F. Stuart Chapin, Presiding
George H. Gallup
J. Stevens Stock
Archibald M. Crossley

MR. CHAPIN: Yesterday Sam Stouffer alluded to the importance of invention. In my opinion the public opinion poll is one of the most important social inventions since the invention of the secret ballot. Now, despite the fact that it is such an important invention and we know that it has worked in the main, some of the criticisms with respect to the last election predictions (which have been so fully discussed) have gotten a response from the people out of all proportion to the stimulus—an explosive response. This suggests the conversation that took place between two charwomen in London during the bombings of 1941 when there were many explosions. One said to the other, "Isn't it dreadful? The bombs fall and they explode, and they blow you into the middle of maternity?" (*laughter*). And the other one said, "Aye, and the worst of it is you'll never know who done it." Now I suppose the association we have with the phrase, "who done it," is "Who-dun-its," or mystery tales.

The subject this afternoon deals with the great mystery of the future of opinion sampling. And I am not going to follow the precedent of one or two other occasions in calling on the speakers alphabetically, so I shall first call on Dr. Gallup, who needs no introduction.

MR. GALLUP: I have a feeling that I am doing a marathon job of speaking here today. I want to talk to you about "The Future of Public Opinion Research," as I see it.

We in the field of public opinion research know that this work of ours is destined to grow and to become more important every year because we know that in reporting public opinion on the vital issues of the day we are performing an important function in our democracy, and we know that there is no better way to gauge public opinion than by sampling procedures. There is resistance to every new idea, but if an idea is basically sound and useful a whole army of critics can't stop it.

It is my sincere belief that polls constitute the most useful instrument of democracy ever devised. And I am certain that the record of the last fourteen years fully substantiates this belief.

Long before we appeared on the scene, our greatest political leaders and students of government recognized the need of a better and a more accurate way to know what the people were thinking.

Abraham Lincoln said: "What I want to get done is what the people desire to have done, and the question for me is how to find that out exactly."

Woodrow Wilson expressed the same view in a speech before the National Press Club in Washington. He said to the assembled newspapermen: "The people of the United States are thinking for themselves. . . . And you do not know, and the worst of it is, since the responsibility is mine, I do not know what they are thinking about. I have the most imperfect means of finding out, and yet I have to act as if I knew."

James Bryce, who has been described as the patron saint of us pollers, made the classic observation some sixty years ago in his book, *The American Commonwealth:* "The obvious weakness of government by public opinion is the difficulty of ascertaining it."

I do not believe, nor have I ever said, that a political leader should follow public opinion polls blindly. But I do say that to the extent that he does take the public's views into account, he should have a reasonably accurate appraisal of their opinions.

Polls of public opinion provide almost our only check today on the increasing strength and influence of pressure groups. They provide the only sensible way of defining the mandate in any election. Finally, they make possible the exploration of areas of ignorance.

This brings us to the question as to how well present methods and procedures do report what the public is thinking. The basic method used by polls—that of sampling—is as old as man. It has been developed and applied in almost every field. There is no science in which it does not play an important part. Finally, and I think few will disagree, no one has yet discovered a better way of finding out what people are thinking than to go out and talk to them.

It seems incredible to me that so many persons still think of polling as something mysterious. Actually we follow the same procedures which political writers and political observers have followed through the years. The only real difference between our method and that of these observers is that we go about the job more systematically. We talk to a great many more persons than any one man could, and we take greater precautions to get a representative sample.

I am talking here about basic procedures. Among students and practitioners of polling there is much argument as to the best way of selecting a sample, and the best way to put questions to persons selected in a sample. But even the crudest methods would represent a great advance over methods used in pre-poll days.

Whether polling has been useful and sound, whether it has indicated correctly the trends of opinion in recent years can best be determined by looking at the record. To me it is significant that our critics have never yet dared attack us on the whole record of polling. Isolated cases have been singled out, but no one yet has had the courage to show that on any major issue of the last fourteen years we failed to indicate the true direction of public opinion, as proved by subsequent events.

In my opinion the public has not only been right on most, if not all the major issues of the last fourteen years, but it has been ahead of our legislative leaders. This is a personal judgment; but I am certain that the majority of you will agree with me if you examine the record.

In 1935 we found a large majority of persons in our polls in favor of re-arming on a vast scale. They particularly wanted the air force built up, and this at a time when our military experts couldn't decide whether airplanes would be of great importance in the next war! In this year of 1935 Congress was actually cutting down military appropriations.

A majority of persons favored a peacetime draft before any person in Washington had even stated the necessity of such a step. Later, when the issue was debated, Congressional mail was running 95 to 5 against the draft, while polls were showing a majority of the public in favor of it.

The public approved lend-lease long before Congress adopted it. They favored pay-as-you-go taxes long before this measure was adopted. Likewise they favored broadening the tax basis when many Congressmen thought it would be suicidal to take such an extreme step.

Polls on the Marshall Plan showed those who were informed about this issue favored it long before Congress got around to adopting it. The present policy toward Russia is firmly grounded in public support.

The public favored universal military training and the draft. An overwhelming majority indicated their support at an early stage for the United Nations.

In the matter of social legislation the public has likewise taken an advance position. A majority favored control of syphilis and other venereal disease at a time when most newspapers refused to use this horrid word in their news columns. Polls, in my opinion, helped open up discussion on this problem.

The public has favored social security and its extension. The people have approved federal aid to education, increasing minimum wages, and government housing plans.

I could cite dozens of other cases. But these will give you some idea of the *quality* of public opinion and will, I believe, show that polls have caught the major trends of public thinking, and at an early point of time.

The polling idea has been accepted in many fields. The volume of such research has expanded almost every year. According to present indications more money will be spent for polling research in the present year than in any previous year in history. And I believe it is a safe bet that ten years from now the volume of this work will be double what it is today.

It is just a matter of time until every foreign country makes use of polling. All major cities in the United States will make use of polling research because they will find that these procedures will help them save millions of dollars and will help solve many administrative problems.

I note with interest that many new Congressmen are polling their districts to find out what their constituents think about various issues. In due time I hope to work out the details of a plan which will permit every Congressman who so desires to poll his district quickly and at a very small cost. I am willing to devote my time and effort free to this cause because I am certain that anything which will provide a Congressman with a more accurate appraisal of public opinion will almost inevitably result in better and more efficient government.

Acceptance of polls is largely a function of age. In my own experience I have found that few persons under the age of forty (mentally or chronologically) fail to see the value of polls. On the other hand it is difficult for many oldsters to adjust their thinking to this new instrument.

Young people in our high schools and colleges are growing up with polls. They see how they work in their own school worlds. They use them on their school publications. Is it conceivable that they will not use them more and more?

And now what about the future of opinion research itself? What changes will come in the techniques and procedures?

Improvements will obviously be made in all departments of polling. The election experience of last fall has only accelerated a program that has been going on from the day polls in this country were started. I would estimate that at least one-fourth to one-third of all the revenues which we have obtained through the years has gone into experimental work to improve our methods.

At the Gallup Poll we are setting up a new department whose sole function will be to carry on this experimental work and to try out every new suggestion which we or others believe will improve polling techniques.

In the field of sample design, I believe we can make improvement in both quota and area sampling methods. For the last year or two we have been concentrating on the problem of "call backs"—the nub of the problem of area sampling, in my opinion. We shall be ready to announce a plan in the not-too-distant future which calls for a careful control not only of *place* of interview but also of *time* of interview.

I confess that I get irritated by some of our critics who assume that area sampling is the answer to all of our problems, and especially by one critic who blandly says that "We [the area samplers] can compute with confidence the limits or range of error for any result obtained."

At just what point does this confidence begin and end? If half the persons in the sample are missed in the first and in subsequent calls, can we "compute with confidence" the range of error? Do the laws of probability apply when a third of the total sample is missed and substitutions have to be made? Do they apply when ten percent of the sample is missed and ignored?

It seems to me that there has been a lot of loose thinking about random sampling. It has certain definite advantages under certain definite conditions. It is not a cure-all. We believe that when our studies are completed on the problem of which members of the family can best be reached at which hours of the day and on which days of the week, we shall have made a real contribution toward making area sampling more efficient and at the same time more "scientific."

An important part of our research through the years has been devoted to the problem of responses. Many years ago we developed the "split"-ballot technique, and two or three years ago the quintamensional plan of question design.

We now have had occasion to use the five-way approach on the most complex problems. I have yet failed to find one issue which could not be approached in a practical and meaningful way by this type of question design.

The quintamensional plan of question design provides the framework for probing five facets of opinion. It answers most of the criticisms voiced by those who say that single questions are inadequate, that we have not examined into the problem of question meaning, that we ignore the "why" of public opinion, and the "intensity" of opinion, and that we do not report or take into account informed opinion.

Most of our critics like to charge that we ask only "yes" and "no" questions. Actually this has never been true. In many studies that we have undertaken in the past, and many that we are currently doing, interviews consume more than an hour. In one study that we made many years ago, the questionnaire required some eighty mimeographed pages. A total of 384 questions were put to respondents, not counting parts. Interviewing time was approximately five hours. But there is a danger in going too far, I think, in the direction of multiple questions. I am fearful that the day may arrive when we may think it necessary to put a man through a psychiatric examination to find out whether he has a match.

In this respect I have observed that many persons in the academic world struggle to make simple things complex, whereas in the cruel world outside many persons constantly struggle with the problem of making complex things simple.

No one believes in cooperative research more fervently than I do. Up to this point we in the field of public opinion research have had to carry the ball ourselves with comparatively little help, but with plenty of criticism, from the social scientists.

The Social Science Research Council has laid the groundwork for a healthy and continuing partnership. I for one am ready at all times to work with any social scientist or any group of social scientists on any problem of public opinion research.

MR. CHAPIN: I now introduce as the next speaker Mr. J. Stevens Stock, of the Opinion Research Corporation, Princeton, New Jersey. Mr. Stock.

MR. STOCK: I brought my lunch [indicating package wrapped in newspaper], but I already had lunch so I'll put it out there on the table. Actually, that's some "public opinion" there. I brought it along because we've been talking about it, but nobody has had any. It's not quite as volatile now as it used to be a few months back. [Unwraps package and displays a hunk of black material.] Notice, it's hard; it's malleable. Oceans of water and most acids won't affect it in any way at all. If you get it hot, it melts; it can burn you. It splatters when it boils; it could set fire to everything in this room. *That's* "public opinion." It looks like a piece of tar.

Now I've got to talk about the future of opinion sampling. Being an *entrepreneur*, I sure hope Ted Gallup is right that we are going to do more business this year than ever before. My future in opinion research started at nine o'clock on Black Tuesday, in the evening. Those first results began to come in and my wife was reading, and she looked up at me, and I said, "Now, wait a minute. Wait. Those are just early returns." About three o'clock I had my pencil sharpened, writing notices to my clients, explaining. By nine o'clock I gave the notice to the girl in the office to type and at the same time the phone rang. It was a client. He said, "WELL?", and I said, "Wait a minute. I've got the stuff being typed. I'll have an answer for you, and it will be ready in fifteen minutes. I'll call you back."

Well, it didn't look as good at nine o'clock in the morning as it did at three o'clock earlier in the morning, so I changed it and kept changing it and rewording it, and finally the phone rang again. I looked at my watch and it was ten o'clock. The same client. And he said, "You predicted at nine o'clock that you'd have an answer in fifteen minutes. You're already 300 percent wrong."

I don't know what the future of opinion research is. I just hope Ted Gallup's right. But Barnum was right on several things (*laughter*). Once a woman was going to sue Barnum, and when her suit failed, she said she was going to get a lot of bad publicity for him, and she was just going to fill the newspapers with what a horrible guy P. T. Barnum was. Barnum said, "That's all right. Whatever you do, spell my name right!"

I think some of this bad publicity is going to help us. At least more people have heard about opinion polling now than did three months ago. But we have been getting some publicity which I don't think is doing us any good—either we, the commercial pollsters, or people in government or university life—and this publicity has been coming from our colleagues. This publicity has been coming from the one-man-social-science-research-councils who have been writing for the press just what is wrong with the pollsters—the Johnny-one-notes—who have one technique and that one technique explains the whole problem, be it sampling or interviewing. They hit the press and say, "That's why the pollsters are wrong." This is foolish.

How much actual data have we to show? Sam Stouffer says we have none. That really ties down what made the pollsters wrong. Where do we get these Johnny-one-techniquers who come around and say, "If you had done what I told you to do, you'd be scientific like me." For goodness sake!

You know there are many techniques in polling, and if we concentrate on just one and let the rest go, well—I've told this story before, but it's like the time I had down in Washington about six months ago. I was there on business. And I had this suit on—it wasn't as well pressed as now even, because I'd been traveling for days—and a friend called me up and said, "Do you know we're going to have a big banquet tonight?" I said, "No." He said, "Well, I'm in trouble. We were going to have a great speaker," and he told me the name of a very famous orator. "He's not going to show up and it's now four o'clock in the afternoon." I said, "Don't tell me your troubles. I didn't know about your banquet." He said, "How about your taking the speech?"

Well, it must have been a "five-o'clock shadow," or something, and I agreed in a moment of weakness. I didn't know what I was going to say, but I went out and hired a Tuxedo—and in that short time it didn't fit very well—and I bought a paper collar and a tie, which I had to tie without the help of my wife. And I went to the banquet. I sat down next to the master of ceremonies, who had never seen me before and I had never seen him. But what was bothering him was that he had to introduce me. He had to get up and give the audience some reason why I should talk to them instead of this great orator who had been scheduled. All during dinner he kept questioning me about who I was and what I was going to talk about, and so on, and I didn't know what I was going to talk about.

It was one of those hotels—not like the Jefferson—but one of those hotels where at a banquet they bring you one course, you pick up a fork to start eating, and they take it away before you can eat it. The master of ceremonies was talking my arm off. I was trying to think of what I was going to say, and I felt uncomfortable in that Tux. The fork was bent, and the knife was dull, and you know what you do in those situations. You just look out across the room and throw your mind out of gear. But presently, coming in the door— just like that one over there—was a waiter.

There was nothing peculiar about this waiter except that he was pushing a great big chromium-plated cart with rubber-tired wheels. He pushed it down to the center of the room, up between the tables, up in front of the master of ceremonies. Then he threw back the top of the cart, took out a long pair of forceps, put on a pair of white gloves. [Pauses to put on white gloves.] He reached down into the steaming interior of this chromium-plated cart, and put one on the master of ceremonies' plate, and one on my plate—a roll! And the roll was *cold!*

Now there's a hotel that goes to all that trouble to sell you a roll. What do they do with them in the kitchen? That's your Johnny-one-techniquer, putting on white gloves, and worried about one detail of technique, but what happens in the kitchen?

Recently I have been looking at some of our problems of sampling. I've been reviewing some of this work that Ted Gallup has been doing in time and place interviewing. This has great promise for the future of opinion polling. The basic problem of sampling is the problem of availability of the respondent. If we can find some measure of the availability of the respondent, some measure of the probability that that respondent will be selected, then we have a probability sample no matter how it is.

Recently we have been experimenting with the idea, interviewing in the homes and asking the respondents, "Were you home last night? How about the night before that?" And we ask about six preceding nights and then use the results of this first call to weight up our total results. Since a person was home only one night in six, the night we happened to call, he would have a weight of six, but the person who is at home all nights in six gets a weight of one. This gives us some measure of the probability of selection without call-backs. But this is disappointing because, for most of the things, the people that are home one night in six and the people that are home six nights in six give us the same answers.

It's like this problem of interviewing. We did elaborate studies to check on our cheaters. And after we had put the cheaters into one column and the non-cheaters into another, and tabulated all the results, this was terrible. We got the same results from both!

Recently I have been looking at the variability among interviewers. (These are all delivered—little white rolls—to you, cold. See?) I've even been looking at what happens when we sort our sample by interviewers and study the difference by various interviewers. This is terrific. Because when you take out the variation due to respondent, and due to location, you still have a variation as big as all you took out.

Some of the work that has been done on questions—this I hope is in the future of opinion polling—showed that question worries were the most serious problems. We made a mistake in one of my recent studies of asking a question early in the ballot and asking the same question later in the same ballot, and got a 40 percent difference. We had to explain to the client what happened. I still don't know what happened for sure.

Well, I can't go into all the technical problems that we must work on in the future. We have a long way to go on many fronts. All I'm trying to say is these Johnny-one-notes are not helping by giving us some awful bad publicity in this business. They are like doctors who prescribe aspirin for everything.

Since it is appropriate now to say that you liked or didn't like the Social Science Research Council report, I want to take one thing out of this report that I don't like. I guess it's the same thing that Paul Lazarsfeld mentioned. "The failure of pre-election forecasts successfully to pick a winner in no way constitutes a yardstick for measuring either the accuracy or usefulness of sampling surveys in fields in which the response does not involve the expression of opinion or intention to act." What it says is that, if you have factual data, like consumption of coffee in pounds, or opinion data—"What kind of coffee do you like?"—one is very precise and the other isn't.

This is a very limited way of looking at data. Of course, one may be very precise in telling how many people had bought such and such a kind of coffee. Sure, that's precise. But that isn't what you're interested in. What you want to know is how to make some decision as to what to do about the sale of coffee.

Now, it's when you take data and make a prediction as to what to do about it that you are out of a statistical problem and it doesn't matter whether the data is opinion data or factual data. You still have the problem of prediction.

Unemployment went up last month terrifically. That we know with great precision. But do we know what to do about it, with great precision? It doesn't matter whether that is opinion data or factual data. Opinion data is, for many purposes, more accurate than factual data because it comes closer to measuring basic causes and motivations.

Here's where we are probably at our weakest. We have so few mathematical models in social psychology. I hope the future of research will bring more of them. We need mathematical models for interpreting the psychological phenomenon which we measure, for predicting what will happen because of these data we have. The engineer with his data predicts what his bridge will do, because he has mathematical models on which to base this. We haven't. We have very few.

For instance, when an opinion shifts from 90 percent to 92 percent, is that the same kind of a shift as opinion shifting from 50 percent to 52 percent? We need a mathematical model to interpret this. Much of the data that we get we seem to be perfectly satisfied with if it be statistically precise, but what good is it if we do not know how to predict from it what is the best thing to do, what is the best policy, what will happen. Here we need an awful lot of work toward making our data more useful. Here we are barely scratching the surface. Let me tell one old story again and I'll sit down.

Down where Ted Gallup and Arch Crossley and I live, we have quite a neighbor. He's a very modest sweet fellow who walks around town in an old pair of blue jeans and long gray hair, and speaks to people on the street—a very pleasant sweet fellow, particularly modest because he is probably one of the greatest men living and maybe the greatest mathematician that ever lived. Albert Einstein, like so many great men, is modest but he has one immodesty. Do you know what that is? He thinks he can play the fiddle. Now Einstein has a friend, a great man who comes to see him every two weeks—the greatest living musician, Arturo Toscanini. He is cut of different cloth than Einstein, but he is a modest man too, and being a great man and a modest man, he has one immodesty. Do you know what that is? He thinks he is a mathematician.

There is an apocryphal story that some months ago Dr. Toscanini came to visit Dr. Einstein, purportedly to tell about his recent mathematical studies. And Dr. Einstein welcomed Dr. Toscanini— Why? Because he could play the fiddle. Toscanini started in on mathematics, much to the boredom of Dr. Einstein. For two hours he went on. Finally Einstein got him to shut up and got him down to the piano; set him down to play the piano while he squeaked on his fiddle. He had waited so long! He took out a very difficult Mozart concerto—the middle section of it has three-four time for the piano and four-four time for the fiddle. Toscanini started off bravely; Einstein even more bravely, squeaking on his fiddle. At the end of that second movement—and Einstein was doing a horrible job, just horrible—and Toscanini is not noted for his patience— finally, his face flushed, he banged on the piano and said, "But, Albert, WHY don't you learn to COUNT!"

We of social science have got to learn to count.

MR. CHAPIN: We come now to the last speaker, Mr. Crossley.

MR. CROSSLEY: Steve Stock lives about a block away from me in one direction, and Einstein lives about a block away from me in the other direction. I have been wondering what Steve has been doing at night, and now I discover he has been prowling around looking in Einstein's windows.

I would like to say just one or two things about this subject of *Future Trends of Opinion Sampling.* We have been talking a great deal about political polls and I sincerely hope we do not lose sight of the fact that there is a great deal to public opinion besides political polls. We had some interesting examples yesterday.

I was particularly impressed by Mr. Kennedy's contribution, giving a lot of the details in the use of public opinion sampling in law. I talked with him a little bit afterward and told him of some of the work which we have done. We have testified in various suits, and we feel that there is a great field there, and that a way must be found to use sampling in law. I asked him, incidentally, if the census material would be admitted and he said he thought so, even though of course census material would be hearsay also (*laughter*). You have a difference between, as Morris Hansen said yesterday, I think, a 97 percent sample, sometimes a hundred percent sample, and a five or three percent, or whatever sample we might take in ordinary marketing and public opinion research. But in any case, the census enumerator is asking questions and reporting what he hears. In law there is a great need, I think, for admission of public opinion sampling as evidence.

Just to skip very quickly—one of George Gallup's special interests is the use of public opinion sampling in education. I haven't heard you sound off on that, George, in a long while. But I'm sure you still feel the same way, that there is a great need to study the attitudes and opinions of people and to revise our educational system to conform with what we may find out.

Now, certainly in crime we have a great need, an opportunity into which I think we ought to go a great deal more. We are beginning to make studies of juvenile delinquency and that sort of thing by the use of public opinion sampling methods, to find out causes, to find out what can be done. We haven't begun to scratch the surface of the public opinion sampling tool in the study of crime. I believe there are various ways in which we can use area sampling and certain sampling principles which are in their infancy right now to do a lot more in the study of crime.

Considerable is being done in labor relations; Steve's organization is doing quite a bit, and I imagine that right now that is rising very rapidly. Elmo Roper is doing a great deal, and you hear quite a lot about studies of labor relations. Elmo is also doing something in the way of studying public opinion on economics. You may have seen his *Fortune* poll on the public's attitude toward conditions of the day.

There is the whole field of public relations, and that covers a great deal. Hotels, for example, railroads—well, not only public opinion toward railroads but how are the railroads going to plan their future? We are doing some work for railroads in which we are trying to help them in their future planning. Should they allow for more traffic in this direction, or what?

Entertainment—George Gallup is doing, as you know, a great deal of work in movies, very fine work incidentally, and under the toughest of conditions. We have done a little ourselves in studying public opinion in the theater in cooperation with others, and we have been able in the very small amount of work that we have done to discover certain trends that were coming up and trends that seemed to be counter, at the moment, to box-office sales, but which later proved out. In one particular case we were instrumental in keeping a show on the stage which was about to fold up. Our evidence indicated that it had a future, which later turned out to be the case.

There are a great many more facets of public opinion research. I am not going to take your time here to try to express all the different angles in which opinion sampling can be used. I think that if I could succeed in getting you to think along those broad lines, it might be of some help.

We will naturally develop a lot of new methods. Paul Lazarsfeld this noon mentioned particularly in connection with future attitude research the use of correlations and scoring systems and filter questions and other things. I feel we haven't gone anywhere near far enough with information which psychologists and social scientists and various others have in the effort to work out correlation plans.

One of the most interesting examples I have seen was in a job which we did for the federal government during the war, on the subject of inflation. As we made the study, Paul and some other men got together to analyze the results by the use of the correlation system, and worked out individual scores and combination scores. The additional amount of valuable information which was brought out that way opened my eyes to the potentialities.

I think that the way is open for all of us in the various lines of public opinion study to get together and I hope that we do.

DISCUSSION—Morris H. Hansen; General Discussion

MR. CHAPIN: The discussion will be led by Professor T. C. McCormick, Head of the Department of Sociology at the University of Wisconsin.

Mr. McCormick: The topic of the program reads *Future Trends of Opinion Sampling.* In dealing with this topic, the previous speakers (I think very properly) departed somewhat from that assignment, and have largely told us what they intended to do in the way of improving their methods in general, not just in sampling. Whether this should be called a prediction in sampling is a question. Rather than comment directly on their papers, I will take the risk of making a few offhand predictions about the future trends of opinion sampling. I do that with the comfortable feeling that anything that I may say will be forgotten long before time can show that it was wrong.

In the first place, I think that the trend of sampling methods that will be used for public opinion polls in the years ahead—this may not be too popular—will be in the direction of stricter conformity with the fundamental theory of sampling that has been worked out by mathematical statisticians. More specifically, this means to me that opinion pollers will come to approximate more closely than they have in the past, as far as I know their work, purely mechanical or random methods and will avoid to a somewhat greater extent everything depending upon personal judgment. I haven't gathered that from the speeches; that is a wild prediction of my own.

I believe that a second important source of improvement in sampling methods, not only in opinion polling but in other social research as well, will be an increasing knowledge of the population to be sampled. I foresee that more effective sampling controls will be established throughout this country, applicable both to urban and rural places, chiefly as the result of the work of such big federal agencies as the Bureau of the Census, the Bureau of Agricultural Economics and so forth, which have already made an important start in that direction. Any other research organization I think will one day be able with confidence to tie into some already tested master sample suitable (or readily modifiable so as to be made suitable) for its particular purposes.

It is my own opinion that the kind of master sample that will come to prevail in opinion polling in the near future as well as in most other social research will be of the type known as the area sample. Since the suitability of the area sample for opinion polling has been dealt with already this morning, and as it is the special topic of the next session and since the next discussant, Mr. Hansen, of the Bureau of the Census, is one of the chief devisers and users of the area sample, I shall not go into any discussion of it.

Still better than the master area sample would be something approaching a complete population register of the nation, by its various political subdivisions, something like what they have had in a number of European countries. That is barely worth mentioning at present because apparently there are only very dim prospects of any such register, any such list. However, it seems to me that probably the best of all sources for sampling voters would be one that is already at hand, namely, the lists of registered voters that are kept in every voting district or precinct. An adequate sample of these precinct registers obtained by some type of area approach would, I think, offer a very promising prospect for setting up sampling controls superior to any we have been using in the past. I expect that more use will be made of these voting registers in the future.

I further venture to say that regardless of any favorable developments in sampling methods that may occur, it is certain that sampling troubles enough will remain to upset now and then the best predictions of opinion pollers, as well as those of other and lesser men. There is little chance that any master sample will achieve in practice all ideals set up by the mathematical theory—if you have any respect for that theory; some do not have much. Even so, there will still always be some over- and under-representation of this or that part of the population. And at least occasionally these sampling errors will happen to be serious.

The difficulties to be overcome are especially great in the case of opinion polls intended to predict voting behavior, because in such cases one is required to sample a changing universe or population. I mean, of course, a population that may change after the sample has been taken.

It would be getting off the subject to mention the idea of making election forecasts from a study of political trends, or anything of that sort. But it is very much on the subject to say that a great deal still needs to be done, both in the theory and in the practice of sampling one of these shifting universes, a job that I understand my friend Fred Stephan of Princeton has been working on.

Personally I am convinced that no improvements in methods of sampling that can be foreseen or, I may say, that seem possible, can make the business of unequivocally naming the winner in a close election so scientific that it won't still be pretty much of a gambler's risk.

I hope that nobody will infer that I believe all the errors, if any, in the November polls are chargeable to faulty sampling. I don't know. I don't think anybody knows. Nothing short of a recheck of the sample polled in November might show—would be needed to show—just how much the sample was to blame, and how much other factors were at fault. I don't think it likely that such a recheck will be made, or could be now made. No doubt future studies will throw more light on what the probabilities were, but I am not sure that we will ever know just what amount of error to attribute to this or that cause.

MR. CHAPIN: Again I am reminded of something by the speaker. Apparently I should never have used the word "mystery" when I introduced the speakers as going to speak on the great mystery of the future of opinion sampling because it has been noted that they showed great adroitness in sidestepping this mystery. One might almost say "all similarities between my paper and the topic of discussion are purely coincidental."

MR. HANSEN: There are two sorts of questions under consideration that I might comment briefly on. One is samples in the polls, on which there has been a good deal of discussion, a good deal of discussion of probability sampling versus other methods of sampling. It is my own view with respect to probability sampling that most of the discussion I think has been directed in perhaps not the most fruitful manner. That is, not whether we are going to use probability sample or not, but rather what is the best way, what steps do we need to take, to adapt probability sample to use in opinion polls. I have little doubt that is the direction we will move in more and more, and that there are numerous problems of adapting sample methods for the most economical use in opinion polls that need to be worked on.

Second, that probability sampling, properly carried through—and I think that second point is exceedingly important—properly carried through, the design of the sample, and it must be carried through in accordance with reasonable performance in accordance with the specifications, will not be any sort of a cure-all for the problems of the poll. I think the sample problem is much the easiest problem, the one in which we have the least distance to go.

The major problems have to do with response, getting accurate responses, getting techniques of formulating questions that can get meaningful responses, and the whole set of problems of getting information relevant to the problem at hand that one could get by either a sample or a census. The same problems that I talked about yesterday in the census are the problems in opinion survey, attitude survey work, problems of getting meaningful results on questions— formulation of questions that deal with the issue at hand.

MR. CHAPIN: Any questions to any members of the panel?

QUESTION FROM THE AUDIENCE: I'd like to hear Dr. Gallup discuss the relationships of the technique to the question of public health.

MR. GALLUP: I have been greatly interested in the application of polling techniques in this whole field of public health.

I believe that it may sound a bit extravagant when I say that one of the great advances that the medical profession could make at this time would be to apply polling techniques in this field. I say this on the basis of experience in England where the Ministry of Health has carried on a regular health poll for a couple of years. One of the men who used to be connected with the British Institute of Public Opinion, Louis Moss, has carried on the work there. The Scandinavian polling organizations have also done a great deal more in this field of public health than we have here.

I became interested in the subject when, as a member of the Cancer Committee, I discovered much to my amazement that nobody in this country could make even a crude estimate of the number of cases of cancer. The highest estimate was at least three times the lowest. And for a great many diseases common to mankind— T.B., heart diseases—there was little information that was very useful or valuable on the incidence of these afflictions.

Also, we need to find out what people know about different diseases. Believe it or not, we find people who think that cancer is contagious; a great many more think that cancer comes from using aluminum utensils, and so on. We find a great many strange ideas about various diseases. That information is needed to direct an intelligent educational program.

We do not know, at any given time, how many people are ill, what kind of medical advice they are getting, or whether they are getting any. In England such a study goes on every month. Health authorities know the health condition of the entire nation. One of the interesting things, incidentally, that the British Institute of Public Opinion does is to weigh people, 12,000 people every three months, to help guide rationing policies.

I believe there is a possibility, by gathering a great deal of information about people, to get at some of the causes of disease. I need to qualify that very carefully. I think the extent to which disease is a factor of living conditions, food, lodging, possibly even of soil conditions, could be brought to light by the right kind of polling research.

I have talked to many doctors about interviewing problems. The first thing that such people think of is "Well, how can you send some interviewer out to discover whether people have some obscure disease. Of course that's insane; no one would even think of it. But it would be possible to bring to the hospitals, to doctors, or to clinics a sample consisting of some 10,000 families—a true sample of all the families of this country. We could bring them to the best clinics, or send a doctor to each family and get all members examined. Then for the first time we'd begin to know just how many people are really ill in this country, how many people have diabetes, how many have almost any affliction!

Miss CROSSLEY: I don't have a question to address to anyone but I'd like to make just a comment, a matter of emphasis I think, because the matter was brought up by Dr. Gallup and I guess some of the other speakers, and it is a matter that is the subject of areas of ignorance. I feel rather strongly about it, having tried desperately to write a Master's thesis last year about it, but I know, having done that, that people have done a lot of talking about it and there hasn't been a great deal of research that goes very far down into it. It is the question of what people know about all the different subjects that we have investigated in opinion surveys.

And I'd like to suggest as one of the future trends in opinion sampling that surveys, analysts, and everybody else give special attention to investigation of how much people really do know, and what does that opinion mean if they just heard of the issue when the interviewer first mentioned it.

It's just a matter of emphasis really, particularly important in the medical field, which we were just talking about, particularly important I believe for the public officials such as the State Department's and various other people. And if anybody knows of any over-all studies that are being done on it, or have been done on it,

I think they should be given wide publicity so that everybody can learn of them.

MR. BEILER: Mr. Chairman, I hoped that someone would make this point but nobody has made it. I foresee that the whole business of opinion sampling is approaching a dead-end unless some new avenues are opened up.

Now we are about to go on into a session of studying the actual sampling methods. I think we know a good deal about sampling methods. I think that while some improvement is going to be made there, no great improvement in the whole business of attitude and opinion polling could really be expected from improvement in sampling methods. And we know furthermore, on the other hand, through experimentation for instance, that when questions are presented in different lights, so as to involve the prestige of the respondents and so on, you can get differences in response up to fifteen, twenty, or twenty-five percent. This means that the sample problem is essentially a very small part of the problem.

Well now, I suspect one reason that the questions which are directed in each of the interview instruments are rather blind questions is that so little research has been done on the public opinion process itself. We do a great deal of counting of heads, a great deal of gaining simple responses, and very little research, pitifully little research, on the whole question of how those responses, the attitudes producing those responses, came to be formed.

It seems to me that the whole field of public opinion sampling will head into this dead-end and we will find further research yielding less and less in the way of real new results until more of the research is directed at the public opinion process itself. That's the question, and—well, I think communications analysis can contribute there a considerable part, what symbols are in the channels of communication, who responds to them, some studies which will very closely relate the content of communications to the spoken responses to communications and in that way determine the basic attitude structures and the attitude content that are in the minds of the different audiences which are polled.

Only when that information is available will it be possible to construct interview instruments which will be really precise, really incisive, really get at the attitudes which are in the minds of the respondents. It seems to me that the basic problem of public opinion research now is in presenting a stimulus to the respondent in such a way as to derive a response related to the attitude which you are actually trying to measure.

I'd like to ask as a question whether Mr. Gallup or Mr. Crossley expect to do anything further in the field of investigating the public opinion process, the process by which these attitudes are formed, than they have done to date?

MR. CHAPIN: Will you gentlemen comment on that?

MR. CROSSLEY: I think Dr. Gallup has answered that to some extent by saying—How was it, George? A third of your money that you put into public opinion is on an experimental basis? Didn't you say that—some statement of that kind?

MR. GALLUP: Yes.

MR. CROSSLEY: There is a great deal being done by all of us in trying to work out those techniques. Frankly, we have a terrific job. There are many unsolved problems and I think you are quite right that the sampling problem is the easiest of the bunch. There are lots of ways to carry on samples and you can very easily find out whether your sample is right or not once you can isolate the other problems. The other problems are much tougher and they do need a good deal of work.

Yes, we are all trying to work out some methods and techniques for the individual studies as they come along. I don't suppose we are doing enough of the pure research type, and I think we do need the help of the universities in that respect.

MR. GALLUP: I'd like to add this footnote. I agree that is needed, but we in this field of polling have so many other and immediate problems that crowd in on us that we just never have the time to do very much of that particular type of research. I say it very much needs doing, and I think that is the place where the social scientists of the country and people in academic fields can be of the greatest value to us. That is the kind of information that we would like.

MR. CHAPIN: That suggests certain areas for cooperative research, does it not? And I was interested this morning when Mr. Bachelder in his excellent discussion stressed the same point and spelled it out point by point, to the number of seven or eight different points on which more research was needed, wholly apart from the matter of sampling.

MR. BACHELDER: I hate to take this time, but the topic is the future of polling and I'd like to speak of the system at the Public Opinion Laboratory in Washington.

The system very briefly—and I promise to be brief—the system was set up by an act of the state legislature, financed completely by the state. There is a setup at State College of Washington and the University of Washington. The purposes are divided briefly in this way: fifty percent of the time and money goes into what we roughly call civic research for the state, one-quarter into technical research, and one-quarter into basic social science research.

The functions of the laboratory are to serve the legislature, the governor, and various organizations in the state of Washington, to train graduate fellows in the field of polling, and to get the various social sciences together in the laboratory to get away from this one-man polling idea.

But I just wanted to get off a few comments as to the development of state polling, supported by State Legislature, for the people of the state. And to show you the gamut of things, we have run one on old-age pensions in the state of Washington, another on the attitude of the people and their knowledge concerning the state school system, another study on adult education. Dr. Dodd has done some studies, some very fine snap studies or emergency studies of racial situations in the city of Seattle, in which there was a call practically overnight to go down and determine whether or not there was a critical situation. We are running another one on food consumption in the state of Washington, and so on—many different topics on civic research, but on each one we can take time and money for technical playing around with different types of experimental work, and particularly with Dr. Dodd's work in the development of basic social science through the use of a poll.

And I'd like to point out now, you can develop data for basic social science by asking people how many quarts of milk they consume, or whether they like the school system. If it's well worked out you can work basic social science from a type of civic research.

MR. DODD: I still think one of the trends of the future is in the relation of adding to the present polling fraternity more university laboratories.

Within the last four months we have received notices from four different universities that are starting such laboratories, asking us for information on budget and administrative policies and all details for getting under way. This may be one of the trends of the future, thereby backing up the practitioners with more leisure and opportunity to go into some of these theoretical questions that we have all been realizing need to be investigated, but which the various practitioners with the various pressures on them don't have the opportunity to do.

I want to raise not so much a question to the panel as an invitation to the conference here to develop a trend of the future in using polling for basic research in the social sciences for the development of laws of human relations. It is a dream we all have and many of us have had our fingers burnt in trying to do it. We are rather cautious perhaps in seeing how it can be done and so I want to just take a minute to suggest to the practitioners here and to the students who perhaps have Ph.D. theses, one way in which a law of human relations can be developed in the next year or two by a group here, if they get interested in working on it. This is a principle that is known in psychology as the Weber-Fechner Law. It is briefly that the sensation goes up in arithmetic units as the stimulus goes up in geometric units. Another way of saying it is that the sensation equals the logarithm of the stimulus times a constant. Thus, for instance, the interval from one octave to another on the piano is subjectively about equal, whereas actually the stimulus goes by a ratio doubling the number of vibrations from C to the next C, and so on.

Now the question is, Does that apply in the field of attitude and opinions? Does the intensity of the attitude go up as the logarithm of its content, pro to con? It is an excellent hypothesis that can be tested by any of us that are making a poll on any subject whatever in market research, or anything else. We must measure the intensity along with the measurement of the content, and we must measure both of them in at least five degrees or five points so as to get enough points to fit curves to. We must measure them in cardinal units, such as making a Thurstone sort of scale, or we must measure the degrees of content of an attitude, if the variable doesn't happen to come in cardinal or equal units. With that simple addition to our ordinary techniques those curves can be fitted. We may find a U-curve, relating intensity and content of the attitude. Or we may explore further to see what kind of a curve fits those data best.

The significance of this sort of a law is tremendous. All progressive income taxation is based on the assumption that the law holds good. The percentage rate of tax goes up as the different income brackets go up, assuming that will make a constant burden on the taxpayer. That means a constant subjective response to a geometrically increasing stimulus, the amount of the tax.

Is that Weber-Fechner principle valid in polls? Is polling based on this psychological law? We don't know. But we can test it by polling. It would mean, for instance, that in any field of human engineering where you want to predict the public's response in any way; if you want to get them to buy war bonds, or some advertised product; if you want to educate them to anything different in their behavior than they are now doing—you would have to have the stimulation go up in geometric progression. The numbers of hours of radio time, or the inches of newspaper space, or the units of any other form of stimulation would have to go up in geometric progression in order to get an arithmetic progression, if this principle holds true, in the attitude or opinion or behavior of the respondent. If it holds true in the peripheral nerves, why may it not hold true in the central nervous system for attitudes and opinions?

We have the techniques employed for measuring those things and it seems to me we have here a beautiful case of a possible fundamental law of human relations that can be tested out by our techniques. All we need simply is, first of all, a knowledge of hypotheses possible and just what the techniques would be, and we can get on with making contributions to a basic science in our field.

18

TECHNICAL PROBLEMS: METHODOLOGY AS RELATED TO THE REQUIREMENTS OF PUBLIC OPINION MEASUREMENT

Clyde W. Hart, Presiding

Norman C. Meier

MR. HART: I have been struck as I have sat through this series of conferences at the difference between the character and quality of the performance here and that of some professional societies with which I am identified. There is a kind of unity and progression of thought in the program here which I find not only very pleasing but very stimulating. I wondered to what it might be attributed, aside from the superiority of the planning committee that is in charge of this particular conference. I am sure all of us from the outside, if I may rate as one from the outside, appreciate the excellent opportunity that has been provided all of us for free, full, high-level discussion of important problems both of a substantive and methodological sort that have been provided for us here.

But I suspect that one of the reasons for the superiority of this meeting is that most professional societies pick a chairman and then leave it up to him to go out and pull in all of his friends and people with whom he agrees—once in a while one with whom he disagrees that he wants to put on the spot particularly—to come in and be on his program. Here the committee arranged everything and they proceeded quite logically in the development of the program.

I am sure that on a subject as vital and important as the one that is assigned to this session, there will be no difficulty about participation. I have been interested many times during the conference in hearing it said that we are now at the point in the sampling phase of our survey-type researches where emphasis needs to be shifted markedly to the problems involved in executing a sample regardless of its design. All of us realize that the sample in any study is not the sample that is laid out on paper, but it is the group of respondents that we ultimately succeed in getting.

I hear very frequently claims that a probability sample of an area type has been used in a particular study. Right after the November elections it was frequently said that the area probability samples were as badly off as were the quota samples that were used.

As far as I have been able to ascertain there wasn't any strict probability sample used in the November elections. In one of the instances a probability sample was set up, but in the execution of it eighteen percent of the people who were in the sample as designed were never worked into the actual sample of people who were interviewed about their intentions and preferences. Thus it was not, strictly speaking, a probability sample, at least until that eighteen percent had been systematically sub-sampled and the original sample corrected accordingly.

I mention that as an illustration merely of the importance of the problem of executing a sample design so that the group with which you come out fulfills as precisely as possible, absolutely precisely if possible, the requirements of the design.

Now I don't know to what extent that is the aspect of the problem which will come up for discussion here. I am certain that it is an aspect of this whole sampling problem to which very considerable attention needs be given. We in our agency now are logging all of our field experiences in connection with the execution of the sample design, keeping track of all the places where we go wrong, or may go wrong, and of the methods that have been devised in the field to prevent our going wrong. And we are preparing that material so it can be shared with the other people who are confronted by the same problem that all of us who are working in this field confront. And I think it is important to have that kind of work done because, as I say, regardless of the kind of sample design, it is no better than its execution in the field.

I think it is appropriate at this juncture in the conference that we should get into the technical aspects of sampling. Here in Iowa I understand a cooperative study has been going on that involved parts of the research units here at the University of Iowa and research units at Iowa State College at Ames, particularly the Statistical Laboratory at Ames. That study has been under the general direction of Professor Norman Meier, in collaboration with Dr. Charles Haner. I understand that the results of this study are now fairly final and the session is to begin this afternoon with a brief report of the problem involved in this study and of its implications from the standpoint of sampling.

I am pleased to introduce, if he needs introduction at this juncture, Professor Norman Meier, who for a good many years has been active and interested in research in the general field of attitude and opinion. He was involved in some of the early ventures of Ted Gallup and others in this field, as well as in regional projects that have developed into the Iowa State Poll and the Bureau of Audience Research here. Mr. Meier will report on this project, following which the question will be open for general discussion.

I must apologize because I can't complete this role that has been assigned to me. As many of you know, I spent nineteen and a half years as a member of this faculty. I have an appointment I do not want to break, and I have arranged with Mr. Saunders to take over the chairmanship at that time.

I am very pleased to present Dr. Norman Meier, who will open the discussion with a report on this study.

MR. MEIER: To clarify my position before I start, let me say that the general policy in organizing this Conference was to bring together at one time in one room diverse types of individuals who have been contributing to or interested in the technical problems of public opinion and attitude measurement. It was my feeling that statisticians meeting with like-minded associates, psychologists meeting with psychologists, and sociologists with other sociologists could never arrive independently at any comprehensive envisagement of the full nature of these problems; because so frequently they are considered only on a theoretical basis, without testing the theory in the field. In this session in particular we wanted to have representatives of different viewpoints on methodology; we wanted them together and to get better acquainted with each other's views.

We now have here a representative group but not the full number we had hoped to have had. Rensis Likert, who was urged to attend; Louis Bean; several from the SSRC Committee, particularly S. S. Wilks, Phil Hauser, and Fred Stephan, could not be here.

The subject of the session is the question of *the adaptability of the area methodology for public opinion measurement.* Can a method that has worked well in agricultural experiments and has been found serviceable for census estimates and other uses, be suited to the special requirements of public opinion measurement?

Since 1944 the main research interests of the speaker have centered around the problem of whether for public opinion measurement area methods are as good as or better than good quota methods. I hope we may keep *that* question in mind throughout this discussion. As a basis for discussion we shall examine three studies made over the past three years, which attempt to follow the method of experimental science, of keeping all factors constant while varying only one which is the factor under study, in this instance the method of selecting and contacting respondents for opinion polling.

It is assumed that all of you know the basic differences between the two methods. The area method in brief is a special form of simple random sampling in which the universe area is divided, subdivided, sub-sub-divided down to a number of sampling units, all by randomizing devices, and these sampling units only are covered completely or sampled. The quota method has its interest in *types* of individuals who, taken collectively, make up the universe and a specified number of each type is interviewed, in the proportion as they are found in the universe. Check data are also obtained which provide a means for checking internally the sample against characteristics of the universe.

The goal of all sampling concerned with human traits, with attitudes and opinions, is that the sample be representative of the universe under consideration, which in opinion sampling is the universe of politically-cognizant citizens, frequently a universe of attitudes and opinion.

In area sampling, which is based on land areas, on geography, the universe is the total area, or rather all items contained thereon.

But in public opinion measurement the referent is usually *the effective citizen,* often the person who votes (though he may not at times). It cannot be equally interested in minors, the aged, the feebleminded, the insane, those incarcerated in institutions, and those completely disinterested in public affairs.

Moreover, people's attitudes and opinions are tied in with affiliations, with church, ancestral extraction, with labor organizations, economic class levels, age groupings, sex, and perhaps other minor determinants of attitude and opinion. Such affiliations do not exist in a perfectly uniform spread over any geographic area. There are even heavily saturated "islands" here and there where people are nearly all Catholic, or old females, or Republican farmers.

It is hence conceivable that psychological and social stratification assumes an importance in the opinion survey far beyond any function it may play in agricultural or general population surveys.

Representativeness, then, for a public opinion survey, must refer not to the whole population but to the effective adult universe whose attitude configurations can be roughly stratified. From previous work in the field we can say that these more significant attitude configurations are to be identified roughly with (a) socio-economic status, (b) age, (c) sex, (d) ecological setting (urban, town, rural), (e) occupation, and to a lesser extent with (f) religious affiliation, (g) ancestral stock.

It is apparent that any considerable excess in a sample beyond its true proportion in the effective adult universe would tend to produce distortion in the opinion estimate, where such opinion was related to the attitude configuration.

I shall now present the studies. The first two were made with the primary objective of testing the representativeness of samples drawn by each method on the same universe, where the characteristics of the universe are known. This method is known as the "laboratory method" of testing samples and requires that results of a previously-made survey be available in files. By use of maps and aerial photographs the universe was divided into count units and sampling units for selection of the area samples by random number tables. The quota samples are simply locations on plain maps much as a quota interviewer would select respondents after becoming familiar with the community. For public opinion objectives, the first study turned up results that tended to favor the quota method. In fact, in 25 points of comparison using samples of five different sizes, the quota samples were closer to the *known* control characteristics in 16 instances; in 6 the difference was slight and in 5 the area was favored. In the second study made jointly with Dr. Cletus J. Burke [1] the representativeness of the quota samples were found superior on socio-income status, which is perhaps the

[1] Meier, N. C., and Burke, C. J., "Laboratory Tests of Sampling Techniques." *Public Opinion Quarterly, 11*, No. 4 (Winter 1947-48), pp. 586-593.

attitude-configuration of greatest single importance for public opinion.

The third study, the one which is of direct interest to us here today, was a cooperative study requiring a year of planning with the field work done in August-September, 1946. So far as known, it is the only elaborate field study made under adequately controlled conditions permitting direct comparison of the quota and area methodologies *in actual public opinion measurement.* The universe was the state of Iowa. The state is highly literate and the population is more or less uniformly distributed over the whole area and has an absence of extremes of wealth and class consciousness.

The procedure was basically this. We had the Ames Statistical Laboratory provide the area sample, an adaptation of the General Purpose Sample for Iowa based in part on the United States master sample of agriculture, plus units in the urban and town sections. In the towns we used aerial photographs. The quota sample was the Iowa Poll's regular (quota) sample.

The *Des Moines Register and Tribune's* Research Department supplied, as a contribution to scientific advancement, the entire cost of the field work of the experiment.

The interviewers were given adequate instruction in the area-interviewing requirements, which include ability to read maps. These instructions were worked out in great detail from the Bureau of Agricultural Economics instructions, which we had to revise considerably to make them fully comprehensible. The same interviewers therefore were used, after they had become familiar with both methods. Identical questionnaires were used.

A series of four surveys were made—one by quota, then one by area, then one by quota, then one by area—four, for the reason that with four we would have a chance to get a better comparison as to what kind of control items each one would turn up. We wanted a repetition of each also so we could measure consistency in each method.

Under these equated circumstances and conditions, the results generally favor the quota method. It showed up somewhat better on most counts. There was no election at that time except a gubernatorial election two months hence, and in the political indications in late August and the first half of September, the area would have indicated the election of the Republican Governor by a very slight figure, and the quota more nearly what the election figure showed.

It also indicated that on past voting preference, had the two surveys been made in 1944, the area would have indicated the election of Roosevelt, whereas Dewey carried Iowa. This is the reverse of the Washington situation, though the two studies are not strictly comparable. The area sample showed a heavy Democratic population in this definitely Republican state.

Plates 1 and 2 show the two samples. The area sample used was a part of the Iowa general-purpose sample, worked out as a part of the master sample of agriculture, Iowa section, dividing the state into five units with about twenty counties in each, and then dividing and subdividing by random procedures on down to selected sampling units—located in about twenty towns, twenty open country areas, and about eighteen cities.

Here I'd like to point out two or three things that our analyses disclosed. In the "town" unit that represents the four counties of Linn, Benton, Iowa, and Johnson, the town selected by random methods to represent all the towns came out by chance to be University Heights. It is not a town; it is an integral part of Iowa City. Those people work in Iowa City; they go to church here; they go to the university; they are, to all intents and effects, a part of Iowa City, but by area procedures it is a village, a part of the county.

Now that in itself is not necessarily a disturbing thing, but in the city of Waterloo there is another suburb known as Castle Hill; so the town selected by random methods, representing five other counties, is that "town" of Castle Hill, which is an integral part more or less of the Waterloo metropolitan district.

Yet there are other aspects of this particular area sample our study disclosed. In the urban section of Burlington, Iowa, the interviewer correctly located the designated area according to the map—this was checked afterwards—but found nobody living there. It was an abandoned trailer-housing development which during part of Burlington's wartime activities probably was occupied by war workers. The aerial photo showed it filled with housing units.

Again, in Sioux City, one of the designated units happened to be a place where most of the residents happened to be transient, described by the able interviewer there as "flop houses." I am just mentioning these items at random to show that for public opinion purposes, the question can be legitimately raised that if we consider that there is any difference between an urban resident's constellation of

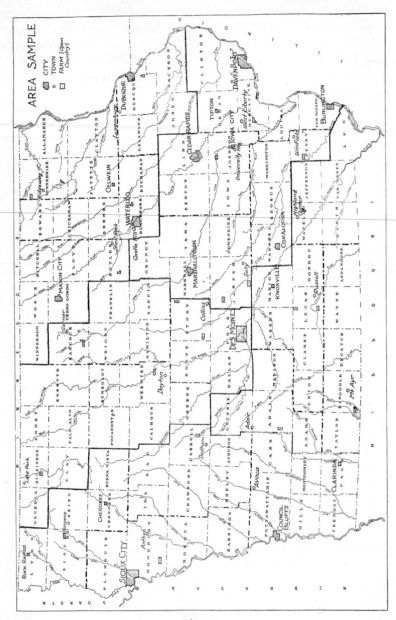

Plate 1

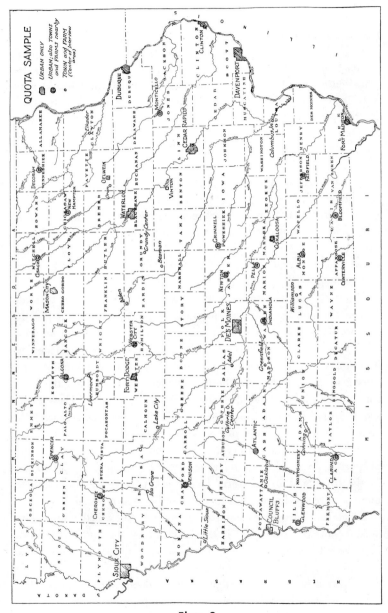

Plate 2

attitudes and opinions, and those of rural or town, there is here something like fifteen or twenty percent misclassified by strict randomization procedures.

Still other aspects of interest are these: in the town of Hospers, the community is almost entirely Dutch and that being the case, its contribution to representativeness of the state of Iowa would hold only if the population of Iowa was five percent of Dutch extraction. In the towns of Sully, Collins, Luxemburg, and Avoca there were almost no male residents found in the sampling units. They were almost entirely older women, unmarried or widowed women. You will see that in Table II.

By comparison, note the quota sample of Iowa, which more or less blankets the state. At points marked with a square within a circle, urban, town, and rural interviews are obtained by the same interviewer, getting those in the city and then going in a different direction each time to get the towns and the farms also. Where there is a single circle it is town and farm only. Where there is a rectangular area it is urban only.

The next slide illustrates something which may be new to most of you in sampling practice: the method used by the Iowa Poll to allocate town and farm residents. Note this interview point and another interview point there. The distance in between is divided in half and a line is drawn at right angles through the midpoint. The same way here; same way here, and here, and here and the lines connected so in that way the state is divided into areas. These areas are measured by polar planimeter which gives the exact square mile area of each. This is not of course an area sample; it is a device for allocating to each interview center and to each interviewer the proportionate number of interviews which that person should get in the town and in the farm categories, to give an apportionate number directly in relation to the size of area covered.

When this process is completed, figures for all the areas are machine-totaled. That total is then divided by the number of town interviews to be made for the given size sample, varying of course according to the sample. The quotient provides a factor which is then divided into each area figure, giving then the number of interviews for each interview area. The same procedure but using the factor for farm gives the number of farm interviews for each interview point.

Now, to sum up the results of the study.

Income. For area, note the comparison of Segment *a* with Segment *c*. *a* and *c* are adjacent to a common s. u. "*b*." In the first survey *a* and *b* are used; in the second, *b* and *c*. One should get little variation. The quota formula followed at that time by the Iowa Poll was based on reasonably good statistics, from the Income Tax Commission, BLS surveys, and other sources. [Note in Table I the distribution by the area method.]

TABLE I

Income Distribution

Respondent Status	Area Segment *a*	Quota I	Area Segment c	Quota II
A	5.22	2.30	4.15	2.50
B	18.87	12.30	20.40	10.90
C	62.89	58.80	61.49	56.20
D	13.02	26.60	13.96	30.40

Because there has been a good deal said since the election that the quota methods do not get into the lower income levels and that an area or probability sample is the only way that can be assured, please notice here that the area samples do not get into the lower income levels to the extent that the quota samples do, and the B group here is very much greater in the area samples.

In Table II we have the sex distribution. One can see very clearly here the actual area bias. Here in the city segment on the *area*

TABLE II

Percents of Males and Females in Area and Quota Samples

Classification	Sampling Method	Ballot 1			Ballot 2		
		City	Town	Farm	City	Town	Farm
Male	Quota	49.8	52.7	50.5	48.4	47.9	55.0
	Area	41.2	49.2	56.9	46.2	37.0	43.0
Female	Quota	50.2	47.3	49.5	51.6	52.1	45.0
	Area	58.8	50.8	43.1	53.9	63.0	57.0

sample we have 41.2 percent male, 58.8 percent female; and we
have on Ballot 2 in town, 63.0 percent of female with 37.0 male;
while on farms we have on Ballot 2, 57.0 percent female and 43
percent male. One can see the consistencies and inconsistencies of
the proportions as obtained by the area method. In our studies, the
thing I fail to understand is why this occurs in so many area surveys. In the *Washington Post* Poll surveys in Washington, D. C.,
they came out occasionally with even 68 and 65 percent female;
and also in the Washington state area sample the sex item was off.
It may be that in some places there are many excess women, but
I am sure that either the census is very wrong or else something else
is wrong because I have checked this for counties in Iowa, I have
checked this for precincts, for statewide figures, and there is no
ratio in this state that indicates a deviation of more than one or two
percentage points. The sex ratio is usually around 50-50. This study
was made more than a year *after* the war was over, and we know
from the Draft Board how many men were in the service and approximately how many returned. So I would point this up as one
of the things which would be disturbing if this particular area
sample at this particular time involved a public opinion questionnaire on anything pertaining to a matter in which sex differences
were important.

In Table III, educational attainment, I'd like to point out two
or three things. This will tend to show, unlike the Washington result we heard this morning, that the educational differences are
not too great. In this case they are in favor of the area sample.
I would like to point out, however, that there is a misconception,
at least so far as I understand this, as to what a public opinion
survey should show in educational ratios. I think Morris Hansen
would check me on that, that the public opinion universe is not the
total population universe nor is it the total adult population. It is
the effective adult population and I mean by that, the effective normal adult population that may vote, and is more or less politically
interested and generally awake to ordinary public affairs. Therefore
persons in institutions for the feebleminded, for the insane, and in
penitentiaries, old people's homes, homes for the aged, should not
ordinarily be included in a public opinion universe because those
people as a rule either cannot vote or seldom vote and therefore
are not considerably interested in matters of public opinion. Hence
the universe would be upped somewhat educationally.

TABLE III

Percents of Respondents in Specified Educational Attainment
Brackets for Area and Quota Samples

Response	Sampling Method	Ballot 1			Ballot 2		
		City	Town	Farm	City	Town	Farm
Grade school	Quota	28.7	31.2	42.8	30.2	29.3	41.7
	Area	30.92	43.08	49.02	33.33	36.11	62.82
High school	Quota	48.0	50.4	41.3	47.0	46.4	45.5
	Area	42.26	40.00	35.30	38.89	41.66	30.76
College	Quota	22.2	17.6	15.4	22.8	23.6	12.8
	Area	26.80	16.92	13.73	25.56	18.06	6.41

Note the number of persons who have had some college education: here the area has 26 percent in the city, with 22 percent shown
by the quota. But the Iowa Poll has repeatedly returned figures
there of 18, 19, and 20 percent with some college and that probably
is inflated but not nearly as much as one may think. One should
not compare that to the figure for the United States because Iowa—
I believe—has the highest literacy, or one of the highest of all the
literacy rates, and it is of course blanketed with small colleges as
well as two major institutions. So it may be near 18 percent, but I
offer this here for what it is worth. It shows what those four surveys
showed on education.

The area figures are involved also in the inverse relation of age
with education. An excess of older people tends to depress the educational levels, and would tend to favor area which has an excess
of older people. This then seems to be the only important respect
where area may be superior. On social and economic-income status,
it seems to me, any question which depends upon income in this
study would have been more properly reflected by the quota sample;
anything referring to sex, undoubtedly more accurately reflected
by the quota sample. Anything related to age would also, because
the area sample was very, very much inflated upward in the age

control; I refer to anything that pertains of course to differences *in age levels,* I mean youth, middle age, and old age, that has been found to be correlated with a great many attitudes on socio-economic problems.

Because in an election year (such as 1948) the interest in political affiliation takes on special significance in opinion polling, I shall add one more segment of the findings, the political affiliation of respondents and their vote for president in 1944. The item has particular significance in view of the recent assertions of a number of persons and known views of others. Tables IV and V show the tendency of the area samples to yield a Democratic bias.

TABLE IV

Political-Party Classification of Respondents

Response	Segment *a*	Quota I	Segment *c*	Quota II
Republican Definitely	18.64	19.8	22.71	22.3
Republican Independent	26.11	35.1	26.27	31.9
Democrat Definitely	22.30	14.3	21.97	17.2
Democrat Independent	23.01	23.7	17.89	20.6
Refused	10.04	5.6	11.16	6.6

TABLE V

Percent of Respondents on Area and Quota Samples Voting for Candidates in the 1944 Presidential Election

Response	Sampling Method	Ballot 1			Ballot 2		
		City	Town	Farm	City	Town	Farm
Dewey	Quota	48.5	51.6	45.5	51.5	51.4	41.7
	Area	39.70	47.17	43.75	43.28	35.42	32.14
Roosevelt	Quota	50.5	48.4	53.1	48.5	48.6	57.7
	Area	60.29	50.94	53.12	56.72	64.58	66.07

In 1944 Iowa was definitely Republican, consistent with her past half-century of political history. The vote was Dewey 52.26 percent and Roosevelt 47.74 percent in the major party division.

Sam Wilks, who is joint chairman of the NRC and SSRC Committee, once remarked to me that the only way progress can be made is simply to put methods to work in the field on actual public opinion surveys.

Where we are dealing with attitude constellations as we are in public opinion work, and face so complex a thing as we learned at the SSRC session, which involves all kinds of ramifications and involvements, this is not a simple matter which can be answered by any one methodology.

In presenting these studies I trust that it be clearly understood that my sole interest is disinterested methodological research. If there are better methods now available for public opinion measurement than those in current use, that fact should be clearly established. The area methodology was developed largely by federal agencies at great cost; it is expensive to design and expensive to operate if done properly. Short-cuts and failure to realize fully its fundamental tenets vitiate its theoretical integrity and does violence to probability concepts. If, however, it proves to be for public opinion work a better method, cost should be a secondary consideration; but if the cost is beyond the reach of most public opinion polls, then it should be demonstrably very much better to warrant serious consideration.

Has anyone yet submitted incontestable proof of superiority *in actual field tests* satisfying to impartial judges? Has anyone conclusively proved its *feasibility* for public opinion sampling on a year-round weekly or biweekly basis at a cost within available budgets? Who has plans for making such tests? Who will finance such tests? Who will judge?

In our work here with the Bureau, we have tested various methodologies for different purposes, on small units, such as eastern Iowa. For some purposes we have found quota methods quite unsuited, for other purposes we have found both area and quota methods unsatisfactory, and have had to develop new methods combining probability with a measure of variable control. We have explored random-point, circular random-point pattern with fixed and with variable rotatable axes. We did that until we found a method suitable for our immediate purpose and requirements. The same attitude should be applied to public opinion measurement. Who knows what methods may in the future be devised that will be superior to these now in use. But whatever they may be they will have to prove their superiority in actual results. I happen to be from Missouri but also my training as an experimental psychologist does not permit accepting anything on blind faith.

The problem is now open for general discussion and I hope we may progress beyond theory and assumption to the real question before us: *Is the area methodology suitable for public opinion measurement?*

DISCUSSION

MR. HART: Thank you, Mr. Meier, for a very clear, simple, straightforward presentation. I will now turn the meeting over to Mr. Saunders and we hope that anyone else who has any similar contribution to make, anybody who wishes to discuss the experiment reported by Dr. Meier, to ask him further questions about it, or in any other way to contribute to the subject matter of this conference, will immediately make himself known.

MR. STOCK: A question. What was the final sampling—people, or families?

MR. MEIER: People.

MR. STOCK: Individuals within a household?

MR. MEIER: Yes; one to a household.

MR. STOCK: How was that person selected within the household? —by the probability method?

MR. MEIER: That gets into complications here because in the process of the two area surveys, we rotated around different methods. We sampled within the household and at other times took the first one that came, doing this for different segments of the samples. That was all prepared by Ames for testing variations of selection. Mind you, the State Laboratory had control over that part of it. We wanted to be sure that nobody would say, "*You* planned this and you didn't have a properly constructed area sample." We just turned it all over to Ames. The Statistical Lab wanted to know answers to many of these questions too, so they even worked out the statistical aspects.

MR. BACHELDER: I'll probably have to share a little bit of time with Dr. Dodd on this thing because we represent a laboratory that's using the area sample in all of its work, except in the test with the quota sample prior to the election. One comment is that there are several ways to draw an area sample, several different ways. The area sample really, as most of you know, but for some who may not be familiar with the terminology, the area sample uses the domal sample and interdomal sampling technique. The Washington Public Opinion Laboratory uses the latter, the interdomal system where randomness theoretically applies and the interviewer has no choice throughout.

Now I am not at the present stage of the game, as I indicated this morning, a proponent of either system on the basis of fact or proof. The answer is, we don't know yet which is best. I can tell you which costs the most, but not too much more. The field interviewing cost of the area and quota systems, we found, differs very little. The administrative cost is much higher for the area. But it is on another basis, other than the data presented by Dr. Meier, which was extremely interesting, that I think we should judge the area and the quota, and withhold judgment until more evidence is in.

I'd like to take up the theoretical point of view, and that is this: that statistically, if randomization operates down to the selection of the individual within the household and you have 100 percent control of the sample with no substitutions, that is the Utopia. A purely random sample will give you the proper proportion within the universe and all characteristics within the universe. That is the theoretical position.

The quota sample cannot possibly in any way ever become representative of all characteristics of the population. It is physically impossible to ask the interviewers to select a person over the age of fifty, who is a Presbyterian, with two years of college, and who belongs to five organizations, who lives in a certain part of the state, who had measles at the age of six and reads so many magazines. It would take them years to locate more than three or four persons with all those characteristics, and unless in the theoretical design you have a system so that after selecting on three characteristics you at the same time are getting a complete coverage of all other characteristics, you are running into extreme difficulty, theoretically.

The problem of the area sample in most places where it has been tried is that we have never gotten to the Utopianistic 100 percent completion. However, as I mentioned this morning, some of the data we do pick up as to representativeness in the area sample is uncanny. In the breakdown of small units—I mentioned only the widowed males, over the age of 65—the breakdown on veterans' status falls right into pattern; the breakdown on this particular study of registered voters falls right into pattern; the breakdown as to the number of registered voters who actually voted in the state of Washington falls right into pattern. By merely selecting at pure random, and controlling randomness down to the nth degree, theoretically the area sample will represent more.

I would like to take up a criticism of the area sample and its inability to measure more items than the few that are selected by the interviewer. True, you can ask fifteen or twenty more items at the end of the interview and relate those to known data; true, you cannot prove statistically that that is still representative. That may have been luck, and you have no way of showing whether it is luck or not, as long as you have randomness stopped at one point in the complete selection of the sample. The quota system in operation in our work in this one particular study we made did get about the same background data, the same other items. The point I was going to make was that as yet we don't know in what items sex is an important factor. We don't know on what attitudes and opinion age is an important factor. We can guess. We can begin with a beautiful rationalization of one sort or other. We don't know as yet clearly on what factors amount of education is an important item. But little as we know about those, on the basis of a little piecemeal study here and there—no universal studies with all the people polling in the United States working on one thing for a period of three months—we know far less about their combinations, the permutations, of age, sex, and education.

We know so little about the parameters of our universes. We take the census data as parameters of our universe and it changes overnight, particularly in our part of the country, the state of Washington, where it is changing so very rapidly. But theoretically the area sample design if controlled 100 percent, permits you to build your parameters, and if your educational data are out of line it doesn't bother you; if your age data are out of line it doesn't bother. Theoretically the area sample is the type which gives you all the factors relating to attitudes, whether you know what they are or not; the quota sample cannot possibly do it.

Why do you get about the same results? Frankly I don't know, and it's going to take a lot of study to find out.

MISS CROSSLEY: I have so many ideas on this, and I don't want to make a speech, just a little comment. First of all, I believe Mr. Bachelder made a point this morning, and it showed up in Dr. Meier's figures on education. And also I believe that in the A, B, C, D distribution your area sample got much less of your D group than your quota sample did, and I think there is one fairly obvious reason for that, which is that they said they took one interview to a household. You've got more people to a household in your lower groups so if you are going to do that, you are representing more people and not balancing for it.

Then I'd like to comment on the point that your quota sample theoretically can't come out with the proper proportion; it's something you haven't control for—and yet it does come out, and it has for twenty-five or thirty years. I think one of the reasons probably is that you are getting your proper age, sex, and anything you do set up, and the other things perhaps are not related to it, not affected by it, and they come out. At least you do make your age and sex come out, and on an area sample you know they are wrong because you don't get the proper people so, so long as you can check back your accuracy for a quota sample, you can use your quota. But I would say there's usually more chance of coming out right than you will on the area where you miss ten percent or more of the people.

Then one other point I'd like to make. It seems to me maybe it doesn't have to be area or quota; maybe you can use both. Certainly you stratify an area sample before you start taking it. A quota sample is another case of stratification. Why can't you stratify both of them? Why can't you, when you get down to the household level maybe, set up quotas to avoid getting too many women? I believe that has been done in Denver. Bill McPhee, if he is here, can probably tell you what luck he had with it. But if you are supposed to get a man, and the man isn't at home, don't allow a woman to be substituted. Make the interviewer substitute a man, or control your substitutions some way so you won't get that bias.

Likewise, another combination you might do is to use perhaps quota sample in the cities. As I remember those figures on education that were on the board a little while ago, it was in the farm sample where the quota was divergent on distribution of education. On the city distribution, if any of you remember—perhaps Dr. Meier can check me on that—the quota sample was as good or better than area; on the farms it wasn't. That indicates that an area sample would be the answer in rural interviewing, whereas a quota sample would be perfectly satisfactory in cities.

MR. SAUNDERS: Was Miss Crossley correct on those figures?

MR. MEIER: Yes, essentially. May I comment on Mr. Bachelder's remarks? If all Mr. Bachelder says proves to be verified in time it will be remarkable. Probability theory will solve all our problems. My research in sampling, however, has not led me to place such complete and utter faith in sheer randomness. It sounds too much like magic. Sample size, objectives, character of universe—should determine basic procedure.

I would like to say also that, contrary to Bachelder's belief that there is no necessary relationship between age, sex, income, and so on, in opinion constellations that Cantril, his associates, and others have studied through the years—the thirteen years that polls have been reporting back on different questions—we do have a considerable accumulation of data showing such relationships, and they are reasonably definite. We do know for instance that as people become older they become less liberal and more conservative—not everyone—but I think about everyone tends to be less liberal as he grows older. On certain things I think we have an abundance of information to show these relationships, and I don't think that it is quite necessary or accurate to make that observation, that there isn't any.

I'd like to say too, that if one examines the accumulated control data of well-organized and properly conducted quota polls, he will find they come out very close on many of these same things that Mr. Bachelder cited about the area. Those he mentioned are easy ones to check out with. There are some of them that have checked consistently through the years, in quota samples, and the correspondence has been in some instances remarkably close. With the well-known and ever-present error in Census data, one should not be too proud of too close correspondences. Both noses may be off.

MR. McPHEE: We have been doing some experiments with this, which would have the value of being very naive. Some of these experiments deal with the practice of area sampling by quota sam-

pling of persons. In other words, we can tell something of what
we will find when we get into it. By and large, our evidence seems
to make us want to get over to a modified probability sampling as
fast as we can feasibly do so.

The sort of things we've been doing are still small experiments.
We too matched an Ames sample against our standard state-wide
quota sample for farms. We did this in small cases of a hundred and
fifty to two hundred samples, all we could afford, but they seem
to reveal a new type of bias, a type of bias in rural areas which is
different and probably more serious, from the marketing standpoint,
than the urban biases. In this sort of thing, the quota sample differs
greatly from the area sample since the quota sample for instance
gets typical farmers—in Colorado, that is farmers that own from
a hundred acres to five hundred acres. It gets a tremendous load of
them and doesn't get the farms over five hundred acres, which are
big livestock and wheat producers, and doesn't get the farms under
five hundred acres, which are marginal farmers.

Then accessibility—that has a definite effect. The area sample,
particularly in that wild country, gets a necessary element of population which is the inaccessible people in communities—at least
that's the way we interpret it.

We find that the quota sample gets many more farm magazines
per hundred homes, many more urban publications such as daily
and weekly newspapers, more radio listening to one sophisticated
radio program. But that was not because of an income factor insofar as we could tell. It was not a factor of income, socio-economic
level so much, because in the value of the farm, in tenant-owner
relationships, the two samples were comparable.

So much for some of those rural biases which scare us on certain kinds of studies. The other experience we have had is in the
urban work with a sort of an area sample of households with quota
within the household, or interviewing a responsible adult. That was
what our particular survey called for, and in this case we did one
in the present election.

The week before election we did a quota sample. Because we
were showing more Truman strength than we thought there was, we
did an area sample which we knew would give us more Trumans.
The two samples were identical within one or two points, right
down from Truman and Dewey, through Governor, Senator, Congressmen, and District Attorney. They were identical with the elec-

. tion results themselves within one or two points, except in one case where they were both off five points.

The remarkable thing to us was—this may be a funny way to put it—that the area sample was as good as our quota sample in an election situation. I think people who have wrestled with the turnout problem will know why we would not expect an area sample to be as good as quota sample in an election. In quota sample that cancels a turnout bias that favors the Democrats and many biases that favor the Republicans. But those two surveys were identical all the way, in all the comparisons we could make, with each other and with the election.

Finally, the cost picture is the one in which I think, and I am glad to hear Washington confirm this, we are finding the astounding thing that for a good many problems, particularly where you can sample household and not clear down to individuals, the costs aren't a great deal more for the area, particularly in urban areas. We have the two urban samples we have done, and in the rural sample we see that the cost was double, but we see where it could be brought down. It was double within counties in which we had no resident interviewer. But if the area sample forces you to go, as it did us, clear up to Morris Hansen's home in Wyoming, and we were working from Denver, then there are of course expenses which there wouldn't have been if we had been able to use our quota sampling on those places.

MR. TICK: A sample is a good sample, only for a specific use. We found a quota sample just as good for household magazines. Well, we probably made use of certain information about which we were sure, and which does not exist in the other cases.

Now, from my own examination of the literature I understand it this way, and I am discussing the use of area sampling for political behavior, not household magazines, or age groups, or this, that and the other thing. Outside of initial combinations made by Dr. Lazarsfeld in his study in Ohio, in which he reported how the voter makes up his mind, we really have very little information yet, very little accurate and good information about what goes into a political decision. Hence all our knowledge about the characteristics of a political population—by that I mean political behavior of individuals—is almost nil, and randomization is a process by which we could hope that all factors about which we do not know stand an equal chance of being represented in the sample.

Now, we do know certain things about age groups, and family size, and so forth, and in drawing a sample say to find out these things, we make use of that information because we are sure of it. But in political behavior we have none, and the only thing we can do to put ourselves on hard ground is to make a complete random procedure and by this we can get some measurement which doesn't exist in any other kind of information.

MR. HORNSETH: I want to make the observation that these problems of sampling have been settled at the theoretical level, and not by comparisons of any two particular samples. The reason is that on measurements of error—and our procedures of estimation of course must be made on a theoretical level—the difficulty with the quota sample, in theory at least, is that we have no way of knowing in advance whether the estimate will be good or bad. In some cases the standard error will be smaller than will be the standard error in the area samples, and in some cases it will be larger. You simply have no control over the size of the error at any one time.

Now in the comparison of these two particular samples, it was perhaps an accident that the quota sample turned out to be better than the area sample. That may very well be true, but we have no way of telling when that will occur. It is for that reason that the area sample is theoretically the better sample to take.

MR. STOCK: First, may I ask a question. Are we limited to political polling in this discussion?

MR. SAUNDERS: We'd like to hold it pretty much on that level.

MR. STOCK: I want to make one point. Many of us in commercial research much of the time are not studying the general public. We're doing a cross-section of clergymen, or a cross-section of mothers of children aged two, or a cross-section of foremen in factories. Now sometimes we can find in the time allowed us and the budget allowed us that we can use the probability sample. Sometimes we cannot. It's pretty hard to get a cross-section of clergymen in the United States, for instance, by probability sample. That is simply because we don't have the background data yet to do it. Our general philosophy is, we will always get as close to the approximation as we can. We can't always do it. We've run many experiments of probability samples where we have had community studies, where we could very safely control all the conditions. Here it has always been disappointing from the standpoint of comparisons, because there is no difference.

The only thing we can compare that seems to show any difference at all is cost and there we find, as you might expect, the area sample running a little higher until we discovered one thing. We had always been taking quota samplers and letting them do area sampling. Then we'd try taking a measure of the cost in quota sampling and taking the cost of area sampling and we find the cost went up. If we take area samplers and then assign them to quota sampling the cost goes up again. It's simply a problem of interviewer cussedness.

Apparently we are experimenting with a technique which looks pretty good where problems of state estimates are required, or detailed estimates for small areas—that is, a limited number of areas in the country. We take a very strict, as strict as possible, probability sample and at the same time cover those same areas with a quota sample. We attempt in that limited number of areas then to get some picture of bias that exists on certain questions in those areas for certain segments of the population. Then we expand our quota samples throughout the whole country, using several hundred interviewers in all forty-eight states. We apply these statements of bias that we get in the limited number of areas to the complete quota sample. It's much cheaper, for making state estimates, to estimate the bias in the limited area and then do your national sample with the bias in.

MR. HAUSKNECHT: I have a criterion which I'd like Dr. Jessen and Mr. Hansen to concur for me.

In the Veterans Administration we have a lot of sample designs done on an area basis and several of them don't look very good when they are done. They are not uniformly scattered over the state. They are patches, and they don't look right. Every so often somebody comes in and says, "Well now, that can't be a good sample. Look at this big blank space here, and you've got a lot of them bunched up over here. It must be a terrible sample. You ought to fix it up a little better so it's spread out more evenly." That bothers us for a while, and Earl Houseman was consulted on the subject and he thought about it, and thought about it, and he said, "Well, there may be a principle involved in this."

This is the principle I would like you to consider: If it looks good, it's bad. You see, the chance of getting a checkerboard display by just drawing a chance sample is not very good; you are not likely to get a nice even checkerboard on the map. There's rather a remote chance of getting it, and if you are going to work with a sample that remote, you're working with a biased sample. So that seems to imply, "If it looks good, it's bad." Dr. Jessen and Mr. Hansen, would you like to agree with that, or would you like to embroider it?

MR. SAUNDERS: Mr. Hansen, do you wish to make a comment?

MR. HANSEN: Not particularly to answer that question.

MR. SAUNDERS: This reminds me of the wake that was being held out in Nebraska. Everything was very quiet about three o'clock in the morning, when one man spoke up and said, "If no one else is going to say anything, I'd like to say a few words on Free Silver" (*laughter*).

MR. HANSEN: Sometimes it might turn out, but I wouldn't want to express a view on it. I did want to make a few remarks on quota sampling and area sampling, the possible illustrations we have had and other illustrations. First, there are many situations in which one would normally expect, at least I would normally expect, a quota or purposefully selected sample to give you results superior to a random sample, depending on your ability and techniques in drawing that sample.

Let me put it this way: if we are in a box, that is, in any jobs we deal with in the Bureau of Census where we have only one or two or three units, a comparatively small job, that is the indication for a quota technique. It's pretty easy to demonstrate that the types of approaches we ordinarily use aren't feasible—the use of this probability sampling, when we don't have the best resources in the world to work with—so we resort to area methods. I might say area is sort of a technique of getting away from taking a probability sample when you don't have a very large sample—I don't know just what "very large" means, it depends upon the problem—but the facts are these. Ordinarily you can purposefully deal with an approach that will have a bias in it of more or less serious magnitude. It usually is not awfully serious on many problems, though sometimes it may be. And then you also have a variance to deal with. Now this bias may or may not decrease as you increase the size of the sample. It will tend to decrease with the increase in the size of the sample, up to a certain point. We don't know too much about how it might decrease in a particular case, but on the other hand, the variance with an appropriate sample will decrease with the decrease in size of the sample. So you have a method in which for very small samples the variance will be much larger than the bias. As you increase the size of the sample the bias goes down and down, so pretty soon you reach a point where the probability methods will give you results closer than the purposive techniques in drawing a sample.

I don't know in this particular case. One thing that may be operating here is that the biases may be comparatively small as compared to the size of the variance, as in the size of sample that was used here. For another thing, there are all sorts of kinds of probabilities, all sorts of kinds of area samples. I can give you a kind of probability sample which gives you very good results for any given size of sample. There are many aspects of this sample here, and I would want to know something more about comparing magnitudes of bias and variance in this particular job.

Let me talk about this thing of bias and variance, and give you another typical illustration. Suppose you could afford a sample of three people, and you want to predict the election in the United States. You want to predict any kind of characteristic that you know a fair amount about, or someone knows a lot about. Or let's take instead a sample of ten people.

Let's consider two ways you might go about getting statistics on this matter as to the number of people that are going to vote a particular way, or the number of people that have a particular attitude, or the number of people employed or unemployed, or something else in the United States.

One way of getting information on that kind of question, if you could afford a sample of ten people, would be to go out and get a probability sample or another quota sample. Another way would be to ask the judgment of a reasonably well-informed person, one person. Now, which of these do you think you'd choose on a sample of ten? I can tell you. I'd choose the good judgment rather than a sample of ten sampled at random, probability, purposefully, or anything else.

This is the same principle I was talking about a minute ago, between the bias of quota and variance. Now one of the problems that is involved and what you often get into, in talking about why area samples will give poor results—Dr. Meier did a little here too —is trying to take the sample and break it down into very small pieces. You can demonstrate normal discrepancies in a very small element which you don't perceive when you get a big sample. When you have a big sample and try to get highly precise results, the biases are what you want to fear. With the smaller sample it's the variances you want to fear.

It's exceedingly important to have in mind those principles in deciding where you are going to spend your money on any particular job. When we spend our money on jobs, we use judgments when the level is low enough; when the size of the sample we are going to be able to afford is larger we use purposive techniques; and we use random when we are really putting the money into it.

MR. SAUNDERS: I think we will permit one more question or statement, if someone so desires.

MR. JESSEN: I might make a few remarks or rather comment on a few remarks made by Dr. Meier here. One rather incidental, but I think rather important, is that I wish he would check into his history as to whether or not the statement is true that the Bureau of the Census followed the Statistical Laboratory with the area type of sampling.

Another one, it is true that the Statistical Laboratory did draw the sample that Dr. Meier described. I would like to point out this, however, that the Statistical Laboratory had nothing to do with the field work. I do not have any knowledge whatsoever as to the accuracy with which that field work was done, the extent to which the work was actually carried out according to the advice that we gave on the matter, and I don't know to what extent they got complete information on these areas, which might explain quite a lot of the discrepancies that appeared in the discussion.

Other than that, I would like to say that I agree very much with the discussion of Mr. Hansen on our general attitudes toward the use of random samples, area samples, and the judgment of individuals; that we too follow pretty much that kind of practice, and I don't think there is much to be said on the matter of which is better in general. It all depends upon the problem.

MR. MEIER: In answer to Dr. Jessen's remarks, I can only say that the field work in the Iowa study was carried out by competent and experienced interviewers well informed on the requirements of both methods. Every detail of the study was planned well in advance, in Ames, Iowa City, and Des Moines. Some of the interviewing *was* checked. The study followed every precept of careful experimental design. It is unnecessary to assume that every detail was carried out perfectly for no field work probably ever is, but conditions were as close to optimum as one can reasonably expect, with no known advantage to either method. Let me reiterate that this was a test of the actual workability of the two methods in actual public opinion sampling under similar conditions and under the usual requirements.

In the field a method has to stand on its own feet. I sincerely hope that there may be more such studies, adequately planned, amply financed, carried out in the field by competent personnel under circumstances fair to both methods, for only in that way can real progress toward clarifying methodological problems be advanced.

I would also like to refer back to Mr. Hornseth's remark that these results could well have been an accident. Perhaps it is not widely known that the Granneberg study, made in Seattle about three years ago, came out with similar results, and that two nation-wide surveys made independently but concurrently in 1946 yielded results that were very similar in findings.

On the other hand would Mr. Hornseth regard the recent Washington outcome as *not* an accident? With about 20 percent of the area respondents still not contacted, and with numerous substitutions (around 40 percent, wasn't it?) ; with a *deficiency* of farmers "who were Republican" and an *excess* of women who were Truman voters —these two last conditions, other things being equal, could alone have produced the "uncanny" results, quite apart from probability sampling. In fact, had it not been for those two biases operating to pull up the Truman percentage on a small sample (four hundred actually contacted) the result could have been a Truman underestimation, close to their quota result as other polls showed instead of being "right on the nose." Hitting an election on the nose has been done many times by quota methods, for that matter.

MR. SAUNDERS: Thank you, ladies and gentlemen. I hope you can continue this discussion elsewhere another time.

(Meeting adjourned.)

19

SHOULD POLITICAL FORECASTS BE MADE?

Virgil M. Hancher, Presiding
Gideon Seymour
Archibald M. Crossley
Paul F. Lazarsfeld
George H. Gallup

MR. HANCHER: Ladies and gentlemen of the visible audience, and ladies and gentlemen of the radio audience. I wish to welcome you to this discussion, to this forum.

The order of the speakers will be: Mr. Seymour, Mr. Crossley, Mr. Lazarsfeld, and Mr. Gallup. The subject is *Should Political Forecasts Be Made?*

The gentlemen who are to speak this evening have been much exposed to polling and to polling techniques. Therefore I trust that they will not resemble the typical college or university president who has once been described as "a man who sits with the slightly detached air of one who had heard all of that somewhere before." Whatever the speakers' familiarity with the subject may be, "this audience has not heard all of that somewhere before," and by its continued interest in the successive sessions of the Conference, has demonstrated its desire to learn more about the general subject of the Conference.

You will note the words of the topic: "Should Political Forecasts Be Made?", not "Will They Be Made?" There is, I suppose, no law by which we could stop the making of political forecasts. And I am sure that political campaign leaders and particularly the chairmen of the national committees would explode in any campaign if they were not permitted to make their own predictions. But what we are talking about this evening is, as I interpret it, political forecasting of a more scientific character, and the effect which that forecasting may be expected to have upon our social organizations and our body politic.

The first speaker on tonight's program will be Mr. Gideon Seymour, Vice-President and Executive Editor of the *Minneapolis Star and Tribune*. We are very happy to welcome him here. His brother is the editorial editor of the *Des Moines Register* and the family is, as you well know, interested in newspaper activities and in public opinion forecasting.

MR. SEYMOUR: I am speaking tonight strictly as a newspaper editor and solely from the standpoint of one whose business it is to publish the news, and not as any kind of an expert in the measurement of public opinion. But I speak as one of a considerable number of newspaper editors who still have great faith in the measurement of public opinion. Dr. Gallup may not know this, but the contract of the *Minneapolis Tribune* with the American Institute of Public Opinion provides that it is cancelable immediately in case of his death or disability, and we have not even put in a claim for partial disability! (*Laughter.*)

I have been communicating in the last few days with our Washington Bureau to ask whom we should nominate this year for the Raymond Clapper Award, which was won by a member of our Washington Bureau last year, and whom we should nominate for the Pulitzer Prize for the most distinguished Washington correspondence, which also was won last year by a member of the *Minneapolis Star and Tribune* staff. In answer to both questions our Washington Bureau said, "We think we haven't anything to submit for 1948." They added, "It's too bad, too, because there aren't going to be very many entries from Washington correspondents, either for the Clapper Award or the Pulitzer Prize." I asked, "Why is that?" "Well, because the election campaign of 1948 was the big news, and every Washington correspondent was utterly wrong on the biggest story of the year."

So it isn't, you see, simply that the pollsters were wrong on the election. Everybody was wrong. The Washington correspondents were all wrong and they were just as wrong as the pollsters. Almost all the politicians were wrong—witness the fact that three, maybe four, of Mr. Truman's cabinet did not get around to contribute to the Truman campaign fund until after the second of November! Everybody was wrong on the election.

All right, the polls should have been right, even though everybody else was wrong. Well, sure, but at least it isn't a case of somebody else having been proved more accurate than the pollsters, in this important business of finding out what the public was going to do on November second.

The general tendency to discredit polls, following the November election, had two chief causes. One was, of course, that the public tends to reduce everything to black and white, to try to find some simple reason for blame. The blame for miscalling the result of the presidential election of 1948 landed on the polls, partly because they were a new scapegoat and partly because they professed to have greater insight, through scientific methods, than the politicians.

The second reason was that the politicians have never liked public opinion polls. Politicians just don't like to have public opinion measurement usurping their prerogative, muscling in on their racket, so to speak, of keeping their ears to the ground. It's the politicians who from time immemorial have said *they* would tell the public what the voters thought. When a Gallup Poll or Crossley Poll or Roper Poll says, "This is what the voters think," the politician is immediately stripped of one of his dearest prerogatives— that of saying, "I know from my mail," or "I know from talking to my constituents what the people think, and only I can interpret the voice of the people." Every politician resents that.

Mr. Truman said the other day, on January 27 as a matter of fact, that even though the Gallup Poll indicated that 69 percent of the voters approve of his actions, he, President Truman, has no use for it or any other polls. He told his White House press conference he has no more confidence in polls now than he did before the election; he never did have any and he still has none; his decisions were made on the basis of what is right or wrong, and the polls had no effect on him whatever.

That's the politician speaking.

I can speak about public opinion measurement in good humor and without bitterness because, as Dr. Gallup can testify, our Minnesota poll did pretty well. We ran a state poll in Minnesota which indicated pretty clearly all through the campaign that Hubert Humphrey, the Democratic candidate for senator against Joe Ball, was going to be successful. It showed that certainly he would be elected if there was a large vote, and that if there was, President Truman was by all odds likely to carry the state, but that Luther Youngdahl, Republican governor, would be re-elected. And those three things happened, so we didn't do too badly. As the French philosopher, La Rochefoucauld, said, "Heaven always gives us the fortitude to endure the adversities of our friends."

I want to make six principal points about the making of political forecasts by public opinion polls. First, let me read a paragraph from the report of the Social Science Research Council Committee on analysis of pre-election polls: "Election forecasts from polls are hazardous. This fact might tempt some polling organizations in the future to limit their political studies to attitudes which cannot be checked up at elections. Thus, they could avoid the spotlight of a public audit of their work. The Committee would view such a step with concern, for all possible tests of opinion studies are needed. Elections are useful for testing the adequacy of polling methods for estimating the percentage of the vote going to each candidate from various groups in the population. No better test is now known."

In the second place, and this in many respects is the most important point, I want to say that opinion studies are eminently newsworthy. Traditionally the news has dealt with two dimensions of social behavior, first, the facts of day-to-day occurrences, and second, the opinions of leaders in the community, expressed through interviews with them in the news columns or through summaries by writers, or reports of the things that they have had to say in public speeches and statements. Public opinion surveying has now brought to newspaper work a third dimension in the coverage of the news. It reflects the impact of ideas and prejudices and events and propaganda upon the people themselves. It is simply news reporting in a new field, a field that has to be studied if a newspaper is to report fully the trends and patterns of the times and of the changing world.

The third point is this: Elmo Roper wrote recently in his newspaper column, "Suppose we grant that election polls do have a scientific purpose. There still remains the problem of their social usefulness." Here he says, "There is some doubt in my mind, still unresolved." Mr. Roper is concerned lest the 1948 polls may have influenced the outcome of the election, even to influencing the choice of the parties' candidates and the campaigns waged by the candidates. But the challenges aimed at the polls since the second of November have been better grounded, it seems to me, in criticisms directed at interpretation of poll data, rather than in criticisms of the relative accuracy of the findings at the time of the surveys.

The Social Science Research Council Committee report says again: "Looking at all the evidence now available, the Committee tentatively concludes that in the last two weeks of the campaign there was a net shift to Truman of two or three percentage points, probably varying quite a bit from state to state. Indeed, there is a remote possibility that the shift could have been large enough to make Gallup's and Crossley's last pre-election survey not too far off the mark, as of two weeks before the election."

A newspaper which is basically concerned with accuracy in news reporting expects that polls of public opinion will, in general, meet the same criteria for accuracy as are imposed for other kinds of news. If the technique is sound but interpretations are faulty, then we need great attention to development of sound techniques. There is every reason to expect that this development will take place, especially with the impetus of the November results to push us on.

One thing seems certain, that future pre-election poll reports will differ from those offered in the past, in that they will confine themselves to facts as established and will suggest only such alternative outcomes as the facts may warrant.

In the fourth place, the wave of shock and disillusionment which swept the country on November third, when it was established that the polls had erred in their appraisal of the election results, would have been nowhere nearly as great if the public had had a fuller understanding of what polling entails. That has been so widely developed in other sessions of this conference that I need not elaborate on it here, but all agencies of communication which are users of poll materials share the responsibility for educating the public far more adequately to an understanding of the strength and weaknesses of public opinion measurement, and for picturing clearly the limitations that operate.

That is one field in which I think the Minnesota poll and all the rest of the polls have been guilty. They got a little too sure of themselves and tended to claim more for themselves than they themselves believe to be true about their own capacities. They just pressed their luck a little too far.

Well, let me correct that statement, because I don't like to use the word "luck" in this connection, but the feat of having hit result

after result pretty well on the nose made them careless about interpretation of their data or even about their techniques, and at the
same time tended to let the public presume that this science was a
more nearly exact one than the pollsters themselves, as evidenced
in such conferences as this, actually believe it to be.

In the fifth place, well, the *Minneapolis Tribune* editorially advo-
cated the re-election of Senator Ball, but it presented Minnesota poll
reports which consistently indicated throughout the campaign that
Humphrey was going to win. Was there social usefulness in presenting factual poll findings running contrary to the editorial position
taken by the newspapers? From the viewpoint of the readers, the
answer can only be, "Yes."

Now, finally, why do we make pre-election polls? Why make political forecasts? In the first place, candidates and campaign man-
agers and other partisans are never-ending in their claims and
counter-claims and predictions during the campaign. The polls, conducted on an impartial basis, seek to bring a factual background
against which such claims and statements can be weighed. They
form another element in the over-all picture and add proportion to
it, susceptible to biases from a dozen different sources.

The score of experts in appraising political tides is substantially
poorer than that of the polls, even if you include 1948. From the
newspapers' standpoint, public opinion polls on non-election issues
may be as important as or even more important than those dealing
with elections.

When election day comes, election issues settle themselves. Perhaps the polls' greatest opportunity for service in gauging public
opinion is to be found in the multitude of important issues that
never come to a popular vote. In many respects such surveys may
serve a more useful social purpose than the efforts to assess the intentions of the voters. The rigid tests to which polls are subject
in forecasting elections do provide a means of evaluating their performance and accuracy. It isn't that they are correct in their findings on all non-election issues, but rather there is indication that the
polls thus demonstrate their ability to grapple with the peculiarly
difficult problems of elections and in so doing advance their methods
of research for use in other fields.

So to my mind the question whether polls should make political
forecasts is hardly debatable. Political forecasts should be made by
means of public opinion measurement if that is the best means by

which to make political forecasts. The newspapers are going to make political forecasts somehow. They have done it in the past by various means. One was by quoting the politicians—if a newspaper was leaning ardently enough in one direction it quoted only the politicians of its own party; if it was reasonably neutral, it quoted the claims of both sides, and the reader had to judge for himself which was able to make the more convincing statement of expected victory. The newspapers have used straw votes, back before the days of scientific opinion measurement, knowing that straw votes didn't mean much of anything. The newspapers sent their political reporters country-wide, state-wide, to attempt to say how the election was coming out.

The public opinion poll superseded these methods of trying to ascertain what the public was going to do. The public demands that a newspaper, as a very part of reporting the election campaign, do its best to tell how the election is coming out; that's part of the news. And if the measurement of public opinion, the public opinion poll, the political poll or survey, by the Gallup method or the Roper method or Crossley method, is the best way of providing that service to the reader, then political forecasts are going to continue to be made. And if Gallup, Crossley, and Roper all go out of business, then other machinery, other mechanisms for measuring public opinion, will be set up to take their place.

So there isn't any question that political forecasting by this means is going to continue until and unless a better means is found. I think everybody, even the ones who made the loudest fun of the polls, is pretty well convinced that public opinion measurement by this means is the most nearly accurate method of telling the public what it is likely to do at the polls. I hope and expect that Messers Gallup, Roper, and Crossley and the rest will be back at it in 1952, to tell us whether the next President of the United States is going to be Franklin D. Truman, William Jennings Dewey or even Ulysses S. Eisenhower.

MR. HANCHER: I should like at this time to tell the audience that at the conclusion of the four talks which are the formal part of the program, there will be an opportunity for questions from members of the audience directed to one or more of the participants. I hope you will be thinking of the questions, that you will make them penetrating, difficult, and interesting. Having seen a great many questions or heard a great many questions answered which didn't deserve an answer, I added that third point.

At this time I should like to present as the second speaker, Mr. Archibald Crossley.

MR. CROSSLEY: Ladies and gentlemen, the question is, "Should Political Forecasts Be Made?" The answer is "No" (*laughter*). I think I might just as well sit down at this point, but the radio people would like to have me use up a few minutes of time so I will take up a few angles of this "No." You probably would like to know why not. Well, they used to teach me when I was a small youngster that it would be a very good thing for me to go up and touch a red-hot stove—and I did (*laughter*).

But entirely aside from the experience factor, there is also the question of what we can do in forecasting. Can we be sure that any forecast we make will actually be safe? The answer is "No." We are by nature, in public opinion and marketing research business, great hedgers. And I can tell you that it doesn't come easy and natural to us to come out and make a definite statement that Dewey will be the next president, or even to make a statement when we submit a report to a manufacturer that this product is going to go and the other one isn't. We just naturally hide behind our figures.

So in this particular case, when we did make a forecast we did it partly because we were importuned on all sides. For the several times that we have carried on polls, you have probably noticed that time and time again in our stories we said we could be three or four points out of the way. As Gallup said today, probably you'd have to go out with a sound truck and announce the fact that you are going to be three or four points out of the way. We seem to have tired people with our three or four points. I guess we tired ourselves too, but anyhow we stopped saying it or we didn't make very much noise about it. Now I wish we had started off all our stories with something like "Please believe this within three or four percentage points."

Trends? Yes. Not forecasts. Trends are a matter of reporting what you see. I think we should do more of trend reporting and less of saying what those trends may lead to. If it should develop as it did in the polls that Truman was rising, fine. Let's show that. It doesn't necessarily mean you should say Truman would be President, but merely to present those figures as they show up in trends.

Well now, you may say, perhaps, "If you don't feel like making a forecast any more, is that due to the fact that you have had trouble in this one election only?" Yes, that is correct. We have had some pretty good fortune in previous elections and maybe we were a little too satisfied. In the past election, in 1944, we came within 1.6, and in 1940 we came within 1.8, so we thought in 1948 by using similar methods that we would not have much trouble. One of the things that we have learned, and you have heard about that today, is that changes occur during the campaign in the attitude of the people as to their actually voting for President. We were perhaps lulled into believing that campaigns do not change or add votes. And yet as we look back on some of our own figures we see that that is not entirely the case.

During the Willkie campaign we used a question which asked, "When did you make up your mind?" And we followed that along week after week, month after month. We noticed the thing was working, and we noticed it produced a very definite trend. That trend was showing a rise for Willkie. But Willkie was still in the minority; Roosevelt was ahead all the time. Willkie was approaching the fifty-fifty point and then the Roosevelt campaign, with his usual tactics, got started late. Immediately the Willkie curve flattened, started moving slightly down, and the Roosevelt curve increased greatly. We knew from the speed of the movement that Willkie couldn't possibly gather enough votes in that time to be elected.

So we said at the time that there was no chance that we could see that Willkie would be elected. Well, then we carried our interviewing right up close to election time. This time we didn't do it. We stopped three weeks before the election, and didn't gather any reports after that. We should have kept on, and then we might possibly have been able to make a more accurate forecast. I very much doubt in my mind, however, whether we would have forecast a Truman election if we had carried on interviews the night before and wired the story for publication on the morning of November second.

Well, you will have to realize, as many of you do, what is involved in forecasting. You know there are two great questions of which the first is the question of taking a sample of the public. And the second question, which is much the more difficult, is the question of finding out who will vote. And that is the great question which we have not answered.

Now, as for forecasting in general, if you leave out the word "political," I would change my answer from "No" to "Yes." If you said, "Should forecasting of any kind be done?" I would say, "Yes, by all means." Because we are forecasting all of the time. Many things that we are doing in business require forecasting. We are really forecasting continually in our daily lives.

We are asked in our public opinion and marketing research to tell industry what type of a product will sell best. The only thing we can tell them is what type, what brand, what pattern, will work best right now, before any advertising or any salesmanship comes into the picture. From that point on, the manufacturer must discover what is going to happen when salesmanship and advertising are introduced. Whether that promotion is going to be of his own origination or whether it is competitive doesn't matter. There are those impulses which have to be taken into account.

One of the reasons why we have carried on polling has been that we feel very strongly that we must find a way to do forecasting. We feel it is very important to find that way for industry. We don't yet know how to do it; we don't yet know how to measure the impact of oncoming advertising and oncoming salesmanship.

In this particular campaign we feel that the one thing we didn't know how to do was to measure the impact of the salesmanship that was brought to bear. We feel that this is a subject to which we must devote a great deal of effort. We are working on it. Gallup is making great strides in it. And we think we are. Many of us are working along that particular line, to try to measure the imponderability of the impact of advertising and salesmanship. We are going to continue to that end.

Mr. Hancher: I shall now present as the third speaker on this evening's program, Dr. Paul F. Lazarsfeld, Director of the Bureau of Applied Social Research of Columbia University.

Mr. Lazarsfeld: Ladies and gentlemen, I am at this moment in a very strategic position. Mr. Seymour's address said that there should be forecasts; Crossley was against it. So the future of political forecasting depends on how I will cast my vote (*laughter*).

A man trained in political science tries to save his vote—he sells his vote as dearly as possible. And my position indeed is that ·I am inclined to vote, and I am inclined to vote "Yes, they should be done," but for a price (*laughter*). The price I shall try to extort from my friend Gallup and others in his position is that my "Yes" vote should be contingent on this: if I let them forecast, if I let them make political forecasts of the future, they should use their prestige and they should use those occasions to contribute, during presidential elections and while they are making such forecasts, to our general knowledge of the problems involved.

And to talk a little bit more seriously, I am very definitely in favor of political forecasts because only by trying and trying over again to make political forecasts will we finally learn to understand what really explains political behavior of people. And to go even further, I find the whole problem a little bit silly.

Suppose you were to ask a natural scientist whether the volume of a ball of iron that is put into a fire should be forecast? He would laugh at you. He would say that forecasting and explaining are really the same. It is just looking at the same phenomenon from two different angles. If I understand something I can also predict what will happen, and if I cannot predict I also cannot understand. It is a triviality of undergraduate courses that predicting and explaining are the same thing in two terminologies, and certainly no one will seriously raise the question, "Should political behavior be understood?" (*Laughter.*)

But you can of course run the prediction business—it is not easy, but you can run it so that it does not contribute to understanding. On the other hand you could raise the question, "In which way could the explanatory, the scientific function of prediction be strengthened?" I think it could be strengthened if during times of political electioneering and engineering of political affairs, we would form the business of forecasting into a more systematic analysis than many of us have done before.

There are a number of ways in which that can be done. I mentioned this morning for instance that much more attention to studies on the state level would be most desirable. I think our emphasis on national studies is not enough. Only if you understand your local conditions in a state as well as do some of the people here from Minnesota and Iowa who talked to us today and explained them to us—only then can you hope that you will make really good analysis. Maybe we should even go down to the community level.

When I came back from Europe, where I fortunately was on November second (*laughter*), I was really dumbfounded when I realized that in a way I had the glory of my life in my hand and lost it. In 1945 when O'Dwyer ran for mayor the second time, and won the election in New York after he had lost it the first time in 1941, I was surprised by a series of studies we made at the time.

The New York newspaper, the *Daily News*, had made a series of polls in 1945. It had predicted O'Dwyer's election with 67 percent and no one paid at the time any attention to the fact that O'Dwyer won only with 57 percent. That is to say, the *Daily News* was ten percent wrong. My own office in New York City had done a study at the same time just for our own interest—we never published it—and we were also ten percent wrong. We had exactly the same figures as the *Daily News*. And no one paid any attention to it. Why? Because O'Dwyer had won anyhow, and what difference did it make? (*Laughter*.) I concluded then that it made no difference in those matters, but as we came to realize later on, the ten percent can make a considerable difference.

So I went back to my data and to my original material, which I fortunately still have to this time, and I think I have a pretty good theory why O'Dwyer lost the election—that is to say, why he won it only with 57 percent and not with 67 percent. And as I am not such a gentleman and scholar as people from the Social Science Research Council, I will not try to keep this as a state document and hedge back and forth, but I will tell you what I think happened (*laughter*). And looking at my simple figures, the situation was quite simple.

Up to practically the last day there was a twenty percent "Don't know" in the voters. The twenty percent of the people couldn't make up their minds between O'Dwyer and Goldstein who was the Republican candidate, and that is very unusual. Those twenty percent were probably mostly Jewish voters in New York who were under cross pressure. The whole Roosevelt tradition, Mrs. Roosevelt and anyone who meant anything in the New Deal, came out strongly for O'Dwyer. But the Republican candidate was a Jew—Goldstein, a Jewish judge—and was definitely selected to be a Jewish candidate in anticipation of such a situation. A large proportion of the Jewish vote, therefore, was squeezed between an ideological adherence to the Roosevelt support, and racial and religious interest in the Republican candidate. In the end they voted for a third candidate, Newbold Morris.

The newspaper *PM* at the time came out for O'Dwyer until about ten days or so before the election and then this liberal newspaper, under somewhat similar cross pressure, shifted to Newbold Morris. So we could have anticipated the terrific catastrophe, an earthquake which actually happened ten days later, only no one paid the slightest attention to it, including myself. If I had even published, or at least looked more carefully at those local figures, I would have precisely foreseen the repetition of this, three years later in the Truman campaign—and I would now be a respected and prosperous man and not have to earn my living by talking four times a day! (*Laughter.*)

Now I have not the slightest doubt—I understood it so clearly when I listened this morning to the Director of the Iowa Poll —how much serious study of local conditions and local situations, including all such factors of which this New York episode is only one of hundreds, would improve our knowledge of political behavior and therewith our ability to forecast.

As a matter of fact, you could go even further. You could go back to times when there weren't any polls—there were such times once in the dim past—and you could look at history books and they are full of such examples. Mr. Blaine lost an election because some obscure minister talked of Rum, Romanism, and Rebellion. Mr. Bryan lost an election because some rich men came together and gave more money than McKinley had ever seen before. The whole history books are full of stories, legends so to say, why elections are lost and won, and that is why it is wise to go back to those stories and look at them with the eyes of a public opinion man. Indeed, one of my students, Robert Bower, has published such a collection in the *Public Opinion Quarterly*, and even this historical material would be a help to this type of work we are doing here.

But in addition to historical studies, and in addition to the study of specifically local situations where you understand all the factors much better and can therefore make much more important contributions, I personally, as some of you know, am a great believer in a third type of poll, another approach to this more detailed study of elections.

Since 1940, first alone, and now we are doing it in cooperation with other universities, especially Chicago and Cornell, we have done this: we have picked a community and incidentally it was not to be a representative community of any kind, it is just a test community. And about six months before the election we have sent staffs of interviewers and analysts into this community and kept the community under observation from about May just prior to the convention until the middle of November after the election.

I rely here on our chairman that when he said the audience doesn't know everything, that was good advice, so I will explain in a few words what those studies were like. You pick a representative sample in this community—a quota sample or an area sample, whatever the fashion is—and you reinterview those people about once a month. That has varied. In one year we made seven interviews; in another year we made five interviews. There are different considerations on how to proceed, but the essence is that you reinterview the same people several times, and by reinterviewing the same people you can pick out those who changed their minds during the time before the election. And those people become your guinea pigs to understand what goes on during the election and how it affects people.

You see, if you were not to interview the same people then you would say five percent more are for Truman, or five percent less are for Truman, but you wouldn't be able to pick out who was for Truman the last time and who is against him now. You wouldn't catch the changes. How do you find out why they change? Partly you can ask them, but much more important, you can plan the study so that if people have changed you have then afterwards enough material to really explain this change.

Let me give you one or two examples from the last study we did —this time in Elmira in upstate New York—to give you just the feeling for the material. Let me say incidentally that we never tried in the slightest degree to forecast. The problem simply was to get a community where we could hope that changes come about that we could study.

We suspected from the beginning that certain issues like price control and the Taft-Hartley bill would play a considerable role. So in August we gave our people a long list of issues like how they feel about housing, about price control, about the labor issues, and so on, and let them vote on it, and we also asked them for what candidate they intended to vote.

Then we cross-tabulated their voting intention with their opinion of issues and it was most interesting and still is interesting to note that in August there was a great difference between people who wanted to vote Republican and people who wanted to vote Democratic. The intended Democrats by and large were in agreement

with the Democratic platform. They were for price control and for
the housing bill and they were all for Truman. But people who intended to vote for Dewey were almost split on major issues, especially on price control.

There were people who definitely said, "I intend to vote for
Dewey, and I have no use for Truman," but when you asked them,
"Do you think the cost of living can go down without considerable
price controls coming back?" those intended Republicans said yes,
they wanted price control. And it was so on housing. It was considerably less so, incidentally, on the labor issue, the Taft-Hartley bill.
In other words, the intended Republicans turned out to have an unstable attitude structure. The vote on issues and vote on candidate
were not in harmony for the intended Republicans, as it was for
the intended Democrats.

We then went back to our data after the election and of course
that is not hindsight, that is what the technique consists of. We
could pick out the people who had shifted from Dewey to Truman
over those five months and it was a considerable number, about
seven percent. The great majority of those shifters who had shifted
from a Republican vote-intention to a Democratic vote-intention
came from that group who had this contradictory attitude pattern,
who on a number of important items were not in agreement with
their own platform.

And my contention is that you can obviously, slowly, develop a
theory of change, a theory of susceptibility to propaganda or whatever you want to call it. It is possible to formulate a theory of political activity, and I think this is essentially what the campaign
does: it brings out underlying contradictions in a person's whole
political attitude pattern, and if the campaign is vigorous enough,
it forces at least a small number of those contradictory patterns to
get harmonized, in terms of shifting politically in the election.

I could go on and give you other examples. For instance, it turned
out during the summer that a lot of workers in Elmira were in favor
of Dewey, partly they were always in favor of him, and partly they
had been Roosevelt voters in 1944 and now intended not to vote for
Truman. We wanted to know, because we found from previous
studies that the class issue is very important, whether we could
codify a little bit their class position. And we asked them the question, "Would you think you belong to the working class or to the
middle class?" We had then two groups of workers—those workers

who called themselves middle-class people, and those workers who called themselves working-class people. They had the same objective position but a different attitude toward their own class position, whether they looked at themselves as up-coming middle class people or as working people.

We then picked out those workers who intended to vote for Dewey in August and divided them as to whether they counted themselves as workers or as middle-class people. And again we found that an intended Republican worker who looked at himself as a worker was more likely to change to Truman in the last weeks of the campaign than a Republican worker who looked at himself as a middle-class man.

You see, in this way again, we could show the element which a definite class appeal in Truman's campaign played, and it didn't consist in changing people's attitude but in bringing people's attitude out. Those workers who called themselves workers were more easily swayed by a campaign which contained very strongly a working-class appeal.

I think such kind of analysis will slowly contribute to systematic knowledge. But it requires hard thinking in advance. If you haven't had good ideas, good questions like this theory of cost-of-living pressures or this theory of class identification, if you haven't had this idea in August, after that it is too late.

You see, you cannot after the election ask the people, "Why did you change in August?" You have to have the best picture of the attitude structure in August, and then you have to wait and see what happens. If you are lucky, then you can explain why certain people change in the light of what you found out about them in August, but only if you were wise enough to think about what to ask them, and therefore those studies have to be of a very cumulative nature. We can very easily show by these studies how we learn from one election to the other. They are very expensive, and financing of the 1952 panel study is only guaranteed now because that was a condition under which I voted for the continuation of political forecasts (laughter).

Now the story has, however, to be ended with a rather serious reminder, not only to you but unfortunately also to myself. There is a danger, especially in the beginning of the studies and the first thirty-forty years you are making them, that you generalize too quickly. And the question of what result is due to special circumstances and what you can carry over as a kind of general knowledge is quite serious. My friend Stouffer today at lunch ribbed me by saying I am the man who said that campaigns don't make any difference. Now fortunately I have almost as good an alibi as George here, who read an article yesterday which he published before the election that said he didn't mean it in quite this way. I too, in an introduction to a book, stressed very much that you cannot generalize. I even said, discussing the last four elections—look at how lucky I am—I said the next election might bring into the foreground labor issues and that might change the situation completely (*laughter*). I said it in 1947, but I didn't exactly take a sound truck. So I am a little in the same boat as my polling friends are, on a somewhat different problem.

We certainly in our earlier studies underrated the whole effect of propaganda. Why did we? Essentially because, since 1940 when we started those studies, probably even earlier, elections were for or against Roosevelt. The 1948 election had many more unstable attitude patterns among the people, and therefore in a way I think the election campaign made a difference. But now the difficulty is that I would have to qualify that again, because we shouldn't think that if you just make enough propaganda you can sway everyone. I think the right solution is that we should slowly, from these studies, find out under which conditions does propaganda make a difference, and under which conditions doesn't it make a difference. I think this notion of finding out in time what kind of cross-pressures and unstable attitude patterns exist will greatly help to slowly specify under which conditions propaganda matters.

In addition to that I think we can very safely say, on the grounds of four or five studies—different studies which we have done so far—that we should never think of propaganda, election propaganda, as basically changing people's attitudes. Propaganda, in my opinion, changes a little bit the balance of elements among those prospective voters who have quite a complicated and inconsistent attitude pattern. Consistent attitude patterns, I still feel, are not changed by propaganda.

Well, however much I would like to lecture to you for two or three more hours on this very fascinating topic, I have now to cede the final decision on the issue to George Gallup. But I hope he will agree with me that we should not look at forecasting as just getting a lot of nice figures and being right or wrong: to boast when we are right, and to find good alibis when we are wrong. I hope he will agree that forecasting elections should be part of the much more general process of analyzing what goes on during elections by considering local situations which are studied for many, many months in often very laborious techniques, so that the poll in the end becomes a part of the analysis of political behavior.

MR. HANCHER: I should like to present as the closing speaker on the main part of the program, Mr. George Gallup.

MR. GALLUP: Ladies and gentlemen, Should political forecasts be made? My answer is "Yes." I like to live dangerously (laughter).

I have said many times that I see no great social value in reporting twenty-four hours in advance of an election how the country is going to vote, or approximately how it is going to vote, but I do think that elections are valuable in providing an acid test for polling techniques. As a matter of fact, it is the best test that we people in research have to measure the reliability of our procedures.

Certainly it's the only time when we have to stand up in public and be counted. Now that is a fairly dangerous thing to do, particularly at this point in the development of polling techniques. When I say I think that we should make forecasts, I am praying that the next election won't be as close as the last one, believe me!

As I said earlier today, I believe we can reduce the error in our forecasts by perhaps one percentage point or even two percentage points, and normally that margin of error would be small enough to enable us to be on the right side most of the time. But I'd like to repeat again the statement that I have made from the very day we started this work, and that is that with the same certainty that we know can be right most of the time, we know that we will be wrong some of the time. It has to be that way. We live by the law of probabilities and we may die that way too (laughter).

As long as we have good friends like Gideon Seymour, we will do our best to improve our methods and to do better the next time. While I see no great social value in making these forecasts—as a matter of fact, I think the only justification for public opinion polls is to report the views of the people of this country on issues of the day—I fail to see any great danger in these forecasts either. Although I fail to see that election forecasts work any good, I certainly see no harm in them, either.

One of the most persistent arguments raised from the very beginning against us and against all election polls, was that we created a band-wagon movement. We have always argued against this theory. I honestly believe that if the political scientists of this country had set up an ideal situation to test the band-wagon theory, they couldn't possibly have selected a better test than the 1948 election.

In 1948, not only did every single Washington correspondent and every political writer say that Mr. Dewey would win, but the polls all said Mr. Dewey would win. And the majority of the people of this country believed that Mr. Dewey would win.

So I say that probably not in the entire history of this country has there been a better test of the so-called band-wagon theory than that provided by the election of 1948. So at least we have destroyed that theory. Even the *New York Times* said in at least one of its articles that the band-wagon theory was thoroughly destroyed in this election.

I believe that forecasting elections presents a real challenge to all of us in this field of research. And I have a sort of sadistic desire to get a lot of other people into this business of forecasting (*laughter*). What I should like to do is to urge that every social scientist in this country make a forecast in the next election. And when I say "next" I don't mean 1952. I mean the very next election in all of the college communities in this country.

We are going to go "hellbent" into the New Jersey elections this fall. We hope to try two or three different systems of forecasting or sampling. This whole business, as I say, represents such a challenge to me that I will never be happy until I know that we have this problem licked.

What I'd like to suggest is this: that every social scientist in this country, who is interested in this problem of public opinion and of political forecasts, make a study in the next election in his own community, send his results to the *Public Opinion Quarterly* or the Social Science Research Council, *before* the election (*laughter*) and let us all see how good these people are.

First of all, it would acquaint a good many of our critics with the problems that we face. And secondly, it is entirely possible that someone, somewhere, would come up with some of the answers, or at least one of the answers, to the many problems which face us in this business of making forecasts. We should not have to do all the experimental work in this field.

I think this suggestion is not at all unreasonable because I believe that every professor in this country can use his own students to do the interviewing. He can make a prediction in the community in which he lives, and probably at little or no expense.

As a matter of fact, I plan to announce at some time in the near future some cash awards for those people who find that they can predict elections within one or two or three percentage points. We have seriously considered this plan of setting up achievement awards for accurate predictions by social scientists.

I'd like to take this opportunity to refute a point of view that many of our critics subscribed to and that is the idea that if you happen to be wrong in an election you should fall dead (*laughter*). Early in this business I said that if at any time in our history we were half as wrong as the *Literary Digest* was in 1936 we would go out of business voluntarily. That still holds.

The *Literary Digest* had an error of nineteen percentage points in the 1936 election. If we are ever half that wrong I will take up some other profession, probably plumbing. The fact of the matter is, it's pretty naive to believe that the *Literary Digest* went out of business because of its wrong prediction in 1936. It was going out of business long before the 1936 prediction. What killed the *Literary Digest* was an upstart magazine called *Time*. As soon as *Time* entered the scene the *Literary Digest* began to lose ground slowly but surely.

DISCUSSION

MR. HANCHER: At this time we shall have questions from the audience if questions remain in your minds. When you address them, I hope you will give me an opportunity to repeat them for the benefit of the radio audience. Are there questions to be asked of these distinguished gentlemen?

MRS. CROSSLEY: I'd like to ask a question about the band-wagon. I'd like to ask Mr. Seymour what he thinks of the effect this does have in reverse, what effect on human nature's tendency to be perverse, the tendency the people have to vote differently? I'd like to know if you saw any of that in your newspaper, what effect the polls have on the general public?

MR. HANCHER: Do polls arouse our human nature so we are inclined to go in reverse?

MR. SEYMOUR: Is that an accurate repetition of your question? Do polls arouse human nature so people are likely to act in reverse, or are you asking whether a newspaper's editorial attitude is likely to make them act in reverse?

MRS. CROSSLEY: No, as to whether the polls do.

MR. SEYMOUR: You get it both ways. If a poll shows Candidate A leading, certain people are going to say, well, they just manipulate that to show Candidate A ahead because they are for Candidate B, so he will get busy and go to work. If it shows Candidate B leading, they want to create a band-wagon vote. I personally can't see any more justification in one theory than the other. I think they are both nonsense.

QUESTION FROM THE AUDIENCE: I'd like to address a question to Dr. Gallup. I can see the purpose of polling in regard to certain issues because you want to know how the public thinks, but I'd like to know exactly what the purpose is of political polling? It seems to me it's a lot of wasted energy and a lot of wasted time to see who is going to get the election when you will know in a few weeks anyway and it doesn't seem to be that important.

MR. HANCHER: The speaker makes the point that he can see the value of polling on political issues but he asks whether or not polling to determine the winning candidate isn't wasted effort?

MR. GALLUP: I think that's a very good question. And I think the only justification for polling is to test polling methods. It has been my experience that we have had a greater urge, we have done more to perfect our methods, we have actually made greater progress because we knew we were going to have to face an acid test, than we probably would have made if we hadn't been making election forecasts. So I think the only justification of an election forecast is to test polling methods.

I quite agree with you that there is no great social value. I think there is legitimate newspaper interest in election forecasts and I am inclined to agree with Mr. Seymour that if we abandon the field, a dozen other persons would move in. I mean, the public will have its election forecasts. As a matter of fact, the first election poll, one of the first, was over a hundred years ago.

Newspapers have made straw-vote polls for the last hundred years and I think that we should make our reports, and I should have said in the talk that I made, I think we shouldn't assume the role of expert as we did in 1948. I think we should report the facts and all of the facts, but that we shouldn't, in the public's eye at least, try to be great experts in this field. Everyone hates an expert. There is a program on the air, I believe, called "Stump the Experts." In this field it ought to be called "Kill the Experts." Nobody likes an expert. If I have anything to do with it—and I don't know whether Mr. Seymour will agree with me—what I'd like to do, if this could be worked out, is to present the facts in 1952 and let the people be the experts. I'd rather have Mr. Seymour be the expert (*laughter*).

MR. SEYMOUR: You've got to answer the question, Who do you think is going to win? Now in line with the question back there, I hope there will be no speculation about who is going to win the Minnesota-Iowa basketball game tomorrow night, because you are going to know at half-past ten. Therefore don't ask. Don't wonder. Just wait. You will know.

MR. LAZARSFELD: Look, that's all very true, but I think one has to advance more serious—not just psychological—arguments in favor of those predictions. It is not that we know things a few hours earlier, but that from the poll type of data we know facts which we have never known before. For instance, how did we ever know how young people vote as compared to old people? You cannot know that from the precinct reports. How did we ever know seriously the difference between voting of men and women? The real values of those poll takers, in my opinion, lies in the greatly extended type of analysis they permit us to do which no election returns, as election boards publish them, ever give us. I think it is a disservice to put it just on the human-interest angle. It is the new type of data and information we get from the polls which really make them valuable.

MR. SEYMOUR: I apologize for putting it on the human-interest level. Talking about this reminds me of the Irishman who said he wished he knew where he was going to die so he'd never go near the place. I was putting it just as a newspaperman would (*laughter*).

QUESTION FROM THE AUDIENCE: Much has been said of the complexity of predicting elections and a good deal has also been said this evening about the futility of polls to predict about behavior of which we didn't know before, but I wonder if the necessities of preparing polls for newspaper columns permit an adequate discussion of the behavior or whether they limit the pollster and make it necessary for him to make his stories brief, and to skip a good deal of the details which Paul Lazarsfeld suggests may come from more intensive studies.

MR. HANCHER: I decline to summarize that question.

MR. SEYMOUR: We devote a minimum of two columns every Sunday, fifty-two Sundays a year, to telling what we find out from public opinion surveys about a wide range of questions. Now our experience shows that two columns to be as much as any considerable number of readers will read, and rather more than a number of them will read.

In other words, we are giving people as much of the sort of thing you are pleading for as they will take and can digest, we think, and we also have some smaller stories during the week. We do our best to popularize the thing but only in order that they will attempt to study and digest what we are finding out about popular attitudes. That two columns is only the Minnesota Poll, and we publish the Gallup Poll findings in addition on a wide range of things, and publish them very fully, so I doubt if that is a fair criticism.

QUESTION FROM THE AUDIENCE: Mr. Gallup, there was mentioned a certain group in which there was a conflict between the attitude toward the party standard-bearer and their ideas on issues, and that group constituted the one which changed. Now I am wondering two things: first, is there something inherently unstable in that group who can name opposites like that in their thinking, and second, if future testing of that group will give you the same unreliable results? Will you get your unreliable results because of sampling that same group who in this election adhered to one party and to the issues of another?

MR. GALLUP: Only time can tell. I am inclined to believe that what you are describing was a phenomenon of the last election only. I think in most elections people feel much more keenly about the candidates than they did in this one. I think there is much more fanaticism in the typical election than was to be found in the election of 1948, so I am not inclined to believe that we will meet that same situation in 1952. At least I can say that I hope we don't.

QUESTION FROM THE AUDIENCE: Dr. Lazarsfeld is the man that discussed that group. I'd like to hear his reply.

MR. LAZARSFELD: I am afraid I didn't quite get what you are asking me.

MR. HANCHER: I think the question was in regard to the elements of instability which would make it possible for people interviewed to name a candidate of one party and to subscribe to doctrines or platform planks of another, as an element that can never be predicted because it is essentially unstable.

MR. LAZARSFELD: But look, I didn't say those were unstable people. I used that as an example for following what you might call a research program. It should be possible as we acquire more knowledge to predict fairly early which people are susceptible to change. And I gave as one example that in this election we know that if a person was for Dewey and at the same time for price control and housing— for a number of important Truman issues—then he was likely to change. I think that if we concentrate on this notion of cross-pressures or contradictory attitude problems, we will become rather keen to notice such things fairly early and then to have a pretty good idea whether something surprising might happen in this campaign or not.

MR. CASEY: Paul, isn't there another factor? You said that these people, unstable voters who said they preferred Dewey but also preferred the program of Truman, didn't change their vote to Truman until Truman projected himself into their consciousness as an aggressive character and a lot of other things. Isn't there another factor there that is involved in that picture?

MR. LAZARSFELD: Your point is that someone has to take advantage of this position. It doesn't work by itself. I think you are quite right.

MR. HANCHER: Question?

MR. MEIER: I'd like to raise the question as to whether there is any validity to the opinion that election polls perform a scorekeeper function, whether this candidate is behind or ahead, and therefore the one behind will make his campaign more aggressive, and the one ahead also feels the necessity of keeping his campaign at a high pitch?

MR. HANCHER: Do polls serve a scorekeeper function to show from time to time the relative positions of the candidates? To whom is the question addressed?

MR. MEIER: Anyone.

MR. GALLUP: The answer to that one is: that certainly was true in the year 1948. Mr. Truman, I think, was helped rather than hurt by polled reports. I think he took advantage of them. I think that the Democrats realized they had to put in a little extra work and I think they did, and that's one of the reasons they won.

QUESTION FROM THE AUDIENCE: Dr. Lazarsfeld made the point that one usefulness of the forecasts was the fact it allows you to analyze more what goes on behind the vote and allows the academicians to do that. I'd like to complain that that material is not used and cite as an example that one leading university—I won't mention which—wrote us this year and said they were doing a study of minority cross-pressures within elections, as I gathered, and would we send them tabulations? So we said, "Fine. We have a Republican running against a non-Catholic Democrat and it will be very interesting and we will add the necessary questions to our polls and provide you with the data." We didn't hear much again, but we went ahead and put those questions in at some small expense and trouble. We got the data and wrote, and they said, "I'm sorry the project has been changed, and we are no longer interested." I think that organization can be named as Dr. Lazarsfeld's Bureau. I think that happened while he was in Europe (*laughter*).

MR. HANCHER: Is that a question?

QUESTION FROM THE AUDIENCE: Dr. Gallup, from time to time you have indicated one of the important things in the last campaign was the intensity of interest on the part of the voters, in a negative sort of way—that is, you felt there was really not much interest. Precisely how did you measure that, or didn't you measure that interest?

MR. HANCHER: The question is, How was interest measured by the polls?

MR. GALLUP: It was measured in a number of ways. First of all, the interviewers who had worked for us in the 1944 campaign in their daily reports to us almost without exception reported the fact that people simply weren't interested in the election. That's the first bit of evidence that we had.

The second bit of evidence came from the fact that almost twice as many persons were undecided. We and the Crossley Polls and many of the state polls added a great many questions asking people about whether they were interested in the election, whether they planned to vote, how certain they were to vote, how certain they were that the candidate they preferred was the better candidate, and from all of that, from all of those questions, we got more evidence of the general lack of interest in this particular campaign.

MR. HANCHER: I recognize there may be many other questions, but the hour is getting late. These gentlemen have been exceedingly generous of their time and I think we should not impose upon them further. May I call to your attention the fact that ballots or polling devices were placed in your hands as you came in, and you are urgently requested to mark those and make them available as you leave this room.

In conclusion, may I simply say that at a meeting about a year or a year and a half ago, I heard a very great architect say that the twentieth century has substituted the theory of probability for the doctrine of the Holy Trinity, and it may subconsciously have transferred to it some of the infallibility ascribed to the Holy Trinity. After all, it is desirable for us to remember that this is not a theory of certainty but a theory of probability. And if probability means anything, it means that error cannot be completely eliminated.

I should like to add my hope to that of Mr. Lazarsfeld that we may have forecasting at the state level, and there are persons here who will appreciate why I feel so keenly on that subject. And I hope that that prediction will lead to understanding in a greater measure than it has so far.

Certainly the problems of American government are far from solution. Those of us who give thought to the mechanism of government and the fact that it seems not to have kept pace with our industrial and social organization in many respects hope that this device and all others that can help us achieve the solution of our problems will be available to us, because the great question of our generation, the sixty-four-dollar question, is whether we have the wit and the wisdom to govern ourselves successfully and democratically. And if these polls will help us we shall be thankful.

(Meeting adjourned.)

Part Six

UNSETTLED
PROBLEMS

20

UNSETTLED PROBLEMS IN SOCIAL SCIENCE RESEARCH

T. C. McCormick, Presiding
Carroll Clark
Hadley Cantril
F. Stuart Chapin
Clyde W. Hart

Mr. McCormick: In addition to Carroll D. Clark and Clyde Hart, Mr. Hadley Cantril of the Office of Public Opinion Research at Princeton, who was invited to attend this Conference but was not able to come, has sent a paper that will be included in the program of this session.

What are some of the basic unsettled problems in social science research? We call first on Professor Clark.

Mr. Clark: I think there are some rather significant things that we might consider at this stage of the Conference. I have been very much impressed in this Conference with the way things have proceeded; the serious, sometimes humorous, but basically objective kind of assessment that has gone on in view of the events of last November; the absence of petty bias; the willingness to face up to a situation that perhaps calls for some reassessment.

And looking at it, we really are under the shadow of a quite momentous event. The biggest news story of the year was of course the unexpected election of President Truman. The reason it was the biggest news story was in part due to the over-confidence engendered by the polls and the public misconception of the reliability of their use for that highly hazardous kind of predicting on the national level.

Now this has resulted in a serious stock-taking. I think it might result in thoughtful consideration of some problems involving the better integration of the kind of research that is going on in this exceedingly important field of opinion polling and of attitude measurement, with some of the basic sociological, socio-psychological, and other forms of social science research, because that integration hasn't been adequately accomplished.

We do have studies capable of broadening our knowledge of the developing uniformities that can be used as bases of understanding and prediction. But too much is still on a level that results more in a useful kind of public information rather than in a system of logical propositions, the systematized knowledge, which we need to build the sound structure of a social science. It is to those problems I'd like to make just a few suggestions.

Now it seems to me that one thing greatly needed is tying in the kind of research that deals with a community in action, considers problems of group dynamics, treats of institutions and of the organized community life as a functional whole, with the kind of knowledge that comes from the cross-sectional survey of opinion (or other kinds of quantitative pictures) that give us highly valuable information for administrative and policy-making purposes. The kind of research that will be needed in the former is a little different from the latter; it can't all be done at the present time solely by quantitative methods. True, statistical measures may be brought in and employed at certain stages most usefully. Effective co-ordination may be made between statistical surveys and analyses of functioning groups.

But we need, I think, continuing case studies of communities, of special publics, of groups in action. An investigation like the Yankee City Series offers such a possibility. We had there an excellent long-continued investigation that revealed a great deal about a community and the people of the community. We have an excellent picture of the stratification of that community. But because of the methods employed, the total findings tend to result in a kind of static picture; it isn't the community in action. You don't see the ways in which those people interact to form collective judgments about matters of common concern to the community as a whole. You don't even see the special groups, the pressure groups, interacting, vying with each other to put across their programs or objectives in on-going community activities.

To get the kind of investigation I think we need, we should have both sorts of things. We need a kind of study—Yankee City or Middletown—in which a staff task force headed by someone like Paul Lazarsfeld, coming in as he did at Elmira, studies that community when it faces some critical juncture of affairs. Thus the group-dynamics picture will be pushed through along with the well-rounded configurational picture of the community as a whole.

That would give us a much more sound and effective understanding than we are likely to get by either of those methods if they are disassociated. I was very much interested in some of the things Paul Lazarsfeld told about that Elmira study yesterday, as indicating the consciousness perhaps of the need for that sort of investigation, because in that way the organic view of on-going activities or group dynamics can both broaden and deepen the understanding of the way people interact in dealing with live issues, critical problems.

I'd like to see even a smaller-scale study of a situation such as has recently developed in so many of our Kansas towns, where they are putting in parking meters. A whole community becomes aroused about that. You could go out and poll them as to whether they want meters or not. What you find out might be significant; it might help the "City Dads" in deciding what to do, but it wouldn't solve the problem. It wouldn't tell you too much about how the community operates to reach a considered view of a problem like that, what interests are overridden, what pressures exerted, and what elements of dissatisfaction further aroused.

All the pressures in the community are brought to bear on an issue like that; in cigar shops and barber shops, everywhere, people are talking. The kind of thing you might get at in a street-corner investigation would help you to understand how attitudes are shaped, would help you understand that decision-making process as it goes on in a community, how wires are pulled, how pressures are exerted, how "fast ones" are performed by this or that group that thinks it is on the inside track and can get "something good" out of this, how public-minded leadership may arise in less selfish groups to oppose them.

Other groups organize themselves to checkmate the devious ways that some of the pressure groups employ to get their programs across for some private interest. I think all those groups—the League of Women Voters, the University Women, and other women's clubs, as well as the businessmen's and labor organizations, and the formal political machinery—all such organizations of a community can be investigated in somewhat the way that an entomologist investigates the functional activities of a genus of arthropods, with the result that you would have a picture of the group dynamics that might be very useful.

Now there is another phase on which I think there are some unsettled problems of social science research. That is the perfection of the interviewing device. We have been interested in that. Sociologists were interested in it long before the Kinsey Report. They directed quite a little attention to that interviewing problem. There are various ways of conducting interviews, there are various techniques, there are various degrees of depths in which the kind of probing that goes on in an interview may bring knowledge to the surface.

We have had one study recently conducted by Mrs. Louise Cochran of our staff at the University of Kansas carrying on different kinds of interviews in dealing with the same topic, starting with about fifty subjects. First, the ordinary questionnaire, a kind of attitude-scale questionnaire interview, was employed and the topic was the attitude toward Negroes. Then these same people were brought in and interviewed. The interviewer first employed the device used by Alfred Winslow Jones in which concrete hypothetical situations were described and the subjects asked to give a scaled reaction to those situations, such as, "How would you act in the case of a Jim Crow situation on a streetcar or bus, with Negroes on it?" Another situation concerned the sort of situation that is happening in some of our sister states where for the first time Negroes are pressing to come into the graduate school and other classes of the University. And another dealt with segregated districts in which Negroes are buying property and moving in. All of these are typical situations to which the individual is invited to react and the information obtained on that is collated and compared with the former reactions obtained.

Then a third kind of interview was employed, and this is relatively new for this purpose. It is the kind of interview that Mayo and Roethlisberger, Dixon and their associates used in the Western Electric investigation, the interview of the non-directed sort. It is a good deal the same sort that, independently, Carl Rogers worked out. This interview is not used for therapeutic purposes, at least that isn't the main aim. In Mrs. Cochran's study it is used for the purpose of throwing light on the whole profile of the attitude, to get a picture that is deeper, and more reliable perhaps as to how the person really feels about the matter at issue.

That kind of interview takes at least an hour, sometimes between one and two hours. The interviewer in this project has the interviewee come in, opens the general topic of the discussion, then the interviewer in a very neutral fashion lets the person talk, listens to what the interviewee says, listens to what he doesn't say, and tries to help him express some of the things he wants to say but can't say without help.

On this race relations topic some very interesting things have been revealed. Not only the ambivalences the individual may feel, not only a fuller revelation of what his basic racial attitudes are, but revelations sometimes of attitudes that he didn't fully realize he himself had. One thing that rather surprised us came out, namely, how unhappy most of the people interviewed proved to be about the way they feel about their prejudices.

We wondered at first if that might come from the desire to make an impression on the interviewer, or a kind of feeling of embarrassment to discuss with someone what that someone in the interviewer position might regard as a prejudice, but we have been rather careful about that. The guilt feeling appears to be real and to lie deep. Further use of this method will be necessary perhaps to demonstrate that further, but it is interesting how the uninhibited, fuller actions of the individual reveal the attitude, and give a line on the intensity factor, a line on the ambivalences and contradictions within the individual himself, a much fuller revelation of how the individual actually feels about things which he may rather glibly and conventionally have reacted to in the scale kind of attitude questionnaire.

Now that suggests only one of many kinds of investigations that are needed in this field. The main problem it seems to me is to develop batteries of investigational techniques that will see the different facets of these problems, set the problem up in such a way that our resources are effectively brought to bear upon the different phases, and tie in this functional kind of approach to the community-in-action with the other kind of investigations that may reveal some of the measured uniformities.

MR. McCORMICK: The next presentation, sent in by Mr. Hadley Cantril of the Office of Public Opinion Research and Professor of Psychology of Princeton University, will be read. I think he also mentions Professor Einstein.

THE PROBLEM OF
SETTING OUR PROBLEMS

MR. McCORMICK (FOR MR. CANTRIL): With the growing interest in techniques for gauging public opinion and the use of these techniques in more and more areas of inquiry, it seems to me increasingly important for the social scientist to take stock of his own particular responsibility in contributing to our understanding of human behavior as he utilizes these techniques for his own self-assigned purposes.

Perspective seems especially necessary at this time. For I have the feeling that the discussion following the November election has been too exclusively concerned with methodological problems and insufficiently concerned with those problems which we might label conceptual rather than technical. While studies concerning sampling methods, the wording of questions, interviewing techniques, and the like are obviously all to the good, in our enthusiasm to create more accurate instruments of measurement we may sometimes lose sight of the problem of posing for ourselves just what our primary problems are anyway and how our measurement devices can be most effectively utilized.

When we begin to ask ourselves why people are thinking and behaving as they are, or when we try to predict how they will behave or think in the future, we are forced—whether we know it or not—to make some assumptions about the causation of human behavior. Thus our progress in getting answers that will help us understand human behavior will depend first and foremost on the adequacy with which we have consciously formulated our problem to ourselves.

It happens all too frequently that in a desire to "get results" we may formulate our problem in such an inadequate way that the resolution of our most pressing questions is impossible simply because the problem as we have conceived or stated it does not contain within it the possibility of resolving our difficulties. In other words, our conceptual scheme must be adequate, must include in the formulation of the problem itself an answer that will be really helpful to us when our study is completed.

The problem of setting our problems, then, seems to me an infinitely more pressing one than methodological or technical questions. This does not in the least minimize the need for their resolution too. But it does mean—relatively speaking—that such problems as quota versus probability sampling or the elaborate statistical treatment of results are of secondary importance *if* our interest is in trying to *understand* human nature in its social context.

The history of great scientific advances clearly demonstrates that progress within a science is not due chiefly to refinements of quantiative procedures but to insights and intuitions concerning *qualitative* relationships which help us understand causality whether in the physical or human sciences. These insights have the effect, not simply of "adding to" our existing knowledge, but of forcing a complete reconstruction of our conceptual scheme so that we can pose our problems in more adequate ways. And once a problem has been structured afresh, then new techniques or refinements of old techniques usually follow in their stride.

This is, of course, not an original idea. It has been forcefully stated by dozens of men whose names will always be associated with great scientific developments. For example, Einstein has written that "the formulation of a problem is often more essential than its solution, which may be merely a matter of mathematical or experimental skill. To raise new questions, new possibilities from a new angle, requires creative imagination and makes a real advance in science."

From this point of view, then, what kinds of problems can the social scientist set for himself which contain within them the possibility of increasing his basic understanding of human behavior and which involve the use of the type of techniques of interest to members of this conference? I can only give one example and it must, of course, come from my own experience.

One of my current worries—far from solution—is a variation of the old chestnut "What is an attitude anyway?" This general question as posed gets us nowhere. But in trying to set problems within the framework of the area the question covers, we can ask ourselves, among other things, the more precise question, "What assumptions does a person draw on when he reflects an attitude in a specific situation?" For it seems clear that every attitude in any "actual occasion" of the here-and-now, to use Whitehead's phrase, is based on assumptions which the individual has and which are out of time and space. This means, then, that if we are to understand the *why* of an individual's opinion, we must get some clues as to his assumptions. And if we are to understand public opinion, we must learn something about the universality of assumptions held by various members in any population group, discover what may be common in the assumptive worlds of nearly everyone, what may be different according to different functional subgroups, and why there are the common characteristics or differences we locate.

Stated quite generally, some of the assumptions underlying any social attitude in any individual might be thought of as follows:

(1) The actual situation has (or doesn't have) some bearing on my learned purposes, *viz.*, my methods of achieving security, my status, my personal development.

(2) The other people implicitly or explicitly involved in the situation have certain purposes of their own.

(3) The purposes of these other people have some bearing on my own purposes.

(4) There is (or is not) some action I may take that will help me to some degree carry out my purposes. My subjective feeling of surety or lack of surety concerning the probable reliability of my potential action is my best guide here.

(5) What I think or do now is essentially a bridge between the past and the future, and I figure that my reaction "now" will have some bearing on my expectancies for the future.

How can we relate these general statements to something specific, in order to see how analysis of a transitory actual occasion can help us get at some abstractions that may be of more permanent scientific value? One might choose almost any actual occasion, any concrete reaction. Take the situation of a certain voter being asked before the last election how he will vote. How would we try to improve our understanding of man's social behavior in general by analyzing the prediction of voting behavior in a particular case? And, since "synthesis and analysis require each other" (Whitehead), how do we also improve our understanding of human behavior by a better understanding of one man in one situation?

Referring back to the list of assumptions that would seem related to the expression of opinion, we would design our questionnaire to find out, for example:

(1) What difference does it really make to a respondent one way or another who is elected? This information would be sought in terms of the respondent's own pattern of personal security or insecurity, his identifications and loyalties, his status, his own ideas of his chances for development.

(2) What does he think the real purposes are of the different candidates and the groups supporting them?

(3) What does he feel are the probable relationships between his purposes and their purposes? Where is there conflict, where is there overlapping?

(4) How certain is he that his own action in voting one way or another will help him accomplish his purposes? What are the conflicts he is experiencing in terms of the effectiveness of his actions in the past that may give him lack of surety concerning the way he will finally vote? What changes might be introduced into the situation that would increase his sense of surety and make it more likely that he would vote and would vote a certain way?

(5) What is the reliability that voting one way or another will help him achieve some of his expectations and aspirations for the future? What are the causes of the degree of reliability he has?

This particular example, of course, boils down to the problem of voter-intention which the practical operators have long regarded as a major headache in election forecasting. My sketchy analysis of some of the factors involved in "intent" may seem obvious enough. I hope it does. My only excuse for using the example is my feeling that if we can intellectualize to ourselves what is actually involved in that word "intent," we may come up with some better answers, better hunches for new techniques, and eventually better predictions.

Whether we use dichotomous or open-ended questions, probability or quota sampling is, in a sense, secondary. The much more important judgment involves posing the right questions to our-

selves and then using the most efficient methods at hand for getting
the answers. If we don't set the problems right, we certainly won't
get the right answers.

I suspect that the best test we can give ourselves as to whether
or not we are asking the right questions of ourselves is whether
or not we have a feeling—and it is much more an intuitive feeling
than a rational, logical analysis—that the questions are intrinsically
reasonable. But obviously we shall experience the feeling of intrinsic
reasonableness only insofar as our conceptual scheme includes our
best rational analysis of all related variables. The major responsibility of the social scientist seems to me to be, then, to strive constantly for better formulations of the problems.

MR. McCORMICK: The next speaker on this program will be
Mr. F. Stuart Chapin, head of the Department of Sociology at the
University of Minnesota.

MR. CHAPIN: Mr. Chairman, ladies and gentlemen, like Professor
Clark, I am to give a presentation instead of discussion, which puts
me in the position of the young theological student who had to
follow the procedure then in vogue at the seminary which he attended. At some time during the course, each man was given a sealed
envelope and in that on a slip of paper was written a text. He then
was to open the envelope and preach extemporaneously on that
text.

It happened in the particular case in this story, the man so selected was the shortest man in the class. And he went up to the
lecture platform, opened the envelope, and said, "My text this
evening is Zaccheus. Zaccheus was a small man. So am I. Zaccheus
was up a tree. So am I. Zaccheus made haste to get down. So will I."
And he walked off the platform.

I am afraid I can hardly do that, but I thought I might describe
a specific research that perhaps is suggestive because it relates to a
phase of public opinion and public opinion polling which as far
as I know, had not hitherto been touched on. So I shall give you in
round figures, because I do not have the manuscript before me, the
substance of a brief study published in the last issue of the *International Journal of Opinion and Attitude Research*, on the subject
of relationship between experimental design and public opinion
research.

It has been pointed out in some of the previous discussions that experimental methods can be used to great advantage in testing questions and working on the formulation of questions and various aspects of the interviewing and field work procedures. This small study does not deal with that. It deals with the question: having obtained a poll and finding a majority, is the public right? Well, in looking about for material I found that Gallup and Rae, in their *Pulse of Democracy*, had a poll of April and May, 1938, which showed in response to the question, "Do you think—" now of course I am giving you this out of memory, so it can't be very accurate—"Do you think that the federal government should provide living expenses for unemployed people?"

Taking those who replied yes or no, the approximate proportions were 69 percent yes, and 31 percent no. Then a year later, in April and May 1939, the question was asked, "In providing assistance for unemployed people, do you think that a work relief program should be used or that a direct relief program should be used?" And there again the vote was overwhelmingly in one direction. That is, as I recall, it was about 89 percent in favor of work relief as against 11 percent in favor of direct relief.

There you have in two successive polls about a year apart, first the opinion of people expressed with reference to a goal, something to be achieved; second, in the second vote, you have their preference for a means to be taken to achieve that goal.

Now, it happened that in April-May 1939, I had done a study in St. Paul, Minnesota, to collect information that might bear upon the question whether work relief contributed more to the morale and adjustment of unemployed people than did direct relief. This was a simple experimental design which involved about 8000 people as the pool of WPA treated, and some 400 on direct relief. We took a five percent random sample of the people on WPA and then had two groups, an experimental group of roughly 400 on WPA, and a control group of roughly 400 on relief.

We then started matching off these cases in terms of the records, which were fairly complete. I don't recall all of the items in the matching, but there were age and sex and nationality and race and occupation and time—length of time on WPA, or length of time on relief. We tried to equate the factor of length of treatment and a good many other variables to about fourteen factors in all. This resulted in a tremendous attenuation of the two samples, and we ended up with eighty cases matched on these fourteen factors in the experimental group and forty-two in the control group.

Of course the matching on any such criteria as those indicated is not a precise form of matching, but because of the intercorrelations of some of those factors you get a good deal of similarity and homogeneity in those two groups. This, of course, is a cross-sectional design. What we had hoped to do and what we asked the WPA if we might do when they asked us to make the study was this: to select the two groups as we did and then allow a year or more of experience on WPA or relief to pass and then measure the two groups again. We would then have had a projected design where we would have had the opportunity of before-and-after measurement to see whether those on one program gained more than those on the other. That, however, we were told could not be done. So we had merely this control-led comparison for the particular date.

The people in these two groups were interviewed by graduate students and social workers who were given some slight instruction, and information was obtained on four scales. We used the Rundquist-Sletto Scales to measure first morale, and then adjustment, and two other scales—one on participation and one on social status. The result was that when we compared the mean scores on each of the four scales of the two groups, the mean score of the WPA group was slightly better than the mean score of the relief group.

Now of course I could go into the minutiae and the technicalities of this but there isn't time for that. In terms of a rough probability test, the chances of finding the small differences we obtained ranged somewhere between one in ten and one in fifty, depending upon some technical questions and what corrections were made for spurious factors. But the net result you see was to show that in the main there was a slight edge that the people on work relief had over the people on poor relief.

If a study of this kind could be done or had been extensively done in other parts of the country under like conditions so that we had samples from different areas, and if we had found similar results, then we could say that the public's judgment in this poll of April-May 1939, their preferences for work relief as against direct relief, was sound and was borne out by certain facts.

MR. MCCORMICK: Our final speaker on this program will be Mr. Clyde W. Hart.

MR. HART: My first undertaking in this Conference was to discuss a paper I had neither heard nor read. Now I find myself in the position of discussant on two papers which were neither written nor read (*laughter*).

I greatly appreciate, however, the insertion into this Conference at this juncture of the very excellent statement by Hadley Cantril, because, following the combination of technical and policy conversations that have gone before, it brings out a point which needs underscoring in all deliberations of this kind—namely, the priority of the substantive problem in all types of research. Except as method in the sense of logic can be abstracted in such sciences as mathematics, it is always subservient to the problem in hand.

There are inherent dangers in the tendency of some students to identify science with method. There can be no science obviously without reliable methods that yield valid data, reliable methods that enable us to collate and interrelate data and to derive insights and generalizations of some applicability beyond the immediate set of historic facts. But the identification of science with method is pervasive in that it makes an end of what is properly a means. It has led some of us to select problems that fit the particular method or skill which we ourselves possess, or which is already developed and available. The procedure which will lead in the long run to the progressive development of science as a systematic body of knowledge about the phenomena of actual life is an interest in problems which is sufficiently great to make us forget everything else and spend hours in reflection, in tinkering, in consultation with our fellows, discovering, adapting, inventing methods that will enable us to solve them.

I think it would be unfortunate if an organization like NORC, just because it has through the years developed some special skills in sample interviewing in the so-called survey type of research, should consider itself limited to that kind of research and not be flexible enough and inventive enough to adapt and use other approaches when the problem warrants. Exploratory participant observation, case studies, intensive prolonged case studies, life histories, even the setting up of social experiments. If any one method may claim superiority, it is experimentation, for it brings the factors involved in any problem under as careful and complete control as possible. Moreover, it enables the student to intervene in behavior as it goes on, so that he is not limited to analysis of the records of behavior that has already occurred or to the mere observation of behavior as it spontaneously occurs without his having any part in determining it.

So I would underscore the priority of the substantive problem in all types of research as I did in the first remarks I made here. However, I was a little distressed by the implications of one or two things in Hadley Cantril's paper. He called methods secondary and techniques secondary. Emphasis upon the priority of the problem should not in any way be taken to minimize the importance of method and technique. If I am seriously interested in a problem and have an objective, inquisitive attitude toward it, nothing is more important to me than the reliability of the instruments I must use in my effort to resolve that problem. In fact, people who are interested in substantive problems ought to be the ones who are most intolerant of sloppy, slipshod, half-baked attempts to define, collect, collate, and analyze data.

I don't think there is any hierarchy here in terms of the value of one over the other. I think rather it is a sequence in time. But with that qualification I would venture the opinion that in the social or human sciences, we are likely to be more successful in working out methods that are applicable, efficient, and reliable if our interest centers in the solution of substantive problems.

I would like to emphasize one other point in connection with what has been said here this morning and also at various times throughout the Conference, by implication at least. I feel fairly sure that during the next decade, or the next two or three decades, interest in the field of social science research is going to center in considerable degree on the question of contributions that the social sciences are prepared to make to the problem of values. Can the social sciences bring to bear results that are reliable and valid, that will provide bases for the choices which society, acting through its representatives, has to make?

This question arises only in part from the conflict in ideologies that besets us at the moment. But, although the problem of values in social science is of longer, more remote origin, the present challenge to a free democratic society highlights it and brings it to attention.

I couldn't get down here on time for the opening meeting of this Conference because last night I was involved at the University of Chicago in an interdepartmental faculty seminar that is seriously

concerned with this problem. Similar discussions are going on elsewhere, encouraged by the Social Science Research Council. In fact,
the Council has been canvassing scholars in this country and abroad
to find out the current state of interest and preparation and to
discover promising ways of attacking the problem, and it is likely
that substantial portions of the resources available to foundations
endowing research will be available for research into the problem.

I believe the development is wholesome, although initially I was
skeptical. Like many of you, I was brought up on the notion that
the problems with which scientists are concerned ought to stem
from the developing body of scientific theory; I did not believe
that scientists should let the practical needs or demands of society
at the moment determine how they would direct their interests and
employ their skills. I still think this view is in the main sound.

However, I am inclined to believe that this developing concern
about values may impose a wholesome discipline on social scientists.
It may be excessive in its pressure for immediate contributions,
but it may also encourage social scientists to put their theories to
a crucial test and emphasize their long-run social responsibility.
If they are not inventive enough to discover principles and methods
which apply to reality as we know it, so as to give some reasonably
precise and reliable answer as to what will be the consequences of
choosing this course of action rather than some alternative one, the
social sciences fail to justify themselves and will not long be supported by social resources. I am inclined to agree with Jeremy
Bentham that, considerations of *long-run* social utility aside, one
might as well play tiddly-winks as concern himself with problems
of theory.

Now, how far can we go, any of us, no matter how abstractly
we set up our problems, in pointing out the consequences that are
likely to follow from any proposed intervention in the social processes by policy makers who are supporting some scheme of social
values? At this juncture I don't think we can go very far on the
basis of assured social scientific knowledge. We have wasted much
time during the years in unproductive argument about the deter-
minacy or indeterminacy of human social behavior, in attempts to
answer on the *a priori* level, the question, "Is a social science possible?" Twenty years ago I debated publicly with Frank Knight
the question, "Is a social science possible?" If we were to debate
the question again, I don't believe we would be much nearer an

answer now than we were then, and we won't find an answer as long as we attack the question on that level. The only way to find out whether or not a social science is possible is to try to derive scientific knowledge and to test it experimentally—ultimately to test it on the level of practice.

If I'm right in my surmise that social scientists will have to come to grips with the problems of values confronting society at the present time, the implications for attitude and opinion research are obviously of importance. Certainly students in this field will have to give more penetrative, vigorously critical attention to the substantive problems without being any less exacting and resourceful in devising methods and techniques; and we should not hold back because of present inadequacies in our equipment. We'll learn more about these inadequacies and ways to remedy them if we use this equipment under conditions which impose a high degree of responsibility.

The main thing is to set our problems up in such a way that the findings will give more insight into the values people seek, their reasons for seeking them, and the relevance of alternative courses of action to their realization. These are matters about which we know all too little in all areas of human experience, even the most homely ones. Ted Gallup, for instance, cited one such homely area yesterday when he was suggesting how the methods we command could be applied to the pressing problems of health. We do not have much systematic information about people's awareness of their health needs; about their efforts to deal with problems of real or imagined ill health; about their information, misinformation, superstitions, worries, and fears concerning health, etc.

I have recently given a little attention to programs of urban redevelopment. In the early days of the present century these programs were concerned mostly with slums and blighted areas in our cities, but they have gradually grown into movements looking toward the rational planning of not only the physical plant, but the transportation, recreation, and other facilities of the city as a whole. Yet we know little about the incongruities and conflicts in value systems that will have to be modified if these programs are to succeed. We readily assume, for instance, that nobody living in a blighted area could possibly be attached to it or feel at home there. We know little also about the profound effects—economic, psychological, and social—in the lives of the disturbed or displaced people affected by the carrying out of one of these programs. Consequently the resistances encountered are often puzzling and frustrating, and entire programs are abortive.

It is in areas of this kind that the problem of values may be attacked by the students of attitude and opinion, as well as in the larger but more difficult areas of high policy as in the international conflict of sharply opposed ideologies.

Perhaps what I have just said makes it clear why I think we should take cues from Cantril's paper and begin to behave like students of attitude and opinion, behave a little less like imitative mathematical statisticians, on the one hand, or like a special kind of news reporter, on the other. Again let me say that I do not underestimate the need for methodological improvements or the utility of reporting the current state of opinion with respect to popular issues. I only lament the relatively small amount of attention we are giving to pressing problems, both theoretical and practical, of grave, long-run importance.

21

UNSETTLED PROBLEMS OF THE SAMPLING SURVEY METHODOLOGY

Robert R. Sears, Presiding
George H. Gallup
Stuart C. Dodd
Paul F. Lazarsfeld
Norman C. Meier

MR. SEARS: The topic now is *Unsettled Problems of the Sampling Survey Methodology*. There are three speakers listed. We are going to introduce a fourth who, as Dr. Gallup said, obviously has something to say. We will start with Dr. Gallup.

MR. GALLUP: Mr. Stuart Dodd has an interesting story that he'd like to tell; so I am going to make my remarks very brief. I think the first problem—the first and most important unsettled problem of sampling survey methodology—is this problem of how to identify voters and nonvoters. I am speaking now of political polls. I think that is our number one problem and I think that a great deal of work will have to be done before we get the final answer.

I'd like to say once more that this particular problem probably can be solved best by experimentation carried on in small communities. I am sure that Paul Lazarsfeld would agree with me that you people here, working in college communities, are more likely to get the right answer—more likely to find things that we have overlooked—than we have been in working on a national scale.

As I pointed out yesterday, I think that it would be an interesting experiment for every one of you to undertake a poll with the help of your students. This wouldn't involve any great expenditure of money. It would be an interesting experiment to see if you can forecast turnout in the next local election.

Turnout is more important in my opinion than the problem of deciding whether Candidate A or Candidate B will win; but if you take the two problems, turnout and the prediction of the vote of leading candidates, I think you may discover things that we have overlooked.

Another problem is that of measuring prestige. Let me give you an example. When we attempt to forecast the sale of a Bantam Book, we know that one of the most important problems that we have to control and measure is the problem of prestige.

If we were to take a poll of the people present here we might ask you individually whether you would be interested in buying a book called "Tom Paine," and we'd probably get a great many answering "Yes." If we came along with a book called "The Tonto Kid" we know very well most of you would say "No." But that wouldn't be any index at all of the sale of the book amongst those present.

As a matter of fact, we have had to work out a half dozen different ways of measuring prestige, and it frequently happens that a book that comes out, let us say, with fifty points on a hundred-point scale has to be multiplied by three, whereas the "Tom Paines" may have to be reduced by the same weight.

I think there is still a lot to be done in this whole problem of measuring the intensity of opinion. I think we have made real progress in this direction. I am grateful to Stuart Dodd again for some of his ideas. He has suggested that we add to our "quintamensional approach" two more categories of questions, one which he calls "Connectedness" and the other one "Action." Both tie up very closely with intensity. So that is certainly another whole area for experimental research.

Of course you could include almost every phase of research, every aspect of it under this general subject, *Unsettled Problems of the Sampling Survey Methodology*.

I think there are very few problems that have been solved and I think that is likely to be true for a good many years, but these three that I named are the ones which concern me most at this time.

MR. SEARS: The next speaker will be Dr. Stuart Dodd.

MR. DODD: The beauty of a topic like "Unsettled Problems" is that you can talk about anything you want to talk about anyhow and call it an unsettled problem.

One of the unsettled problems of sampling methodology, I think, is concerned not so much with the methodology itself in building questionnaires and doing sampling or supervising interviewers and so forth, as it is with what to use it on. And I am going to tell you of a use for the sampling techniques which are being applied to basic research in the social sciences, to the fundamental attempt to search out laws of human relations. This will have a reflex action on developing the methods necessary to solve such substantive problems, and I think it will be the most effective way of getting on with better methods as a necessary step in solving substantive problems.

This particular substantive problem we are working on is an excellent field for M.A. or Ph.D. theses for a score of students. It is one of the most wide-open and accessible researches that I know of anywhere. It is in a field which is very similar to the law of gravity in physics, and is practically the same formula applied to human affairs. It relates to the *interaction* of human groups, of which all processes of conflict, competition, cooperation and so forth are simply special forms.

Let me just give you the background for a minute of the situation we had to seize on in Seattle to work out this bit of basic research exploring for laws of human relations. There an emergency situation arose in one of the housing projects which was made up of 30 percent unsegregated Negro families, where a Negro pervert was loose in the community and had forced his way into two homes and raped white women. These events had set the whole community on fire and the police and housing authorities called us in to make a quick survey to try to diagnose the situation and see what could be or should be done about it immediately.

We had to make the survey in ten days from the time we first heard of it till the report had to be in, so there were many weaknesses in the methodology because of the haste. I won't go into the civic side of it—the ninety-seven different "gripes" we found in the community with the frequencies of each which we turned over to a dozen different organizations that got to work on reducing them. They are getting on with building a healthy interracially integrated community in that housing project. The civic outcomes of the thing are another story. What I shall describe here is simply the scientific aspect of one bit of basic research that we were able to carry out along with that rather hasty inquiry on the interracial tensions spreading through that community.

Essentially the problem I am describing here will be to measure a rumor running through a community, to measure its spatial pattern and temporal pattern and causal pattern. The rumor was the knowledge of a rape that happened in one house on a date ten days before the survey took place (with all its interviewing done in one day).

In our questionnaire we were asked to keep off the subject of the rape directly and that handicapped us a good deal. We had to ask indirect questions, such as, "Has anything happened here that makes people worry more than usual in the last month?" (*laughter*). There were other tensions, also. There had been a long strike at Boeing, and thirty percent of the people were unemployed. They were losing the strike. And there were a great many other things to bother them besides this one pervert that I have told you about.

So we asked some seven indirect questions of that kind, and we put down as a unit of tension each mention by one white respondent of one anti-Negro opinion. These were counted and made up the "tension score" for this purpose, as part of our "tension theory" and our definition of a "tension."

Then one of the steps was to make a spot map of the tensions for the police, as shown here [indicating map on blackboard]. This was to find out if there were dangerous pockets, or any concentration of tension, which the police patrol cars should watch especially for expected outbreaks of violence.

There were no particular pockets. But in looking over the map I sensed a set of gradients going up to a peak, and charted tentative circles and spotted the highest part of the peak right about there [indicating]. We went back to the housing project and found that was the house where the rape had occurred. We didn't know the location of it before. We can be encouraged by that sort of indirect measurement of a change in interracial tension which can actually spot the location of the event that caused it.

We went ahead and measured the tension in these trial zones. A great deal of statistical work went on for months exploring the data. We arrived finally at hundred-yard zones, seven in number, and worked out the frequency of the tensions zone by zone, from nearest the rape site to furthest away. The tension started at one and a half mentions of anti-Negro feeling per family, approximately, near the rape site, down to half that number at the perimeter. Then we fitted theoretical curves to the data and we found fifteen different types and worked from them so as not to assume anything but to start with finding out what kind of curve might fit best. Having determined the best-fitting curve, the next job was to see how *good* a fit it was and how close a fit. The "closeness of fit" was measured by the correlation between the observed amounts of tension in each zone and the theoretical amounts given by the curve. All the correlations were up in the nineties, showing a very close fit. To check the "goodness of fit" from a sampling point of view, we found a very high probability from a chi-square test that the observed discrepancies from the curve could occur by chance. All this means we had found a hypothesis expressed in a curve, which used distance and population co-ordinates only, and which described our data well.

Now what hypothesis were we trying to test? Let me go back to that as shown in this chart here. This is what we call our "Interactance Hypothesis." It goes back to Zipf and Stewart and others. By it we reduce interaction between any two communities to a product of seven dimensions or factors that could be objectively observed ahead of time, and so predict the expected amount of the kind of interacting. The seven dimensions are time, space, population, and indices of specific condition. I won't have time to go into those indices of specific conditions, but they are definitely observable things like sex, education, income, and things of that kind.

Having observed those seven dimensions or factors, they can be put together in a formula, and the expected interactance between communities calculated. The "interactance" is the expected amount of any kind of interacting between human beings, such as migrating between towns, telephoning between towns, sending railway-express parcels between towns, attending college between towns, choosing friends, marrying between towns, passing a rumor along from zone to zone in a community. In short, almost anything that human beings do to each other that you can go out and count in some fashion, and locate in spatial zones of some kind, can be brought under this hypothesis. It states simply how masses of people interact with each other—the quantity of interaction of groups.

But it isn't limited to human beings. The same hypothesis, with an appropriate shift of definition, applies to any animals, or to molecules, which are simply other particular illustrations of this universal principle of interaction.

Then for testing the hypothesis one tries to isolate each of the seven factors, measuring them one by one first and then in combination. We were able to eliminate and control five of the seven factors, leaving the varying of the other two to be measured alone. These two were the population and the distance from the rape site.

The ratio of the population to the distance is what we call the Population Potential. It is very comparable to potential in gravity or in magnetic affairs in physics, and it measures the effect of a population at a given distance from a point. It is a special case of the Zipf's "PP over D" hypothesis that the effect of any interaction between any two groups will be in proportion to the product of the two populations, and inverse to the distance between them.

In this case, as shown in the chart here, one of the two groups was a single person who started the rumor—the victim of the rape—who went out and immediately blabbed about it. All the other interactants were the hearers of the rumor, who then told it to their neighbors, and a chain of reactions was sent rippling through the community. So of the two populations, one of them, consisting of just one person, reduces to a constant for all zones. Therefore our three hypotheses become identical, or include one another. Our major "interactance hypothesis" with seven factors boils down to the "PP over D" hypothesis, and since one of the populations is unity, this boils down further to simply P over D, or a population divided by a distance.

So then we set out to test whether the observed population-over-distance ratio [1] agreed with the actual amount of this interaction,

[1] *Editorial note:* For the benefit of the reader who does not have before him the charts the audience saw, these hypotheses may be formally stated here in equations.

$$\text{Peo?} \doteq 1.0 \pm \sigma_p \quad \text{an hypothesis}$$

This is a questioned assertion that the index of correlation P, between an observed frequency variable, 0 (here the tension score), and its expected amount, E (here the "interactance" which is calculated from the factors on the right in the equations below), will approach unity, within limits of the standard error or estimate:

where $\quad E \equiv \dfrac{kI_aP_aI_bP_bT_t}{L'T_v} = $ the interactance defined.

Here P_a, P_b are the two interacting populations, I_a, I_b are their "specific indices," T_t, T_v are time factors, and L' is a power of the intervening distance. In this study four factors I_a, I_b, T_t, T_v were controlled in various ways to be the interracial tension, as measured by our poll. That amount of agreement is shown in this chart [indicating] where the different zones, from the rape site to the outermost zone 700 yards distant, are plotted along this horizontal axis. And the amount of tension as observed is plotted along this vertical axis. This rough broken curve is the actual observed tension, zone by zone, and the smooth curve is the best-fitting harmonic curve. The chi-square test shows that it fits the data well as far as sampling is concerned. In other words, it verified the hypothesis. But it did not verify the hypothesis uniquely, for this limited set of data could also be described by other curves.

Then with the hypothesis verifying to that extent the spatial pattern of the diffusing tension, we went further to try to work out the *temporal pattern* of that wave in the community. This is very much like a stone dropped into a still pool, sending a ripple out radially in widening circles but fading in height or intensity as it leaves the rape site, and as the distance and time grows. We couldn't test that hypothesis of the temporal pattern because we had made only one survey on one date and there has to be several surveys on several dates to get a time series. But we were able to work out a hypothesis as to what the temporal formula might be and have it ready to check in any future situation.

The chief point of this paper is that we did not crucially prove the hypothesis from the data in this limited sample. But we developed a methodology ready for use in a future situation. We have a hypothesis so when a situation comes along like this again, we can go in and do a thorough job of testing such a hypothesis. The temporal formula works out to be something like this: that the amount of the tension—that is, the effect of the rape rumor—varies

unities, and the exponent on the distance (L') and the constant, k (which adjusts units), were empirically found to be unity, thus simplifying the interactance to

$$E \equiv \frac{P_a P_b}{L} \quad \text{the "PP over D" in Zipf's hypothesis.}$$

When, as in our study, one population is just one person, this simplifies further to the "population potential" tested here:

$$E \equiv P/L \quad \text{the population potential.}$$

This can be restated by dividing through by P as $E/P = 1/L$ which says that the per capita tension in each zone equals the reciprocal of the radius of that zone. More colloquially: "the rumor fades with distance."

with the population size and inversely with the distance and the time.

A simple way of saying it is that the rumor wanes if there are very few people to spread it through, and it wanes with the distance and it wanes in time. To bring in the time part of it more exactly, the tension wave was found to wane with "1 over T," T being the length of time since the event happened that started the rumor going. If the inverse of time is the exponent on the distance factor, you will have a formula to the first proximation at least. This formula [2] describes the course of that wave radiating out from one date, starting from one person through one channel, going on from neighbor to neighbor through that community. This formula is a hypothesis to test in any future situation. It involves the three fundamental dimensions: time, space, and the population, which when measured will predict the amount of interaction to be expected.

Finally, we went on with a causal analysis trying to test whether, as may seem obvious to you, the increased racial tension we observed was really due to that rape event or to other factors. We isolated the "endemic tension" from the "epidemic tension." The "endemic tension" was the amount of interracial attitude that was there before the rape event. We measured that in three different ways. They all converged to the same answer. We then isolated the epidemic tension or the change in the tension that had occurred in the last ten days since that rape event occurred. And then we worked out a correlation between the observed data and the theoretical curves and found correlation indices up in the nineties. We worked out further evidence of the causation or the linkage, between the rape event and the measured tension ten days later.

What we achieved, I think, with this small sample ($N = 171$), is a technique for the future. We have a questionnaire in which if any event of that kind happened again, we would go in and make a census asking: Whom did you hear this from first? When did you hear it? Where did you hear it? Whom did you tell first? Where

[2] The tension wave formula is:

$$\frac{E}{P} = \frac{k}{L''^t}$$

where E = the tension (i.e. the number of anti-Negro opinions),
     P = the population in each zone,
     L = distance or radius of each zone,
     k = a constant to adjust units, also the maximum tension (in Zone I),
     T = time since the rumor started.

did you tell it? When did you tell it? And so on, until we worked out every single transfer of that rumor from mouth to ear as it goes through a community. Then one can get, not just a total wave, but the movement of each human molecule in that wave developing the whole mechanism of propagating that wave. So that another time we would have the knowledge of how to determine the causation or the mechanism and the mathematics of it, with a great deal of precision, from this exploratory study.

In summary, the study is not one that proves the interactance hypothesis but it is consistent with it; it supports it. It would require thousands of similar studies to prove the hypothesis and prove it uniquely so, as the best possible hypothesis. It is chiefly a study in methodology showing how a demoscope can test basic hypotheses or incipient laws of human relations.

It seems to me that is the kind of thing we, particularly in universities, in public opinion work, have got to try to head for more and more.

MR. LAZARSFELD: I think it is only fitting that the last hours of such an exciting conference are given to prayerful consideration of the future, and I feel that Stuart Dodd made a very good point that the relation of our data to systematic theorizing should be one of the trends we should take.

I would like to get still a little more general and pick up the theme which I think runs through many of our phases of discussion: as one task of the future, we have to keep public opinion work as close to the social sciences in general as possible.

It turns out that there are really two tie-ups which can exist between public opinion research and social sciences. You might call it the two kinds of major integration. The one is more habitual. We all know we need psychology and anthropology and sociology to help in public opinion work. In a way that is so obvious that it hardly needs any discussion. The psychologist and the anthropologist deal with techniques we are using here; they can be of very great help to us and we might be of some help to them. But in addition to this relation with the "technical" social sciences like psychology and sociology, there is another integration possible, desirable, and worthy of some consideration: the relation to the "atavistic" social sciences, especially political science and economics.

If you ever have looked into a textbook of economics or political science, you will find that they deal with terribly crude methods, that their data are very weak, that they are not at all like psychologists and sociologists—method-conscious. On the other hand, those atavistic social sciences have for hundreds and perhaps thousands of years dealt with broad problems of society, have been listened to in one way or another, and in the close relations of attitude or public opinion research to political science and economics lies an important topic. I don't think it makes at this moment much difference that I am the mouthpiece of this idea, even if I know nothing about either of the two sciences.

Actually, this relation of public opinion research to political science and economics presents a very irksome and very serious problem. Remember, I committed myself on Thursday evening to come back to the paper of Professor Clark and to the introductory remarks of Professor Albig. I think we assisted there in a very characteristic situation. Here was Professor Clark from the University of Kansas, not only presenting his own thinking and writing for many, many years, but quoting in his paper eminent thinkers like Cooley, and what impressed me especially, even being able to quote from a letter which Robert Park had written to him on the problem of how can we possibly find out what we mean when we talk about "the public" and "public opinion." There is a great amount of intellectual civilization behind this serious concern with society and the community and its problems, which has been going on for many, many centuries. And then a bunch of barbarous people come around—it's always the same fifty-sixty people who meet always at the same conference, talk to each other about area sampling and probability sampling, and discuss whether we should ask the question this way or that way. It is not surprising that conflict develops between a kind of methodological barbarism and a humanistic mind—inexperienced in technical problems.

You get it in very many ways. Herbert Blumer, e.g., wrote in the last *Sociological Review* a blasting condemnation that everything you have ever done in public opinion research is wrong. I don't think the paper is right, but it presents a criticism that is quite serious. The same situation develops when you come to a European country as a social research man. This fall I was invited by a European University to teach young Norwegians social research, which they are very eager to learn—it's almost a religion for them. After some time they got a feeling of conflict and danger. All right, they are very interested in those things. They wanted social research. But they have been brought up in their schools, in their gymnasiums and their universities, in philosophical contemplation of society. They get the idea they need empirical data, but still they don't feel that you can substitute empirical data for Nietzsche or Kant or any great philosopher. There ought to be some link between the two. While, as I openly confessed, I didn't feel that Professor Clark did justice to the problem he raised, I was impressed by the fact that he had the courage to come to a group like us and to talk in the terms he talked in.

Now let me therefore make a few remarks on the relation between political science and what you might call social philosophy and the actual work of public opinion research. I think it is quite possible to put the matter into a few simple sentences, and then any of you can go from there. I think that the relation between the tradition of political science which we may know from books, and our own technical work which we know from practical experience, is a two-fold one.

Modern opinion research can bring great clarification to the thinking and problems of the political scientist, and in turn the political scientist can bring great richness to our work. It is a trade between clarity, which we can provide, and richness and depth, which they can provide, and I think it is needed badly both ways. They need the clarity and we need the richness.

Now, let me first talk of what I mean when I say we can provide clarity. Professor Clark echoed the great question of what is "really" public and what is "really" public opinion. I think the answer is very simple, and Professor Clark has intimated what it will be. Public opinion research has provided a very simple screen against which the problems of the political scientist can be easily seen—poll research. The typical result of a public opinion poll is a table which gives the distribution of answers to a number of alternatives specified to a given question. This information comes from the whole community and it is ascertained by sending interviewers out.

Now, this very trivial reproduction of a poll result immediately permits a large number of variations. You can, for instance, ask the question "Whom have you interviewed?" Well, a poll result is an interview whether with a whole community, or with a representative sample. But you don't have to do that; you can, for instance, inter-

view the highest educated group in the community, or you can interview the experts in a community, and so on; and this gives
you the first large variation of whether "public opinion" is the
opinion of all the people, or the experts in the community, or
the leaders in the community. This isn't a real problem. Each sector
of the universe might have a different distribution of answers. If
you prefer to call "public opinion" what all the people answer to
such a question, it is one way to get along. Another is to pick a
specific sector of the population—Professor Blumer has a preference
for archbishops. You can easily specify public opinion polls as to
the sector of the population whom you have interviewed and you
get a great variety of information.

There is an excellent book, the first great European book on
theory of public opinion, which was written by a German, Professor
Tönnies, who lectured before the first World War, a six-hundred-page
book. He has a very interesting chapter there on the reaction of
German public opinion to the growth of the German labor movement. Now what does it imply for this German professor? The opinion of labor, the workers who want to organize, is not a phenomenon of public opinion in itself. It seems quite obvious that the people
he would have polled would be the people with an income of more
than five thousand marks or with more than a certain amount of
education. The "reaction of public opinion to the growth of the
labor movement" would sound grotesque in George Gallup's
mouth. For him, the growth of the labor movement would itself be
a *part* of public opinion. But it was for the German professor an
object of public opinion because for him implicitly the sector he
polled was an upper-class sector, an educated sector.

The second great group of discussion has to do with the title
of tables, reflecting the content of questions. The way the political
scientists put it is again to ask what is public opinion. But this time
they do not mean "who holds the opinion" but "what is the opinion
about."

If a poll were taken whether this country should be a republic or
a kingdom, everyone would agree that this is a matter of public
opinion. But how about the star-rating polls which George Gallup
takes when he wants to find out whether Lana Turner has more followers now than six months ago. Is this part of public opinion research? Obviously this is again a mere matter of terminology. You
can choose your questions. You can either call everything on which

you take a poll "public opinion," or you can say only those questions the title of which have certain words pertaining to public affairs should be called "public opinion." Therefore, for instance, movie rating, star rating, would not be part of public opinion. Again, it isn't a very serious problem because it is a discussion of classifying the content of questions.

We come now to a third, a little more complicated matter, and that is, how these poll results are ascertained. In a modern poll, usually personal interviews are being made. As a matter of fact we spurn anything else. We have shown, for instance, that mail polls are not reliable. Mail questionnaires do not give the same results as personal interviews, because they cut out certain people. Suppose, however, that someone is interested only in the opinion of those people who are eager enough to write a letter to a Senator. If the Senator feels that only people who want to write letters should be listened to, then the result of tables ascertained by counting letters to Senators is public opinion, and what Crossley and I are getting together in personal interviews is wrong because it asks the wrong people, who shouldn't be asked.

There was a time when political scientists identified public opinion with the content of newspapers. The French social psychologist, Tarde, wrote a book on *Mass and Opinion* where this point of view is taken for granted. It also shows up interestingly in political history. The diplomatic correspondence in the beginning of the nineteenth century is full of such statements—"His Excellency, or the Minister of Foreign Affairs, is not able to agree with your proposition because public opinion in his country would not stand for it." And it is very clear what he means by this statement, "public opinion wouldn't stand for it." Some editor would write unpleasant editorials.

In this sense every person really has his own public opinion. It is the opinion of those people who are important for him. This brings the notion very near to the idea of mores. But even if we can say who is important for us, how do we know what they think? Our sources of knowledge are occasional observations and they might very well be illusions and projections. So it turns out that a third source of confusion is that political scientists don't specify how their brand of public opinion is ascertained. According to the various ways in which we get information on "public opinion," quite different concepts can emerge.

Let us return once more to our paradigm of a table taken from a public opinion poll. It is, so to speak, the most general scheme, and because it can vary in three ways we have three areas of dispute as to what constitutes public opinion: according to *whose* opinion, opinion about *what*, and *how* ascertained. But a table from an empirical study has also a final frequency distribution. And even this has led to discussion among political scientists. Some feel that only that is public opinion on which the large majority agrees. Others feel, to the contrary, that only that is public opinion on which controversial positions are being taken. Now we know that the distribution of answers can either be unimodal or bimodal or have even more complicated shapes. So it turns out that shapes of distribution curves are behind the fourth type of controversy among political scientists.

It can be shown that the variation of these four factors in a poll table can account for most discussion which has so far come up in the literature of public opinion, and that is very clarifying indeed (*laughter*).

Now unfortunately, I have now no time to go to the second part of the speech. I wanted now to show inversely that if you read political scientists, you get thoroughly ashamed of how meager and stupid and unintelligent our own thinking is on political matters as compared with the really great writers on such matters. We are so concerned with our special problems that we just don't think about political matters any more. We just take polls! (*Laughter.*)

You can take any of the classical writers on political science and you will find wonderful suggestions for interesting polls which no one has taken. At one point, for instance, de Tocqueville says he noticed that Americans are much more interested in little affairs than in big affairs, and the question of a new bridge really excites people much more than a question of a new foreign policy. So some colleagues of mine asked people before the presidential election, "Are you more especially interested in local affairs?" Yes. No. And, "Are you especially interested in national affairs?" And then they correlated that with whether they voted or whether they didn't vote.

The voting in the presidential election was much higher among the people who said they were more interested in local affairs than among the people who said they were more interested in national affairs! The statement, "Are you interested in national affairs?" is a phrase which doesn't lead to action. If you are, however, interested in your local affairs, then the prediction that you will turn out for a presidential election is much better.

There are a large amount of such concrete examples which you can get out of those old writers, things which really give good results if you just put the student to reading books which were written at a time when people were really still thinking. And don't believe that they haven't thought about our kind of problems!

One good source of ideas for public opinion polls is St. Augustine. He also had methodological problems, and just because he meditated in his *Confessions* so much about "How do you influence people?" and "How does one become a leader?" and all those things, he very much wondered how he could find out. They are so intangible and still, as he put it, he can measure them; and how is it possible that social issues and matters of the soul and relations between people can be found out and measured?

He was very much concerned with our problem, and at one point he puts it in the best form in which we can put our whole stage of thinking on the matter. He said: "For so it is, O Lord My God, I measure it and I know not what it is that I am measuring." (*Laughter.*)

Mr. Sears: Next we will hear from Dr. Norman Meier.

Mr. Meier: I shall review what seem to be some of the more obvious unsettled problems arising out of the experience of the last decade or so, which have been sharpened up considerably of late.

At the meeting last night, by a vote of three to one, Mr. Crossley dissenting, it was agreed that political forecasts will be continued. With that in mind the urgent task is to tackle the problem immediately of how such an event, how such an objective, can be attained. And that seems to require some kind of new methodology or technique or operation that can be widely applicable to the study of and the measurement of *continuing public thinking;* in contrast to the static record of the public at a given time (which of course we know now is what the polls should have reported). That would have been safer with the public: a simple indication of the plain and concluded fact that on such and such a date the public opinion was such and such.

Hence if forecasts are to be made and if we are to learn more about voter behavior, it seems clear that there must be some means of conducting polls at perhaps three-day intervals during the final two weeks right up to the election and for two weeks after the election.

In no other way can we increase our knowledge of voting behavior, so that information gained in 1952 can then be applied toward the solution of the problem in 1956. Through such repeated experiments will be gained an accumulation of information and insight into things we now have to speculate about, such as to who changes his mind, when, and in what numbers; who decides not to vote after all; and who previously uninterested later became interested and voted.

In addition to polls made at short intervals, considerable value might be derived from spot checks made in areas which are known to be more or less stable one way or another as to population characteristics, concentration of labor or of foreign population, or any other significant segment of the voter population. A close repetition of those spot checks over a period of time might provide a basis for some kind of check function on the regular polls and hence aid in making a more dependable forecast.

In the preparatory planning of polling strategy there is much to be gained by a pooling of the views and judgment of social scientists. The number could be expanded to include, among others, psychologists and sociologists who can tell the poll-takers more about the population characteristics of the area sampled. Cooperative endeavor in social science, the main theme of this Conference, offers real possibilities for advancement. I think Paul Lazarsfeld pointed out that that can best be done in a limited environment like his Elmira area and the Erie County, Ohio, area, or such as Iowa, the state of Minnesota, state of Texas, or the state of Massachusetts and now in Washington where there are established and regularly functioning polls. It would seem that only through such limited-area checks could one get the information needed to base any kind of a deep insight into what trends are in progress, if any.

Turning now to another unsettled problem, I would offer the view that despite the remarks made about excessive attention given to methodology, it would seem that since polls have to be made by *some* kind of methodology, they have to be made either by what we now have or they can be made by some method or methods which can be experimentally developed in the future. It would seem that one of the constant unsettled problems of sampling-survey methodology is simply constant experimentation on present survey methods.

I am quite cognizant of the disposition of some individuals (and among these are some experts) who decry, yes, who view with alarm, the current difference of opinion regarding what method is best for what purpose or whether a given method is scientific and hence superior for all purposes. To me such divergences reflect a wholesome condition in a growing and new field. There can be little progress by abject conformity, by uncritical acceptance of theory without theory-testing, and of unwarranted *a priori* assumptions regarding applications of theory to problems where applicability may involve unforeseen complications and difficulties.

Nor can there be much real progress in a situation where theoreticians sit in judgment on practitioners. The theoreticians should sit down with the practitioners at least long enough to gain a more adequate comprehension of the latter's problems, and also to give adequate hearing to those few "academic acolytes" who have both the theory and practice, albeit in limited measure yet with a reasonable understanding of both angles. Constant experimentation with working methods, experimental designs set up to test methods and their variations in the field, and creative imagination applied to devising new methods or combinations of present ones so as to eliminate weak or unworkable features and refine promising trends will all pay dividends in methodological progress. The research designers who will ultimately contribute most to social science methodology will be those who are not satisfied with present methods whether area or well-designed and -administered quota.

It is necessary, as was indicated yesterday, to observe exactly how a method works under difficulties.

Good theory is fine and a method may appeal to many people, particularly those new in the field. The thing we have to keep constantly in mind is what is going to happen in the field. If a method requires an interviewer to go out at set intervals to meet a dead-line in a regularly recurring poll, every week or every two weeks, and the weather does not permit contact with designated interviewees, that is an important matter if the method is to be used for public opinion measurement.

There are methods, as yet inadequately explored, that could be pursued further for the purpose of ascertaining what they do yield.

Variations of and innovations in the random-point method may have fruitful possibilities. It has been used in some instances but has not been pushed very far, for the reason that it did not appear to suit the conditions required for the purposes to which it was applied, but that does not say that with some modification it may not be found to be eminently suited for other types of surveys, even better perhaps than anything we now know.

More unsettled problems lie in the realm of modifications of the panel. The panel is not a true sampling method. A distinction needs to be drawn. A panel is a fixed collection or aggregation of interviewing areas in which the interviewer returns at intervals to the same respondents over a period of time, such as was done at Erie County and Elmira. But in many other types of survey, such as routine opinion sampling, that is not desirable for several reasons. One is that the interviewees in the course of a year or two would become satiated, very much annoyed by being repeatedly interviewed. Furthermore the panel would be frozen, and if it has psychological or social bias that would be frozen, too. Therefore the working sample or a true sampling method should be one which can obtain a different sample each time for the obvious advantage of having a different public and the chance of seeing how valid and consistent they are by their performance.

At the risk of being somewhat misunderstood on this, I would like to see, as a carefully controlled investigation, the hypothesis explored that a good quota sample, done according to the very best practices known today, might not turn up a random sample *more random* than some of the better known probability methods. I think that is a distinct objective that would make very worth-while research and would settle some of these problems which I think are bothering a great many people in the field.

As another suggestion may I propose that much more attention be given to attitude probing. This is a difficult and a delicate problem. Distinct progress has been made but very much more is in order. It will mean that less attention be given to the data collected and more to the underlying meaning behind the data. And that is applicable particularly in the political poll. The answer to a dichotomous question or to any simple form of question does not always tell us what is going to happen to that subject, that respondent, two weeks hence. But if the deeper attitude is probed, some clue to his potential behavior may be disclosed.

The depth interview has been suggested as one way of spot checking the probabilities of trends developing in that interviewee's thinking, perhaps indicative of his probable response later on. In that way there would be provided better means of spotting early, identifying the direction of, and doing something about measuring the potential trends in individuals, and also the patterns of political behavior shaping up in a given region.

We saw in this election in Massachusetts that if you connect up two things with the political election, the political election's complexion is changed overnight. There is almost no telling what the change would produce, but you could almost predict it if you knew the population. Boston is about sixty percent Irish. A great many Irish are Catholic. If a constitutional amendment legalizing the dissemination of birth-control information is injected, you have an extraneous factor which is going to affect the respondent's behavior, the potential character of trends of behavior in every person of that descent and of that religious faith. Also if you have in the same election an extraneous factor like an amendment to the state constitution, regulating the closed shop or some other labor practice which draws out a great deal of affective reaction of those in the labor ranks, you have another extraneous factor which you can probably identify and calculate its significance politically.

Therefore the social and political configurations of the respondent, the attitude constellations, the regional constellations of a person of specific extraction—all of those are challenging studies for the future and represent some of the unsettled problems of the field.

Furthermore and lastly, all methods of respondent selection should be reviewed to determine what are the most dependable general practices in respondent selection. There is the perennial problem of interviewer competence and training. All those things, while fragments of the whole picture, are in themselves extraordinarily important, as the Census Bureau has been finding out very much to its surprise, and in many cases these things have accounted for more error than any other one factor, including sampling.

DISCUSSION—Don Cahalan

MR. SEARS: We will now ask Mr. Cahalan to comment on the four papers.

MR. CAHALAN: It is impossible to comment on all four papers in any detail. Instead of talking about methodology I'd like to make a few remarks about the future of the social sciences.

The way I feel is akin, I think, to what Paul Lazarsfeld and Ted Gallup said: there can't be any basically new methods developed unless the climate for further development is right. And it seems to me that if we look back to the Black Tuesday in last November, academic social scientists themselves were as wrong as the pollsters were. This may be a surprising remark, but the failures of the basic social sciences were the reasons why Gallup and Crossley and Roper and others were just not in shape to have that twenty-twenty hindsight beforehand.

A digression about the magnitude of the error in prediction, a story I am dragging in by the heels, it must be admitted: the leading pollsters here have not minimized the error, but others have. Some have talked about the "deviation" (I think that was the term) rather than calling it "error," and some said that after all it was a very small error. Which reminds one of the girl who happened to have an illegitimate child, and her father was chiding her about it. Her response was, "After all, Father, it's such a tiny little thing!"

But back to the need for basic reforms: it seems to me there has been a mass illusion—the great "Children's Crusade" of 1948—in which everyone was taken in about the election. Everyone was wrong in advance, and this shows how little courage and imagination most social scientists had. You have heard a lot of smart answers since; but just who among informed persons, *before* the election, went on record as saying, "There is not sufficient grounds to make a prediction," or "The prediction will be wrong"? I don't know of any, except some who were partisan Democrats who just didn't like the findings.

As far as promoting a climate in which the social sciences can develop, the social science laboratories are growing, and I believe they should continue to grow along the lines described by Mr. Dodd, Mr. Bachelder, and others; but there still seems to be a gap. Whereas we do say and mean all these fine things about unity, and we have arrived at a good many basic understandings at this conference, there is the risk we will all go home and do the same doggone old things, be in the same old ruts, and talk about the other fellow and his work—and that nobody's work is good except our own. What we need are some devices whereby the practitioners and the academic social scientists will be encouraged to work together on problems of common interest.

One possibility would be to have social scientists directly associated with the staffs of the various pollsters. It would be a small step, to be sure, but at least one step. I think it might tend to bridge the gap, because if there were a good social psychologist (with some other abilities) working regularly with, say, the American Institute of Public Opinion, he would be more effective because he would be familiar with what might be derived from the data. Such a person would not waste the AIPO's time with silly questions that arise from not understanding the point of a given survey or its recognizable limitations. The same type of social scientist might be able to work effectively with Mr. Crossley's organization or Mr. Roper's staff.

The various national pollsters have been most cooperative in making much of their data available to outside analysts. However, it seems to me that if we had a social scientist right in the research organization, he could provide ideas and think up research projects and could analyze data in new ways, and then go to foundations to get them to pay for the further development of basic methods whenever he found promising "leads." The right kind of man could keep up a continuing flow of publications on new research applications. Thus, it seems, a great deal could be accomplished in a relatively short time; whereas the way it is now, you (the practitioners) do make your data available to outsiders, but there is a slippage because there isn't a close enough liaison between the practical people who just don't have the time to analyze everything, and the academicians—even the best-informed ones.

(Meeting adjourned.)

THE LOCAL SURVEY
AND SOCIAL SCIENCE

22

THE USE OF LOCAL FACILITIES IN POLITICAL SCIENCE RESEARCH

Norman C. Meier, Presiding

Ross C. Beiler

MR. MEIER: Professor Ross Beiler of the University of Miami, Florida, will present a study made in which a prediction was accurate. It is a limited study of Dade County, which includes Miami.

MR. BEILER: I came to the Conference with an idea, and the hope I might find an opportunity somewhere to bring it out.

Professor Meier seemed quite interested and suggested that I appear at this time. It concerns the prospect of co-ordinated research involving depth and intensive interviewing, possibly the use of panel techniques which would co-ordinate a number of universities and colleges where some work in this field could be done across the whole country. By such cooperative research we might possibly supplement the type of work being done by Lazarsfeld and his associates at Elmira and also formerly in Erie County. Possibly we could get, not on such a large scale at one place but at a great many *more* places, similar work done at very low cost or possibly no cost at all through the use of students who have at least some type of elementary training in public opinion research techniques.

Now, from some points of view this isn't worth your time, and since some of you will take that point of view when I am through (*laughter*), I will try not to be too long. But from other points of view, I think possibly it may be: first, as to the technique, and then as to the findings, and thirdly, as to the possibility of extension of a modification of this idea on a large scale in integrated fashion across the country.

The technique used in this study was exceedingly simple, and in any integrated co-ordinated project I doubt that it would be used. It was used because of the very odd situation which we have in Miami, where everything is in such an uproar that almost any sampling method is inadequate. It is really a boom town again, if you haven't been down there lately. Consequently in casting around for ideas on which to base sampling we finally determined on the absurdly simple one which has of course been disproved in certain applications, the idea of using a pilot or pinpoint precinct.

For that purpose we simply charted the election behavior or the voting behavior of all the likely precincts in Dade County over a period since 1940. And from that, not by any close statistical method but simply by inspection, we chose a precinct partly because it seemed to be very representative and was studied through the period, and partly because it was convenient for polling purposes for the university students, who did all the interviewing after they had received a certain amount of instruction involved in the course of their instruction in the public opinion course.

It seems to me that this type of thing could be done in a great many places. One of the main points I wanted to make was its great *educational* value. It was certainly an eye-opener to me. The enthusiasm of the class was considerable, considering the large number of persons who are usually uninterested in almost anything (*laughter*). And also it proved quite educational to the students as the data was brought together and they were able to study weaknesses in the instruments used and so on. It proved very concrete and quite valuable to them in helping them to understand the weaknesses in polls and ways they could be improved. So that, I believe, would be the excuse for exploiting students in this way for purposes of research, for social science generally, and for pollers in particular.

There are two or three things about the technique I did want to mention because I think they are unique. I wanted to say first, this isn't unique—in plotting the election behavior since 1940, we found this one precinct had gradually tended to drift toward the Republican side. If you have one of these reports you will find on Table 1, at the bottom, the figure for weighting the percentage of Republican vote in the precinct.

Since the Democratic vote was so badly split in '48, we used the Republican vote as the basis and we found that it had reached dead center in 1946, and had been gradually going to the Republican side. But instead of weighting the sample data on the Republican side in '48, we left them at dead center because we found the proportion of the registered Republicans in the precinct was slightly higher than the proportion on a county-wide basis, which was not true formerly. And of course that decision, which was to some extent luck, proved to be very desirable.

We got considerable publicity on this because it was published as a forecast of the Dade County vote, with full information about the sample, and the percentages turned out to be almost exactly right. The Republican vote for president was absolutely on the nose. We predicted 36.8 percent, and it came out 36.8 percent.

This result is in one way just amusing, but if you have one of these reports, glance at Table 4. Unfortunately we have the tables of the first and second surveys run together, but in Table 4 of the pre-election survey you will see some interesting things about that. You will find that the percentages as you go down through the different samples show considerable reliability, both for Dewey and Truman, and even for Thurmond and Wallace. For instance, we actually anticipated the precinct vote, not the Dade County vote, but the result was quite valid with respect to both the precinct and the county. The precinct did prove to be a true pilot of the county, and you find it not only as to Dewey, but also Truman and Wallace, and we were only one percent off in predicting the county vote for Thurmond.

But the interesting thing really about the technique was this: that for this one single purpose of predicting the outcome of the presidential election in Dade County, we included second-hand information. You will find there on Table 4 under the number A5, "All interviewees and others in household in general category," which was taken as the sample for this particular purpose. You will find immediately above that a line which refers to "Others in household in general category"—that is, others than the interviewed. We asked the interviewees first if they intended to vote; later on, whether they were registered or not, and for those interviewees who did understand that you had to be registered in order to vote—we found that 15 percent of those who were not registered said they would vote anyway—but screening that way we included second-hand information from those interviewees with respect to the voting intentions of others in the household.

Now that sounds like a pretty slipshod method, but it was done for the reason that we did not apply any randomization within households at all. We simply took the person who came to the door. Of course that is a haphazard method. We did get an excess of house-wives and other stay-at-homes. Now that sample proved to be valid. However, we added to that these secondhand choices, "Others in household in general category." That also proved to be valid, and together they proved to be precise.

Now, while this doesn't show much in itself, I think it is an inter-esting suggestion because a great deal of money has been spent on call-backs which perhaps for many purposes would be unnecessary, or at least for some purposes might be unnecessary. It is possible that for this particular purpose it would be unnecessary. It is fre-quently common knowledge in a family what the voting intention regarding presidential elections is going to be. And it did turn out that both the firsthand interviews and the secondhand interviews were valid and that both together gave a sharper answer.

Now my point is this. This type of study shows little, perhaps. But if we had the same thing being done in quite a large number of places at one time we might find out a good deal. Each of the individual universities and colleges could follow an agreed upon plan. It would have to be fairly simple. Probably we would com-bine some area and quota sampling methods in order to meet the exigencies of university situations and keep the costs within bounds.

But I think it could be done. I want to point to the charts, which go on here at some length, just briefly to show the type of thing that could be done.

I think we could get more information, a larger number of inter-views over the whole country and more intensively done by this method, and more cheaply, than any other way.

We had information for instance on the extent to which the voters really wanted the man for president that they said they in-tended to vote for. They didn't want him; they wanted Eisenhower! Only 24 percent of those who said they were going to vote for Dewey really wanted him. Sixteen percent of those who said they were going to vote for Truman really wanted Truman.

All these samples are meaningless on a national scale. They're from an individual local survey. But they would not be meaningless if the same type of thing were being done at a great many places at once. I suspect that many of these things had meaning.

I haven't mentioned several that are very interesting which, if true on a national scale, would in themselves go far to explain what happened in the national election. For instance, we found that the Dewey voters were definitely not interested in issues; they were voting for a change. We asked them, "Why are you going to vote for your choice for president?" That's in Table 7 of the pre-election survey. In the first survey we used a scaled answer-sheet; in the second we didn't. The scaled answer-sheet made it easier to tabulate the results, but the results seemed better with the use of open questions.

The point about the Dewey voters ties in with something we heard from Mr. Lazarsfeld yesterday when he spoke about the people who were voting for Truman being interested in the Roosevelt—the Truman program—yes, the Roosevelt program! But the Dewey voters, it appears here, were not interested in issues; they wanted a change. I wonder—I thought probably that propaganda research had been carried on by the Dewey forces and they had found out what appeals would be most acceptable. Apparently they hadn't because Dewey had a slogan in 1944, "That's why it's time for a change," and that was the thing his supporters were waiting to hear. But he never touched it in '48.

The Truman voters on the other hand were much interested in the issues. Such a "finding" in an individual small-scale study like this is only interesting, but it might show a great deal if these questions could be projected on a national scale.

There are other questions here that go into intensity and depth interviewing to show the type of concern which was of interest to persons who intended to back Truman or Dewey, and in the post-election study likewise the shift in attitude which had occurred.

The tendencies here are extremely interesting. For instance, over 50 percent of all of our sample before the election thought that big business was the most politically influential major interest group in the country. Table 5 in the post-election survey shows that labor has come up to over 50 percent and big business has dropped down to 22 percent, which reveals that there was a time there when a great deal of public opinion was formed, when the propagandists might have been at work overtime forming public opinion because it was in process of an intense overturn.

If you have a copy of this report you may be able to peruse it at some greater length. You may get some ideas there as to the value of this type of research, if it could be done at a great many places at the same time.

There are just two other things I want to mention. One concerns this question of intention of voting—who actually is going to vote. We found that 93 percent of the persons who were registered said they were going to vote, but we found that the number of persons who said they were certain their choice for president was the right man corresponded exactly to the proportion of persons who actually voted. That may or may not mean anything. But it seems to me that is the type of thing which could be followed up, if somehow we could set up co-ordinated research at a number of universities and colleges on this type of problem, and possibly panel studies which would follow through a political campaign in a lot of cities at once, doing this sort of thing that Lazarsfeld has done.

I am deeply interested in this not because I am primarily interested in polling. I am primarily interested in the public opinion process and I feel that in order to find out what the public opinion process is we are going to have to develop new techniques for measuring intensity and for depth interviewing on a much larger scale through co-ordinated research than we have yet done.

DISCUSSION

MR. MEIER: I presume you still have other copies in Miami, Mr. Beiler. The name is Ross C. Beiler, Assistant Professor of Political Science, University of Miami.

I think we are particularly happy to have Mr. Beiler's report for two reasons. In the first place it helps the conference because we had participants from the Pacific Northwest and Massachusetts, and now from the Southeast, so it leaves just two foreign countries unrepresented—Texas and California (laughter).

The other reason why we should be happy to have heard this report is that here is a teacher of Political Science who is so much interested in polling methods, techniques, and operations, that he sees in this a useful tool for increasing our knowledge of voting behavior, the political process, influence of news, propaganda, and other things, and has realized in this study a fruitful and suggestive body of information for the guidance of anybody interested. It seems to me that suggests an excellent outline of a program for the future. He hasn't just been talking about political theory. He has really come to grips with the actual operation, and I think that is going to benefit political science.

MR. GALLUP: And polling.

MR. MEIER: Intensity studies and all these other things, the attitude constellations, and all sorts of interests in society.

Does anyone have any questions they'd like to direct to Professor Beiler? If not, next I'd like to ask if there is anyone here who has any kind of data, any kind of observation, any kind of additional report he'd like to bring to the attention of the Conference at this time?

Mr. McPhee, have you said everything you'd like to say here?

MR. McPHEE: I would make this comment, that the sample method he proposes has been explored by Louis Bean in a book, *How to Predict Elections.* If you took every university in the country, beginning with the letter "N," such as Nebraska, New York, North Dakota, and then a professor in each took a precinct equivalent in number to the number of letters in the university name, and then there were bisecting lines drawn, Louis Bean has demonstrated that you have a sample. In that type of sample you get a perfectly good national sample by the sampling policy known as "As Kelly goes, so goes the nation."

MR. LAZARSFELD: There is one serious question, whether there is a danger that if you pick those counties near universities you will have a certain bias. The amount of reading near a university is so much higher, you get a completely wrong picture. Have you any feeling as to whether there is a danger that around the universities the vote is usually different than in more outlying districts?

MR. BEILER: Yes, I have a feeling about that. I think that really could be overcome for this reason. The universities which are not very powerful might not have much influence in their immediate vicinity. The universities that are powerful could afford to do something a little more ambitious in the way of getting their interviewers out away from the university.

CONCLUDING COMMENT

MR. MEIER: At this time I would like to introduce to you two men you have seen very busily engaged around the meeting, who are responsible largely for the easy way in which I believe the Conference was run. I think they deserve a little recognition, a note of appreciation from all of us. The man who represents the president's office, the head of the University Information Service, Mr. James Jordan. (*Applause.*)

MR. JORDAN: I have to get in the program somehow. I want to tell you at this time that this has been a cooperative venture in all the stages of this Conference, cooperation that we are very proud of here. In this case we have transcended a good many academic boundaries in order to put this Conference on for you. I can't take any personal credit for it.

I am reminded of what happened not long ago on the campus. We have a wife of a faculty member who is very witty—the wife is very witty (*laughter*). And on one occasion, one of our deans who had grown old in the service, just a couple of years ago—I don't want to identify him too closely—retired. They were having a testimonial dinner for him and in complete humility as he was being toasted from all sides, he waved his hand and said, "How could I have failed with all of this help?", pointing at his colleagues. The lady said, "It wasn't easy" (*laughter*).

MR. MEIER: Now, also the young man who has been working very assiduously and arduously, through all the multitudinous details prior to the Conference, and all through the Conference, so much so that he hardly had a chance to hear any of it, and is jointly responsible for the easy way in which many things were handled, Mr. Merritt Ludwig. (*Applause.*)

Then I'd like to say that if anyone should consider this Conference a success—we hope perhaps somebody might charitably think of it that way—it is due in greatest part to the willingness of all participants particularly, and all the rest of you for that matter, to leave your work, spend the time in travel and the time you have spent here, to make this Conference a success. So the University of Iowa is very grateful to all of you and wishes to express its appreciation for your cooperation, because a Conference is only as good as the people who attend it. We started out with the intention of inviting here the best-informed men in the country. We wanted to get a great variety of interests; we wanted social scientists, poll directors, psychologists, persons from business, industry and the government—men like Francis Russell who were willing to leave busy days in Washington to come here—and others I need not recall. The University is grateful and appreciative of the fact that you came.

MR. CASEY: Dr. Meier, I am sure that those of us who were invited to attend this Conference, even though we did not participate actively but were simply auditors, want to thank you and your associates and Professor Saunders, and people in other departments, including Les Moeller, for your hospitality and the fine way in which you have treated us, and the excellent program which you have made available. (*Applause.*)

MR. MEIER: Again I say I think we were the ones that were favored by your attendance.

MEMBER OF AUDIENCE: Dr. Meier, you remarked in passing that the split last night was three to one in favor of continuing forecasting. That was a split among the speakers. We were wondering if you meant that—

MR. MEIER: I did, but in the audience it was 129 for, 22 against —or six to one. I think that in itself is a very interesting commentary on the trend of thinking both expert and lay. And also it is a commentary on the confidence that you experts have in the entire matter of survey technology, polling practices, and the whole usefulness to society of the subject matter discussed throughout the Conference. If the University didn't think that survey technology, public opinion polls, all related things that go into an examination of the behavior of the citizen in a democratic society weren't valuable, we wouldn't have had this Conference. We feel that it was deserving of any effort we could give to bring all of you together for this purpose.

MR. GALLUP: May I make just one observation?

First of all, I do want to tell you, Norman, and everyone else here, how grateful I have been for this opportunity to be here and to discuss these problems. And the observation I wanted to make is this: that this Conference is unique in my experience. It is the first one I have ever attended where the people *wanted* to hear what was being said. I have attended thousands of meetings and usually you find a speaker talking to five people with five hundred others milling around in the corridors. But everyone here seemed to be interested in what was going on and I think, as I say, it has been one of the most helpful, useful conferences that I personally have ever attended in my entire life. (*Applause.*)

MR. MEIER: Anyone interested in the World Association for Public Opinion Research is invited to a meeting as soon as we disband here. Stuart Dodd and Mr. Lentz will outline some of the material which they'd like to bring up for consideration toward the development of professional polling on a world scale. I think we are all aware of the fact that one of the hopes of the late war was to bring about a better understanding among nations and also to make the democratic principle operative and functional in other countries that have not witnessed the development of democracy, as we think the United States has developed it at least, and we would be inclined to favor the whole idea of extending the public opinion poll to other countries as rapidly as possible—possibly also to Russia eventually.

Inasmuch as there appear to be no further announcements, we will declare the Conference adjourned, and again, thank you.

(*Conference adjourned.*)

INDEX

INDEX

Adaptability of area methodology to public opinion measurement, 243-256

Admissibility of survey findings as evidence, 99 ff.; bases of, 102-108

Albig, J. W., on nature of public opinion, 111-114

Ambivalence of candidates in 1948 election, 197-198

Area sample, and quota contrasted, 165, 244; in Washington state, 174; in Iowa study, 247; relative workability in public opinion polls, 247 ff.

Attitudes, Army studies of, 17; study of, 17; measurement of, 29; Guttman concept of, 30; multiple-question approach to, 31-32; formation of, and ego-involvement, 123; lack of knowledge about, 170; of Iowa voter, fluid nature of, 187; and communications analysis, 236; formation, need for deeper study of, 236; and opinions as conditioned by affiliations, 244-245; configurations, 245; class, and voting intention, 283; of public toward experts, 289; concrete situation as method of studying, 300; social, assumptions underlying, 304; constellations of, 332

Availability of respondents, research on, 222; as primary problem in polling, 226

Bachelder, J. E., on polls, 171-176, 237-238; comments on sampling theory, 256-260

Ballot scratching in Iowa, 186-187

Band-wagon theory of poll taking, 287

Basic research, in universities, 8; in social science, 8-10

Behavior, political, at local levels, 19-20; theory of, 22; forecasts as providing data on, 290

Beiler, Ross C., 236-237, 337-342

Berelson, Bernard, on mass communication, 58-67; on events as influence on opinion, 148-152

Bias, education, etc., in samples, 165, 181; alleged Republican bias in polls, 1936-1948, 196-197

Bureau of Audience Research experiments in sampling design, 255

Bureau of the Census. *See* Census, Bureau of the

Cahalan, Don, 333-334

Campaigns, effect of, 196-197, 207-208, 285

Cantril, Hadley, on setting issues in social science, 302-306

Casey, Ralph D., on pressure groups and the press, 124-139

Causes of disparity between poll findings and election returns, 159-199

Census, Bureau of the, problems in sample surveys, 77 ff.; checking quality of surveys, 78; problems of accuracy in total enumeration, 78-79; response errors, 80-82; experiments with field practices, 83

Chapin, F. Stuart, on unsettled problems in social science, 306-308

Clark, Carroll, on public opinion, 115-123; on problems, 297-302

Coat-tail riding in 1948 election, 187

349